Disability, Normalcy, and the Everyday

Many critical analyses of disability address important 'macro' concerns, but are often far removed from an interactional and micro-level focus. Written by leading scholars in the field, and containing a range of theoretical and empirical contributions from around the world, this book focuses on the taken-for-granted, mundane human activities at the heart of how social life is reproduced, and how this impacts on the lives of those with a disability, family members, and other allies.

It departs from earlier accounts by making sense of how disability is lived, mobilised, and enacted in everyday lives. Although broad in focus and navigating diverse social contexts, chapters are united by a concern with foregrounding micro, mundane moments for making sense of powerful discourses, practices, affects, relations, and world-making for disabled people and their allies. Using different examples – including learning disabilities, cerebral palsy, dementia, polio, and Parkinson's disease – contributions move beyond a simplified narrow classification of disability which creates rigid categories of existence and denies bodily variation.

Disability, Normalcy, and the Everyday should be considered essential reading for disability studies students and academics, as well as professionals involved in health and social care. With contributions located within new and familiar debates around embodiment, stigma, gender, identity, inequality, care, ethics, choice, materiality, youth, and representation, this book will be of interest to academics from different disciplinary backgrounds including sociology, anthropology, humanities, public health, allied health professions, science and technology studies, social work, and social policy.

Gareth M. Thomas is a Lecturer in the School of Social Sciences at Cardiff University, UK. He is a sociologist interested in medicine, disability, stigma, reproduction, and place. His first research monograph – *Down's Syndrome Screening and Reproductive Politics: Care, Choice, and Disability in the Prenatal Clinic* – was published by Routledge in March 2017.

Dikaios Sakellariou is a Senior Lecturer in the School of Healthcare Sciences at Cardiff University, UK. He is interested in health inequalities, experiences of disability and disablement, and the intersubjective nature of care practices. He has co-authored and co-edited the volumes *A Political Practice of Occupational Therapy* and *Occupational Therapies without Borders* (with Nick Pollard and Frank Kronenberg), and *Politics of Occupation-Centred Practice* (with Nick Pollard).

Disability, Normalcy, and the Everyday

Edited by Gareth M. Thomas
and Dikaios Sakellariou

Routledge
Taylor & Francis Group

LONDON AND NEW YORK

First published 2018
by Routledge
2 Park Square, Milton Park, Abingdon, Oxon OX14 4RN

and by Routledge
711 Third Avenue, New York, NY 10017

Routledge is an imprint of the Taylor & Francis Group, an informa business

British Library Cataloguing-in-Publication Data
A catalogue record for this book is available from the British Library

Library of Congress Cataloging-in-Publication Data
A catalog record for this book has been requested

ISBN: 978-1-138-21421-7 (hbk)
ISBN: 978-1-315-44644-8 (ebk)

Typeset in Bembo
by Apex CoVantage, LLC

For Ellie (GT)
For Apostolos (DS)

Contents

Figures

Contributors

Darshini Ayton is a Research Fellow and Lecturer at Monash University, Melbourne, Australia. She leads qualitative research undertaken by the Health Services Research Unit at the School of Public Health and Preventive Medicine. Dr Ayton is experienced in designing innovative methods to understand complex health issues and interventions. Previous and current areas of research include dementia, falls prevention, Parkinson's disease, stroke, hepatitis C, HIV, and depression. Dr Ayton is also involved in the development of patient-reported outcome measures, using methods to ensure genuine patient engagement, for clinical quality registries.

Maria Berghs is a VC2020 Lecturer at De Montfort University, UK. She is an anthropologist with a PhD in sociology and social policy. She works in the fields of medical anthropology and sociology, specialising in disability studies. Her research interests include disability, global health (sickle cell), humanitarianism, ethics, gender, and West Africa (Sierra Leone). She is currently working on projects linked to sickle cell in the UK and Sierra Leone. She is one of the editors of the forthcoming *Routledge Handbook of Disability Activism*.

Christina Buse is a Lecturer in Sociology and Social Psychology at the University of York, UK. Her research interests include embodiment, ageing, dementia, material culture, and design. She is currently working on an ESRC-funded project – 'Buildings in the Making' – with Sarah Nettleton and colleagues, exploring the practices of architects who are designing care homes and housing for later life. Her recent research includes the 'Dementia and Dress' project with Julia Twigg, exploring the significance of clothing within the everyday lives of people with dementia, their families, and careworkers. She also co-organises the research network 'Materialities of Care' with Daryl Martin.

Edmund Coleman-Fountain started as a Lecturer in Sociology at Northumbria University, UK, in 2016. His research is broadly concerned with social identities and embodiment. He has worked extensively with queer youth and young disabled people in exploring experiences of inequality and notions of difference. He has worked on a range of research projects addressing questions related to disabled embodiments, mental health and autism, and disability and citizenship in the European Union. He received his PhD from Newcastle University in 2011. This work was published in 2014 by Palgrave Macmillan (*Understanding Narrative Identity Through Lesbian and Gay Youth*).

Tillie Curran is Senior Lecturer and Programme Lead in Social Work at the University of the West of England, UK. With Katherine Runswick-Cole and Kirsty Liddiard, Tillie co-edited the book *The Palgrave Handbook of Disabled Children's Childhood Studies* (Palgrave Macmillan, 2017). She is currently a member of the ImaYDiT (I made it) research team with young disabled people researching their futures in a fast-changing society. In her role in professional education, she involves experts from experience and is interested in the challenges students face in learning how to bring about change.

Helen Errington is a self-funded retiree having spent 23 years working in the public sector. She has a Diploma in Fine Arts and a degree in Social Work (Curtin University, Australia). She was 1 of 5 people who established the Western Australia (WA) advocacy organisation Disabled Advocates and Self Help, now known as People with Disability Inc. In 1985, Helen was a member of the State Steering Committee under the auspices of the Hon. Graham Edwards to draft amendments to the WA Equal Opportunity Act to include the ground of impairment. In 1989, she secured a position with the Equal Opportunity Commission as a Conciliation Officer resolving complaints of discrimination. In 2000, Helen was seconded to The Western Australian Department of Education and Training where she developed a policy for those with high support needs to attend TAFE. Helen was a founding member of WA Disability Collective and past Chair of DADAA Ltd, an arts organisation for people with disability/mental illness. As Chair, she drove their 10-year vision and introduced the Affirmation Model of Disability, which aims to redress the balance of power for people with disability in the arts.

Faye Ginsburg is the Founding Director of the Center for Disability Studies and the Center for Media, Culture and History at New York University, USA, where she is also the David B. Kriser Professor of Anthropology. Recipient of numerous awards and grants for her work, including MacArthur and Guggenheim Fellowships, Faye's research focuses on cultural activism and social transformation, from her multiple award winning book, *Contested Lives*, on abortion activists to her long-standing work with indigenous media makers, and her current project with Rayna Rapp: *Disability Worlds*.

Goli Hashemi has been an occupational therapist working clinically in Canada and the United States with some international experience in low- and middle-income countries. She is currently working as an Assistant Professor in the Occupational Therapy program at Samuel Merritt University in Oakland, California, USA. Goli is also pursuing her PhD in Public Health at the London School of Hygiene and Tropical Medicine in London, UK, focusing on access to primary healthcare services for adults with disabilities, specifically in Guatemala. Her interests include access to health and rehabilitation for people with disabilities and community based inclusive development.

Hannah Kuper is the Director of the International Centre for Evidence in Disability at the London School of Hygiene and Tropical Medicine, UK. She is an epidemiologist by training, and her research focuses on disability in low- and middle-income settings.

Kirsty Liddiard is currently a Research Fellow in the School of Education at the University of Sheffield, UK, and a co-leader of the Institute for the Study of the Human (iHuman). She is a proud disabled feminist and public sociologist who believes in the power and politics of co-production and arts methodologies. Her research and scholarship explores disablism and ableism in the intimate lives of disabled people.

Janice McLaughlin is a sociologist who studies childhood disability; her work looks at how practices associated with fields such as medicine, welfare, education, family life, and cultural representation influence their lives. The work looks both at the barriers disabled young people face and their creative capacity to shape what happens to them. Her latest book (co-authored with Edmund Coleman-Fountain and Emma Clavering) is *Disabled Childhoods: Monitoring Difference and Emerging Identities* (Routledge, 2016).

Rayna Rapp is Professor in the Department of Anthropology at New York University, USA, specialising in gender and health, the politics of reproduction, science, technology, genetics, and disability in the US and Europe. She has contributed over 80 published works to the field of anthropology, including her 1999 book *Testing Women, Testing the Fetus: The Social Impact of Amniocentesis in America*. She has co-authored many articles with Faye Ginsburg – including 'Enabling Disability: Rewriting Kinship, Reimagining Citizenship' – a topic the pair has continued to research. For the last decade, Rayna and Faye have researched and written about the rising public presence and consciousness of disability as an aspect of US culture since the passage of the Americans with Disabilities Act of 1990.

Katherine Runswick-Cole is a Professor of Education in the School of Education at the University of Sheffield, UK. Her research focuses on the lives of disabled children, young people, and their families. Her work is influenced by her own family's experiences of disablism. She has published extensively in the area. With Tillie Curran and Kirsty Liddiard, Katherine co-edited the book *The Palgrave Handbook of Disabled Children's Childhood Studies* (Palgrave Macmillan, 2017).

Russell Shuttleworth, a medical anthropologist and social worker by training, is currently Senior Lecturer in Social Work at the School of Health and Social Development, Faculty of Health Sciences, Deakin University, Australia.

Dr Shuttleworth was a social worker and personal assistant for disabled people in the United States for many years. Major research interests include disability and sexuality, disability and masculinities, and disability ethnography. Recent published chapters include 'Conceptualising Disabled Sexual Subjectivity' (2014), 'Critical Engagements with the Politics of Care and Disability' (2018), and, with Helen Meekosha, 'Accommodating Critical Disability Studies in Bioarchaeology' (2017).

Louisa Smith's research interests centre on the relationship between experiences of disability and social policy and social change. Her research works across the disciplines of sociology, disability studies, and policy studies. Louisa leads the education and training arm of the Intellectual Disability Behaviour Support (IDBS) program at the University of New South Wales in Sydney, Australia, which aims to increase understanding and awareness about intellectual disabilities and complex support needs both in the university and in the service sector. In Louisa's research and teaching, she utilises arts-based methods, knowledge translation, and universal design to make her work as accessible as possible.

Karen Soldatic is an Australian Research Council DECRA Fellow (2016–2019) at the Institute for Culture and Society, Western Sydney University, Australia. Karen's DECRA, titled 'Disability Income Reform and Regional Australia: The Indigenous Experience', draws upon two previous fellowships: British Academy International Visiting Fellowship (2012) and The Centre for Human Rights Education, Curtin University (2011–2012), where she remains an Adjunct Fellow.

Julia Twigg is Professor of Social Policy and Sociology at the University of Kent, UK. She has written widely on age and embodiment, recently focusing on the role of dress in the cultural constitution of age. She published *Fashion and Age: Dress, the Body and Later Life* that looked at the role of dress in the lives and experiences of older women. With Christina Buse, she undertook a study of Dementia and Dress, exploring issues of personhood, embodiment, and memory. She is currently working on masculinity, dress, and age. Her website related to dress and age is www.clothingandage.org.

Narelle Warren is a Senior Lecturer in Anthropology and Sociology at Monash University, Melbourne, Australia. Her research concerns neurological disabilities, formal and informal care (including caregiver experiences), temporality, ageing, and the role of structural vulnerabilities in shaping people's experiences. She is especially interested in the effects of uncertainty on people's decision-making.

Nikki Wedgwood is a Senior Lecturer in the Faculty of Health Sciences at the University of Sydney, Australia. A sociologist with a passion for social justice, her research interests include gender, embodiment, sport, disability, and life history research. Her current research explores how young people with disabilities meet the developmental challenges of adolescence and emerging adulthood in the context of a disablist society. She currently coordinates a first-year unit on the social determinants of health and a senior elective on disability, sport, and social inclusion.

Mary Wickenden is a Senior Research Fellow at the Institute for Global Health at University College London, UK. Her initial disciplinary background is in Human Communication Science (speech and language therapy). Mary subsequently trained as a medical anthropologist and her main interests are in diverse aspects of disability and chronic illness in the Global South. Specifically, she is interested in the qualitative, predominantly participatory exploration of the lives of ill and disabled children and their families and carers, both in the UK and in low-income countries, informed by theory from the cross-disciplinary arenas of childhood studies, disability studies, and development studies. She has clinical, training/teaching, and research experience in India and Sri Lanka, and has worked on projects in South Asia, and East and Southern Africa.

Acknowledgements

This book is the outcome of a joint effort which began in 2015. We owe a big thanks to Joanna Latimer, who, seeing our common interest in the ways people live with a disability and negotiate their everyday worlds, brought us together. Coming from different disciplinary backgrounds – Gareth from sociology and Dikaios from occupational therapy – made working together on this volume a great learning experience for both of us. This book is the product of a happy process of experimentation which, we believe, has enriched it.

We want to thank each author for their effort, patience, and enthusiasm throughout the entire process of producing this book. Everyone generously shared their views and experiences in their respective chapter, and graciously responded to our feedback and engaged in a dialogical review process. We are certainly pleased with the final product, and we hope readers are too. We are also grateful to those people who generously invested their time in the early phases of the book, but whose work, for various reasons, is not included here. Regrettably, and inadvertently, this has had an impact on one of our primary aims: to widen the book's international scope. Nonetheless, we feel that taken together, these chapters – covering many different locations – identify concerns that will apply across diverse contexts.

We thank our editorial team at Routledge, and in particular Lianne Sherlock for her help early in the process, Georgia Priestley for her valuable support and gentle encouragement, and our commissioning editor Clare Jarvis and Emma Craig for seeing this book to completion.

We have both benefitted tremendously from working with and learning from many colleagues and friends, some of whom have contributed to this book. We wish to thank them all deeply. While it is inevitable that we will be unable to mention everyone, we wish to thank Pam Block, Arseli Dokumaci, Michele Friedner, Devva Kasnitz, Nina Nissen, and Narelle Warren. In particular, we thank all those colleagues who participated in panels organised by Dikaios and/or Gareth in the 2016 and 2017 meetings of the Society for Applied Anthropology, and in the 2017 meeting of the Medical Anthropology Network of the European Association of Social Anthropologists: Lesley Branagan, Tomás Sánchez Criado, Josien De Klerk, Gelya Frank, Lilian Kennedy, Anna

Witeska-Młynarczyk, Maria Milazzo, Sandra Smele, Marie Schnitzler, Heather Howard, Anna Martinez-Hume, Allison Carey, Richard Scotch, Ross Anderson, Molly Bloom, and Thomas Spitzfaden.

Gareth would like to extend his gratitude to the Cardiff University School of Social Sciences for providing him with the time and resources to dedicate to this book. I have also profited from many engagements which have helped to complicate, solidify, and extend my own intellectual commitments. One such moment was a visit to New York in 2016, where I began thinking more critically about the relationship between disability and everyday, mundane interactions. In no particular order, I thank Barbara Rothman, Julie E. Maybee, and Pam Block for inviting me to teach in their respective classes, and for kindly showing me the ropes in terms of local cuisine, transportations systems, and a range of other confusions. I thank Faye Ginsburg and Rayna Rapp for allowing me to attend their fantastic event 'Envisioning Accessible Futures: Disability, Caregiving, and Photography' at NYU. I have been extremely fortunate to discuss my work among supportive and critical (in a productive and kind way!) colleagues at conferences, including the 11th Annual Science in Public Conference at the University of Sheffield in 2017. I especially thank Imogen Tyler for organising and hosting a wonderful panel at the British Sociological Association Annual Conference in 2017, along with Aidan McGarry, Tracy Shildrick, Lisa Morriss, Kirsteen Paton (co-panellists), Tracey Jensen (discussant), and audience members for their contributions, recommendations, and engagement. I thank my colleague Roser Beneito-Montagut for facilitating a visit to the CareNet Research Group at Universitat Oberta de Catalunya, and Daniel López Gómez and Israel Rodriguez Giralt for their invitation to discuss this interest and for their enjoyable company throughout my stay.

I thank Kayleigh Garthwaite who, in co-organising a workshop with me on stigma and inequality, opened the door to another forum for debating concerns identified within this book. My interest in *disability worlds* owes much to Michele Friedner, who invited me to put pen to paper (or fingers to keyboard) about this in 2015. I thank Michele for her vital editorial support in producing the final paper, published in *Somatosphere*. I wish to acknowledge the contribution of *The Sociological Review*, and Jenny Thatcher in particular, for organising a writing retreat which allowed me the time to work on the book's introduction. I want to especially thank Joanna Latimer, whose liveliness, generosity, and investment in my work is a gift I can never properly reciprocate. I am very lucky to have had her encouragement, championing, and critical eye throughout my career. I hope she reads this book with interest and satisfaction. I also want to thank Dikaios. It has been a joy to work with him, and I am already looking forward to future collaborative endeavours over many years! Finally, a huge thanks to Ellie. Without her unwavering support and confidence in me, I would not be writing this book. Her editorial suggestions were, as ever, extremely helpful. Once again, sorry for those that I dismissed out of stubbornness.

Dikaios wishes to acknowledge the supportive environment of the School of Healthcare Sciences in Cardiff University that enabled his participation in this and numerous other projects. I have also benefitted from the hospitality and intellectual discussions in several other institutions. I would like to particularly thank the following: Narelle Warren, and also Andrea Whittaker and Lenore Manderson for heartfelt hospitality and great discussions on chronicity and disability at the School of Social Sciences in Monash University in Melbourne, Australia; Pamela Block for inviting me to Stony Brook University in New York, USA, and for initiating and organising what has become a well-established disability stream in the annual meetings of the Society for Applied Anthropology (it was in one of those meetings, in Vancouver in 2016, that we first presented our ideas on disability and the everyday); and Sadako Tsubota for her unfailing support over the years and for regular invitations to Sapporo Medical University, Hokkaido Bunkyo University, and Japan Welfare University, Japan. Michele Friedner's invitation to contribute an article to a special issue on 'inhabitable worlds' for *Somatosphere* provided a great opportunity to think about the importance of the everyday. Hanneke van Bruggen, Ben Hannigan, Melissa Park, and Nick Pollard have lent their support to my work on disability and the everyday in different ways and I wish to thank them all. I want to especially thank Gelya Frank from the University of Southern California, who has offered unfailing support and encouragement for over a decade now as I explore issues at the intersections of occupational therapy, anthropology, and disability studies. As a discussant in a panel Gareth and I organised at the annual conference of the Society for Applied Anthropology in Vancouver, Canada in 2016, Gelya expertly and kindly saw ways that different ideas could come together to speak to the 'everyday'.

Writing and editing are essentially solitary activities. Working with Gareth meant I was working with a friend, and for that I am grateful, and I look forward to more joint projects! Family and friends have always been here for me, although I have not always been able to be there for them. I thank them all deeply, and in particular the following: Roula Ksaderfoula, Julia Mpolanou, D. O. Richards, Dimitra Moustaka, Erimo Okaasan, Gareth Morgan, Kazuyo Machiyama, Vaso Tzouti, and Elena Mounou Rotarou. Letting me have the best spot at our shared desk, and engaging in daily experiments on the everyday, Apostolos helped more than he knows, and for that I thank him.

Part I

Disability, normalcy, and the everyday

Chapter 1

Introduction

Disability, normalcy, and the everyday

Gareth M. Thomas and Dikaios Sakellariou

This edited collection brings together scholars from around the world to explore understandings of disability, normalcy, and the everyday. Our concern is with the taken-for-granted, everyday human activities at the heart of how social life is reproduced, and how this impacts on the lives of those with a disability together with their family members and other allies. It is well established within the literature that disability, as a form of embodied difference or body trouble, can trigger personal and social consequences, from stigmatisation to discrimination, from embarrassment to resilience and resistance. In its effort to make sense of such consequences, the literature on disability often aligns with the social model of disability. In its simplest form, the social model treats disablement as a social *problem* belonging to *society*; that is, society disables people on account of unequal access to resources. This social model is commonly contrasted with the (bio) medical model of disability which depicts disablement as a biological *problem* belonging to a *person*, that is, there is an emphasis on *fixing* or *curing* a person. The social model, in contrast, argues that disability 'has nothing to do with the body' since 'it is a consequence of social oppression' (Oliver 1996: 35).

Much ink has been spilled over the merits and drawbacks of each model, and a range of alternative models (e.g. critical disability theory) have been presented as possible solutions to the shortcomings of the mutually exclusive social and medical models. In this book, we do not intend (or want) to repeat such ideas – nor do we want to be caught up in debates on language, including whether we should say *people with disabilities* or *disabled people*; both are used interchangeably here dependent on author preference. The social model of disability has been widely critiqued for its alleged disregard for the physicality of impairment, its failure to take account of difference within the broad category of disability, and for being restrictive and endorsing counter-productive dualisms. While we recognise the importance and potency of these well- (arguably over-) rehearsed debates, we intend to avoid the trap of pouring old wine into new bottles.

It is with this purpose that we introduce recent theoretical and empirical contributions from around the world (namely the UK, US, Australia, Sierra Leone, Malawi, and Guatemala) which depart from static arguments of models and, instead, move towards making sense of how disability is lived, mobilised, and enacted in everyday lives. This involves, for us, foregrounding micro and mundane moments in order to make sense of powerful discourses, practices, and relations. Many critical analyses of disability address key macro concerns, yet are often too far removed from an interactional and micro-level focus. Although the following contributions are broad in focus and navigate diverse social contexts, they are united by their drawing upon qualitative data (e.g. interviews, observations, case studies, life histories) and their valuing of everyday, mundane moments to illuminate the world-making, power relations, and affects at stake for disabled people and their allies. Located within, but also deliberately outside, of disability studies, these contributions thrust disability, as a matter of concern, further into the limelight. Disability studies has frequently operated independently of other fields, including the likes of medical sociology.[1] In this book, we are less concerned with staking a disciplinary allegiance. Instead, our hope is that this volume represents a willingness to explore disability from different vantage points and to acknowledge the telling contribution of other voices.

Theoretically, the chapters in this book are united by a concern with the mundane, everyday interactions and practices of daily life – and what disability *is* and *does* in these moments. In this respect, there is a clear affiliation with interactionist concerns and, particularly, with the work of Erving Goffman (1963). A central concept here, with respect to Goffman's corpus, is social stigma. Goffman argues that stigma sets people apart from (normal) others, marking them out as socially inferior and to be avoided, shunned, rejected; 'a blemished person, ritually polluted, to be avoided, especially in public places' (1963: 1). He highlights how a person may possess an attribute that 'makes [him/her] different from others . . . and of a less desirable kind', reduced in our minds 'from a whole and usual person to a tainted, discounted one' (1963: 5). Here, the person departs from ideas of normalcy, possessing an 'undesired difference' from what 'the normals' expected (1963: 5).

Goffman's ideas have formed a substantial component of the lexicon of stigma politics; his concepts have been taken up many times, such as by those writing on disability and courtesy stigma – known as the *stigma of association* (e.g. Gray 2002; MacRae 1999; Ryan 2008; Thomas 2014). However, his work has also been heavily critiqued, particularly for its lack of engagement (at least explicitly) with issues of power and inequality. Yet Goffman's contributions align with a crucial concern of this book: how embodied difference is negotiated in everyday lives. Disability can often present a problem in such moments, for example, people may not have the capacity to maintain a personal front in public interactions; 'nonplussed, out of countenance, embarrassed, experiencing the kind of anomaly that is generated when the minute social system of face-to-face interaction breaks down' (Goffman 1959: 23–24). Disability, indeed, can involve breaking social rules and norms (Gray 2002) and disturbing the subtle scaffolding of interaction, alluding to 'competence in social presentation' with respect to bodily dispositions (Nijhof 1995: 198).

When disabling conditions are visible, or what Goffman (1963: 41) terms 'discredited', social situations can be tense, uncertain, and ambiguous for people – and this can be so for invisible conditions too, in that they often involve strategic management during interactional exchanges. Drawing on ethnomethodological sensibilities, we may interpret this as a 'breach' in 'background expectancies' (Garfinkel 1967: 34–35). For ethnomethodologists, social life entails rule-following to ensure the smooth flow of everyday situations and to reproduce a recognisable and reasonable social order. Such situations are constantly worked at, created by routines and rituals transforming the 'taken-for-granted' into 'natural' and 'moral' facts of life which frame normative conduct (1963: 35). In so doing, people *do* membership, upholding the social order as a socially managed production. Yet this membership or passing may be disrupted by the presence of something which is unexpected, such as – we argue – a person with a disability; '[he/she] who passes will have to be alive to aspects of the social situation which others treat as uncalculated and unattended. What are unthinking routines for normals can become management problems for the discreditable' (Goffman 1963: 88).

This idea is highlighted by Garland-Thomson (2009: 20) who claims that 'disability provides us with one of the best opportunities to understand how we stare'. She argues that social interactions between disabled and non-disabled people are 'tense, awkward, and problematic', the common result being ocular evasion – a form of 'civil inattention' (Goffman 1967: 145). Interactions can be strained; meeting neighbours, attending parties, and introductions, for example, as the zones of first impressions, present possible opportunities for concerns to arise (Davis 1961). Specific empirical examples of this phenomenon have been discussed in relation to autism (Gray 2002; Ryan 2008) and blindness (Måseide and Grøttland 2015; Schillmeier 2007). These contributions identify how people with disabilities and their allies manage public interactions and, on occasion, present a self which is grounded in the normative expectation to repair any possible rupture and disquiet.

Disability thrusts people, then, into a realm of experiments. Here, we may draw upon Mattingly's (2013: 309) metaphor of the 'moral laboratory', that is, a space in which 'experiments are done in all kinds of places and in which the participants are not objects of study so much as researchers or experimenters of their own lives – subjects and objects'. Such experimentations do not happen separately to everyday life, but are in the midst of the everyday 'as the expected or the normative becomes subject to experiment' (2013: 322). These experiments are about being able, for instance, to walk, eat, participate in social gatherings, or be able to share a bed with one's partner. Such experiments are orchestrated by people with disabilities, along with their families, friends, colleagues, other allies, or sometimes complete strangers.

In these experimental moments, people with disabilities arguably become rooted within what can be called an ethic of care. Care is a relational, intersubjective process that emerges in the spaces between people; people with chronic conditions and their allies negotiate and adjust to their situation, often with the purpose of enabling the production of a *good life*. Mol et al. (2010) discuss care as a process of putting together different assemblages, leading to the creation of a good, or better, life. Providing care can prompt the transformation of relationships, and the intimacy within, so that new forms of engagement between people, including family members, often result (Warren and Ayton 2015). These engagements are broad-ranging, from helping with toileting and bathing, to wiping faces or helping people to eat, or with mobility and beyond, both at home and in public spaces (Manderson and Warren 2013; Sakellariou 2015a). Carers adapt their understanding of their role – as wife, husband, spouse, son, daughter, friend, or other – to accommodate these activities of care. For Tronto (1993: 102):

> Care implies a reaching out to something other than the self: it is neither self-referring nor self-absorbing. . . . Care implicitly suggests that it will lead to some type of action.

People with disabilities, and the people around them, negotiate what needs to be done in order to produce an outcome that they recognise as good. This aligns with what Jackson (2002: 13) describes as:

> An ongoing struggle to negotiate, reconcile, balance, or mediate these antithetical potentialities of being, such as that no one person . . . ever arrogates agency so completely and permanently to itself that another is reduced to the status of a mere thing.

The anticipated outcomes of these negotiations might appear to be mundane, yet they are crucial in determining how disabled people perceive themselves and how they are recognised by others. The outcomes we refer to here concern the multiple ways people enact their desires and needs, and how they perform the everyday. Here is what we mean by the everyday: the mundane, familiar, and unremarkable *stuff* of everyday worlds, that is, the routine, repetitive, and rhythmic reproduction of social life, including, but not limited to, attending school, meeting up with friends, seeing the doctor, or going out on a date. Everyday worlds are infused with power and politics; 'what is mundane and ordinary to one person might be quite extraordinary for another' (Scott 2009: 2). The contributions in this book, therefore, prioritise the everyday – the micro practices and taken-for-granted social relations that are co-constitutive of the wider complexities and structures of social worlds. For instance, how do people eat, dress, walk, work, interact with others, access resources, and so on? It is our contention that routine, taken-for-granted micro-encounters in the everyday lives of disabled people can produce both hindrances and opportunities.

Focusing on the former, a clear example is the material environment itself (e.g. Boys 2014, 2016), such as absent ramps for people in wheelchairs to access buildings. In this sense, 'different bodily forms, abilities, and disabilities are not independent of architecture, but are mutually constitutive such that "produced space" also forms "social norms"' (Galis 2011: 831). Extending this focus on space and place, Serlin (2010) and Molotch (2010: 16) suggest that there is a 'general hostility to bodily difference, disability included', and that particular sites become zones of exclusion for some disabled people – toilets being one example of this. A clear design challenge for how disabled people use toilets is the set-up, which must cover the diversity of disabilities and ways through which people navigate that space (e.g. people in wheelchairs, people using crutches or a white stick, or people with *invisible* disabilities, among others). Providing access means considering how social and physical contexts work, or not, as 'ensembles of dignity', affording possibilities for enacted performances (Molotch 2010: 16). Toilets, thus, 'teach lessons about identity, embodiment, and ab/normal ways of being in the world' (Slater et al. 2016).

Such ordinary moments of everyday life 'make up the complex and contingent scenarios of dis/abilities that create enabling *and* disabling practices' (Schillmeier 2010: 127). Using the example of how blind people use money, Schillmeier highlights the role of materiality in shaping sociality; money fabricates enabling and disabling spaces of calculation which link bodies, materials, technology, and sensory practices. Likewise, Måseide and Grøttland (2015) put forward that interactions for blind people in public settings indicate the ambiguities of action, morality, and meanings in social space which often do not unfold according to the (moral) principles of the interaction order. One aim of the book, thus, is to make sense of the multiplicity of everyday practices with respect to disablement; 'how bodies, senses, and things connect or disconnect, enable or disable, provoke good as well as bad experiences' (Schillmeier 2010: 118). This includes attending to how non-human elements are woven into the social fabric, that is, how materials and space share the scene in order to stabilise a social order (Latimer 2004; Latour 1991). Assemblages of people, things, space and place, and talk combine to produce and order the social, a phenomenon seldom discussed extensively in empirical accounts of disability. The role of space, place, and materiality is captured by a small number of contributions in this collection, particularly Chapter 2 (Buse and Twigg).

Many chapters in this book also unpack the concept of normalcy, or normality (the terms are used interchangeably throughout), within a context of how disabled people go about their everyday lives. For Davis (1995: 2), normalcy and disability are 'part of the same system' since disability 'defines the negative space the [normal] body must not occupy' (1995: 157). He suggests that we live in a world of norms and how, despite being a universal facet of the human experience, disability is still perceived as a disruption, a rebellion of the visual, of normalcy (Davis 1995, 2014). He argues that, in order to understand disability, we must revisit the concept of 'the norm, the normal body' (Davis 1995: 23). Drawing upon Foucault, Davis (1995: 129) describes normalcy as a location of biopower, and he is critical of the tendency to classify bodies in binary terms and as absolutes, that is, as 'whole and incomplete, abled and disabled, normal and abnormal, functional and dysfunctional'. Speaking of how bodies are 'coded', Davis suggests that categories, such as disabled, are products of a society invested in 'denying the variability of the body' (1995: xv):

> The term disability, as it is commonly and professionally used, is an absolute category without a level or threshold. One is either disabled or not. One cannot be a little disabled any more than one can be a little pregnant. One must view with suspicion any term of such Procrustean dimensions. A concept with such a univalent stranglehold on meaning must contain within it a dark side of power, control, and fear.
>
> (Davis 1995: 1)

According to Davis, the universalising classification of disability is problematic as it denies bodily variation; 'the category "disability" begins to break down when one scrutinises who make up the disabled' (Davis 1995: xv). Disability, indeed, is a relational category; what counts as disabled in different socio-cultural settings varies and is mobilised in diverse ways (Ingstad and Whyte 1995). The interstitial and contested category of disability also operates in and across different spheres (e.g. family, work, home, public spaces), and both blurs and usurps boundaries between such domains. Chapters in this book operate outside of this rigid model by recognising the complexity of different and distinctive conditions – including learning disabilities, dementia, cerebral palsy, polio, and Parkinson's disease – thus undoing a narrow classification which creates fixed categories of existence. What *counts*, for instance, as disabled? Such 'dividing practices' (Foucault 1983: 208) often become forces of 'normalising judgements' (Foucault 1973: 177), which produce classifications and, so, forms of in/exclusion; 'the mad and the sane, the sick and the healthy, the criminals and the "good boys" ' (Foucault 1983: 208). Here, we can consider how powerful discourses – language *and* practices – produce a sense of normalcy, of what is to be expected (Thomas 2017). So how is the category of disability *made up* (Hacking 1999) and *ordered* (Moser 2005)? How does it come into being, and who or what plays a key role in this? What does the everyday reality of *being* dis/abled mean for those involved? How does this intersect with other attributes; for instance, how do sexuality, gender, ethnicity, age, and income shape disabled people's sense of self? How does the everyday interact with how disability is lived, mobilised, and enacted?

Answering these questions, the book's contributions also consider how structural conditions shape the everyday lives of disabled people. Worldwide, the close alignment of social policies with neoliberalism has produced several effects, including the marketisation of health/social care and an increasingly powerful discourse of responsibilisation (Rotarou and Sakellariou 2017a, 2017b; Sakellariou and Rotarou 2017). In this discourse, people are accountable, and indeed responsible, for making their way in the world. As Manderson and Warren (2013) and Trnka and Trundle (2014), among others, have demonstrated, this discourse is often acontextual, treating people as entirely autonomous units with equal amounts of agency to affect change in their lives. This is problematic, as the presence of disability can form a structural disadvantage, leading to reduced economic and social capital. In a neoliberal context where personhood is tightly wound up in notions of economy and commodity, and where *unproductive* and *dependent* citizens are penalised, we must ask how are disabled people valued (or not), and how do they negotiate access to services?

Finally, the book also includes contributions which recognise the positives of disablement, that is, accounts departing from narratives of pity, tragedy, despair, and mortification (Oliver and Barnes 2012), and towards stories of hope, joy, resilience, and resistance. In popular accounts, at least *conventionally*, disability is perceived as something to be pitied as an unvalued bodily state, conjuring troubling discourses of suffering and loss (Sakellariou 2015a). These accounts focus on living *despite* disability, rather than *with* disability. Alternative imaginaries of disability can present the lives of people with disabilities as being dignified and worthy. Various forms of popular media – blogs, autobiographies (of disabled people and their family members), social networking websites, artistic exhibitions and pieces, television and film (e.g. the Reelabilities Film Festival in New York City) – are outlets for enacting positive, visible, and rounded configurations of disability which counter feelings of misfortune or complete disturbance (Ginsburg and Rapp 2015; Thomas 2015).

We must consider, however, what values and meanings – implicit, inadvertent, or otherwise – are embedded in such configurations. For example, in her analysis of affirmative and cheerful media coverage of Madeleine Stuart, an Australian model with Down syndrome, García-Santesmases (2017) argues that such outlets, by heralding her weight loss, promoted the notion of ideal (feminine) body types, and 'normalised' her way of being in patriarchal and ableist language. In short, her appearance was subjected to processes of *normalisation*. In addition, there may be a sense that a positive public face of disability exists in tension with the general treatment of people with disabilities. For instance, Tyler (2013: 207) describes how the opening ceremony of the Paralympic Games in London, 2012, was hailed as 'a watershed moment in the history of disability rights in Britain that promised to challenge stigmatising cultural perceptions and attitudes to disability'. Yet Tyler also highlights how earlier that day, hundreds of disability activists in London protested the event's sponsorship by Atos, a group undertaking assessments to decide whether disability-related welfare benefits are provided to applicants (i.e. to determine if they are *fit for work*, frequently in the absence of suitable employment opportunities for people with disabilities). Here, we see a clear tension between positive messages evoked at cultural events and in popular media, and the current context of austerity-driven welfare cuts, disability hate crime statistics, and the deaths of disabled people after being deemed capable of finding work (Department for Work and Pensions 2015) or through clinical negligence, such as the troubling case of Connor Sparrowhawk [otherwise known as Laughing Boy] (Ryan 2017). We may ask, then, how positive configurations of disability are perceived by disabled people and their allies, along with whether positive depictions of disability are a good thing in themselves, or whether they constitute modes of objectification, devaluation, or a distraction from contemporary concerns (Grue 2016).[2]

The relationship between positive configurations of disability and the pursuit of normalcy is explored further by several chapters within this book, as are the ways in which people with disabilities produce a life they perceive as *inhabitable* (Friedner 2015) and as *good* or *better* (Sakellariou 2015b, 2015c). In order to understand what constitutes *a good life*, we may consider how disabled people try to locate a balance between what they want and what others want for them, between what is available and what is not, and what is at stake for them and for others (Frank 2000). This pursuit of a balance reflects a tension, as Jackson (2013: 43) claims, 'between life as thought and life as lived' – a tension severely impacted by mundane (but important) acts carried out with the intention of creating a way of living and belonging in the world (Das 2014). Locating such a balance may involve using 'practices of care to construct a version of life [disabled people] are satisfied with', creating 'meaning in their life', and/or reframing/redefining what a taken-for-granted practice *is*, or *was* (Sakellariou 2016: 1902). With this in mind, we must consider what happens when the everyday becomes subject to experiment (Mattingly 2013) and, likewise, we should explore how people with disabilities negotiate the disparities between what they *desire* for their lives and what others *think* they need. How do people with disabilities, for example, respond to existential pressures which shape how everyday life, lived counter to the cultural ideal of normalcy, is understood? How does care, or an ethic of care, figure in this? Asking these questions, as several contributions in this volume recognise, aids us in uncovering the multiple ways in which disabled people co-construct a positive way of living through the everyday practices that they engage in.

Book outline

This chapter has intended to provide the theoretical grounding for making sense of subsequent contributions in this collection. In Chapter 2, 'Keeping Up Appearances', Christina Buse and Julia Twigg discuss how people with dementia, together with family carers, negotiate notions of normalcy via their dress practices. Arguing that dress represents a taken-for-granted, everyday moment, but one which is disrupted by disability, Buse and Twigg suggest that clothes prompt a reimagining of ideas of normality and ordinariness. Their work is heavily grounded in ideas of embodiment, materiality (similar to Schillmeier's work on how people who are blind use money), and interactions, in which bodily adornments are constituted as central to a sense of ontological security and *knowing*. They claim that this body work is more than simply maintaining continuity; they identify the potency of passing and managing a public presentation of self, drawing upon the ideas of Goffman, in order to normalise dementia.

Buse and Twigg also explicate how dress provides an opportunity for carers to explicitly demonstrate their capacity to care and cope. As well as convincingly advocating for foregrounding embodiment, emotions, and the everyday within disability studies, their work is a strong starting point for considering how taken-for-granted, corporeal norms become ruptured by disability – and how normalcy and ideas of everyday practices, interactions, and relations are negotiated by disabled people and others.

In Part II, we introduce three chapters on disability in childhood and young adulthood from the UK and US. Drawing upon their collective work in disabled children's childhood studies, Tillie Curran, Kirsty Liddiard, and Katherine Runswick-Cole (Chapter 3) identify how disabled children's lives become frequently eclipsed by the tyranny of the norm and by the everyday and implicit, but powerful, stigmatisation and discrimination of people with disabilities. Yet counter to such narratives, Curran, Liddiard, and Runswick-Cole celebrate the lives of disabled children, describing how they breach narrow, normative assumptions of childhood and development which trouble current imaginaries of children's lives now and in the future. They argue – by citing several studies with disabled children/young people, their family members, and their allies – for reorienting research away from discourses of deficit and lack, and towards attending to the hopes, aspirations, and desires of young people with disabilities.

Continuing a focus on youth, Janice McLaughlin and Edmund Coleman-Fountain (Chapter 4) capture how young people with cerebral palsy participating in a qualitative study in the North-East of England embody, conform to, and/or resist notions of normalcy and difference. Starting from the position that disabled people, like other young people, are involved in a set of everyday embodied practices influenced by an urge to *fit in*, McLaughlin and Coleman-Fountain outline how regulatory dynamics govern if, and how, young people background or foreground embodied difference. Equally, some young people endeavoured to challenge and resist encouragement by others to pursue a sense of ordinariness, of un-remarkability. Here, McLaughlin and Coleman-Fountain view the relationship between disability and identity as shaped by practices which involve both creative expression and normative constraint. This allows the authors, as such, to ask whether wanting to be seen as *normal* has high costs for young people transitioning to adulthood, or whether the term *ordinariness* has now expanded to include people with disabilities.

The concept of normalcy, or what can be seen as *ordinary*, is built upon in Faye Ginsburg and Rayna Rapp's chapter (Chapter 5) on young adults with learning disabilities (along with their families) in the US who are in the process of attempting to transition from high school to adulthood. Drawing on their long-standing ethnographic research on disability over the life-course in New York, Ginsburg and Rapp argue that the switch from formal education to life beyond this institution is often experienced as a crisis. Entering adulthood without appropriate support mechanisms can, for these young adults, be experienced as a *transition to nowhere*. Citing interview data, they convey young people's sense of a puncture in their life-course, not dissimilar to how medical sociologists describe the onset and experience of chronic illness – namely as a 'biographical disruption' (Bury 1982) and/or a 'loss of self' (Charmaz 1983). The families in Ginsburg and Rapp's study expressed their disappointment and anger about the absence of adequate support and guidance for life beyond the education system. And yet, as Ginsburg and Rapp outline here and elsewhere (Ginsburg and Rapp 2015), alternative social movements are emerging in different outlets across widely distributed networks of people with shared experiences of disability. For Ginsburg and Rapp, these social formations constitute an emergent form of recognition of people who are disabled which moves away from older narratives of pity and shame, and towards newer ones in which new social and public imaginaries of human difference are erected. This process, by creating a *new normal*, enables the creation and occupation of inhabitable worlds for young adults with a disability, giving them a *future* as well as a meaningful *present* (Latimer 1997; Thomas 2015).

The contributions presented in Part III of the book all analyse the notion of *the good life* in the context of disability. Chapter 6 – written by Helen Errington, Karen Soldatic, and Louisa Smith – charts Helen's story as a disabled feminist activist living in Australia who had a childhood diagnosis of polio, to consider what constitutes a good life. Helen's life narrative conveys the differing modalities of reflexive experimentation which allowed her to redefine what is *good* and *normal*. Describing her early years, she explains her experiences of diagnosis, her life in an institution and in school, her transition into adulthood and employment, her activism, and her friendships and sexual relationships. In so doing, Helen and her co-authors distinguish how Helen's embodied practices of everyday life illuminate the ways in which disability can enable the emergence of inclusive forms of citizenship and belonging.

In Chapter 7, Nikki Wedgwood, Louisa Smith, and Russell Shuttleworth tell the life story of Jay, a young woman living in Australia who has cerebral palsy. The authors describe Jay's creative self-management of support workers, namely those who 'do life *with* me'. The authors locate Jay's story in a body of literature which explicates the nature of care and dependency, power dynamics between *carer* and *cared-for*, and the politics of care services (and often the retrenchment of various resources). While acknowledging the value of this literature, Wedgwood, Smith, and Shuttleworth critically consider how people requiring daily personal assistance negotiate their support in a disablist society which treasures and rewards specific forms of autonomy associated with normative bodies. Through presenting Jay's account of everyday life, the authors unpack how the inherent complexities of support are traversed, how this support is infused with an ethic of care, and how Jay's responses represent a creative attempt to navigate the move into adult life.

Returning to the question of how people carve out a good life *with* (not *despite*) disability and the conditions producing it, Narelle Warren and Darshini Ayton (Chapter 8) draw upon their longitudinal research, also from Australia, to determine how people with Parkinson's disease must (re)negotiate a sense of normalcy on a daily basis. With the day-to-day being unpredictable, living a good life requires a constant reworking, in which the embodied experience of disability, and of the subsequent ambiguity, obliges people to reconcile understandings and anticipations of the self. Warren and Ayton's chapter, in turn, examines how people with Parkinson's disease manage this phenomenological uncertainty, as well as how resilience permeates resultant configurations of self.

In Part IV, 'Global Disability Politics', we introduce two chapters drawing upon studies from low- and middle-income countries. In Chapter 9, Maria Berghs outlines her ethnographic research in Sierra Leone following the Ebola crisis. She argues for the inclusion of *ordinary ethics* in discussions of disability and impairment, claiming that ethical practices during the Ebola epidemic were unmade in relation to caring relationships and the social obligations of family members. Berghs illustrates how, post-Ebola, disability is represented as a form of afflictive kinship (as family bonds have been frayed by Ebola). She also demonstrates how a biomedical reconstruction of Ebola – where, for instance, *survivors* are urged to participate in clinical trials – similarly, if inadvertently, discriminates against those with the condition.

In Chapter 10, Hannah Kuper, Goli Hashemi, and Mary Wickenden recognise how the terms *disability* and *health* are commonly, and unhelpfully, conflated. Moreover, they make clear how disabled people are disproportionately affected by poor access to healthcare and often experience worse health outcomes. While not necessarily *ill*, people who are disabled may be more vulnerable to poor health, owing to vast structural inequalities together with complications of their own impairment. This increased vulnerability to poor health creates greater needs for healthcare among disabled people, yet these individuals often encounter problems when attempting to access such resources. Using examples from Guatemala, Malawi, the UK, and the US, the authors capture how certain people encounter, or not, relevant and accessible services. Spelling out the effects which these inequities have upon disabled people's everyday lives, Kuper, Hashemi, and Wickenden end their chapter with a plea for equitable access to health services and for recognising and upholding disabled people's rights to good health.

Taken together, all of the contributions presented in this book are located within both new and familiar debates around embodiment, stigma, gender, identity, inequality, care, ethics, choice, materiality, youth, and representation. This book, then, identifies disability as a concern not simply for disability studies scholars, but for academics from different disciplinary backgrounds including sociology, anthropology, humanities, public health, allied health professions, science and technology studies, social work, and social policy. While work opening-up and enriching the topic of disability continues to grow and flourish, we hope that this book provides strong evidence of the need for a critical and long-lasting dialogue between disability studies and other academic fields.

Notes

1 Thomas (2010: 38) suggests that medical sociology and disability studies have been at 'loggerheads on the disability question' since the 1980s. Acknowledging this acrimonious disciplinary divide, she urges medical sociology to take the disability studies scholarship more seriously and reconsider ideas that she perceives to be 'medico-centric and disablist' (2010: 38). Another example of disciplinary disconnect is disability studies and social gerontology, which have mostly developed separately over the years, but which clearly share many interests.
2 While this has been addressed by some chapters in this book, it is a budding area of interest and deserves further critical attention.

References

Boys, J. 2014. *Doing Disability Differently: An Alternative Handbook on Architecture, Dis/Ability and Designing for Everyday Life.* London: Routledge.

Boys, J. 2016. Architecture, place and the 'care-full' design of everyday life. In: Bates, C., Imrie, R. and Kullman, K. eds. *Care and Design: Bodies, Buildings, Cities.* Hoboken, NJ: Wiley-Blackwell, pp. 155–177.

Bury, M. 1982. Chronic illness as biographical disruption. *Sociology of Health and Illness* 4(2), pp. 167–182.

Charmaz, K. 1983. Loss of self: a fundamental form of suffering in the chronically ill. *Sociology of Health and Illness* 5(2), pp. 168–195.

Das, V. 2014. Action, expression, and everyday life: recounting household events. In: Das, V., Jackson, M., Kleinman, A. and Singh, B. eds. *The Ground Between; Anthropologists Engage Philosophy.* Durham, NC: Duke University Press, pp. 279–306.

Davis, F. 1961. Deviance disavowal: the management of strained interaction by the visibly handicapped. *Social Problems* 9(2), pp. 120–132.

Davis, L. J. 1995. *Enforcing Normalcy; Disability, Deafness, and the Body.* New York: Verso.

Davis, L. J. 2014. *The End of Normal: Identity in a Biocultural Era.* Ann Arbor: University of Michigan Press.

Department for Work and Pensions. 2015. *Mortality Statistics: Employment and Support Allowance, Incapacity Benefit, or Severe Disablement Allowance.* Sheffield: Statistical Services, Department for Work and Pensions.

Foucault, M. 1973. *The Birth of the Clinic: An Archaeology of Medical Perception.* London: Tavistock.

Foucault, M. 1983. The subject and power. In: Dreyfus, H. L. and Rabinow, P. eds. *Michael Foucault: Beyond Structuralism and Hermeneutics.* Chicago: University of Chicago Press, pp. 208–226.

Frank, G. 2000. *Venus on Wheels: Two Decades of Dialogue on Disability, Biography, and Being Female.* Berkeley: University of California Press.

Friedner, M. 2015. *Valuing Deaf Worlds in India.* New Brunswick, NJ: Rutgers University Press.

Galis, V. 2011. Enacting disability: how can science and technology studies inform disability studies? *Disability and Society* 26(7), pp. 825–838.

García-Santesmases, A. 2017. Modelling functional diversity, the case of Madeleine Stuart. *A Montra/The Window.* Weblog [Online]. Available at: http://amontra-thewindow.com/2017/03/15/modeling-functional-diversity-the-case-of-madeline-stuart/ [Accessed: 23 November 2017].

Garfinkel, H. 1967. *Studies in Ethnomethodology*. Englewood Cliffs, NJ: Prentice-Hall.

Garland-Thomson, R. 2009. *Staring: How We Look*. Oxford: Oxford University Press.

Ginsburg, F. and Rapp, R. 2015. Making disability count: demography, futurity, and the making of disability publics. *Somatosphere*. Weblog [Online]. Available at: http://somatosphere.net/2015/05/making-disability-count-demography-futurity-and-the-making-of-disabilitypublics.html [Accessed: 23 November 2017].

Goffman, E. 1959. *The Presentation of Self in Everyday Life*. New York: Anchor Books.

Goffman, E. 1963. *Stigma: Notes on the Management of Spoiled Identity*. New York: Simon and Schuster.

Goffman, E. 1967. *Interaction Ritual: Essays in Face-to-Face Behaviour*. New York: Anchor Books.

Gray, D. 2002. Everybody just freezes, everybody is just embarrassed: felt and enacted stigma among parents of children with high functioning autism. *Sociology of Health and Illness* 24(6), pp. 734–749.

Grue, J. 2016. The problem with inspiration porn: a tentative definition and a provisional critique. *Disability and Society* 31(6), pp. 838–849.

Hacking, I. 1999. *The Social Construction of What?* Cambridge, MA: Harvard University Press.

Ingstad, B. and Whyte, S. 1995. *Disability and Culture*. Berkeley: University of California Press.

Jackson, M. 2002. *The Politics of Storytelling: Violence, Transgression, and Intersubjectivity*. Copenhagen: Museum Tusculanum Press.

Jackson, M. 2013. *Lifeworlds: Essays in Existential Anthropology*. Chicago: University of Chicago Press.

Latimer, J. E. 1997. Giving patients a future: the constituting of classes in an acute medical unit. *Sociology of Health and Illness* 19(2), pp. 160–185.

Latimer, J. E. 2004. Commanding materials: (re)legitimating authority in the context of multi-disciplinary work. *Sociology* 38(4), pp. 757–775.

Latour, B. 1991. Technology is society made durable. In: Law, J. ed. *A Sociology of Monsters: Essays on Power, Technology and Domination*. London: Routledge, pp. 103–131.

MacRae, H. 1999. Managing courtesy stigma: the case of Alzheimer's disease. *Sociology of Health and Illness* 21(1), pp. 54–70.

Manderson, L. and Warren, N. 2013. *Reframing Disability and Quality of Life: A Global Perspective*. Berlin: Springer.

Måseide, P. and Grøttland, H. 2015. Enacting blind spaces and spatialities: a sociological study of blindness related to space, environment and interaction. *Symbolic Interaction* 38(4), pp. 594–610.

Mattingly, C. 2013. Moral selves and moral scenes: narrative experiments in everyday life. *Ethnos* 78(3), pp. 301–327.

Mol, A. M., Moser, I. and Pols, J. 2010. *Care in Practice: On Tinkering in Clinics, Homes and Farms*. New Brunswick, NJ: Transaction.

Molotch, H. 2010. Introduction: learning from the loo. In: Molotch, H. and Norén, L. eds. *Toilet: Public Restrooms and the Politics of Sharing*. New York: New York University Press, pp. 1–20

Moser, I. 2005. On becoming disabled and articulating alternatives. *Cultural Studies* 19(6), pp. 667–700.

Nijhof, G. 1995. Parkinson's disease as a problem of shame in public appearance. *Sociology of Health and Illness* 17(2), pp. 193–205.

Oliver, M. 1996. *Understanding Disability: From Theory to Practice*. Basingstoke: Palgrave Macmillan.

Oliver, M. and Barnes, C. 2012. *The New Politics of Disablement*. Basingstoke: Palgrave Macmillan.

Rotarou, E. S. and Sakellariou, D. 2017a. Access to health care in an age of austerity: disabled people's unmet needs in Greece. *Critical Public Health* [Online First].

Rotarou, E. S. and Sakellariou, D. 2017b. Inequalities in access to health care for people with disabilities in Chile: the limits of universal health coverage. *Critical Public Health* 27(5), pp. 604–616.

Ryan, S. 2008. 'People don't do odd, do they?' Mothers making sense of the reactions of others towards their learning disabled children in public spaces. *Children Geographies* 3(3), pp. 291–305.

Ryan, S. 2017. *Justice for Laughing Boy: Connor Sparrowhawk – A Death by Indifference*. London: Jessica Kingsley Publishers.

Sakellariou, D. 2015a. Creating in/abilities for eating. *Somatosphere*. Weblog [Online]. Available at: http://somatosphere.net/2015/06/creating-inabilities-for-eating [Accessed: 23 November 2017].

Sakellariou, S. 2015b. Home modifications and ways of living well. *Medical Anthropology: Cross-Cultural Studies in Health and Illness* 34(5), pp. 456–469.

Sakellariou, S. 2015c. Towards the construction of a nicer life: subjectivity and the logic of choice. *Anthropology in Action: Journal for Applied Anthropology in Policy and Practice* 22(1), pp. 46–53.

Sakellariou, D. 2016. Enacting varieties of subjectivity through practices of care: a story of living with Motor Neuron Disease. *Qualitative Health Research* 26(14), pp. 1902–1910.

Sakellariou, D. and Rotarou, E. S. 2017. The effects of neoliberal policies on access to healthcare for people with disabilities. *International Journal for Equity in Health* 16(1), p. 199.

Schillmeier, M. 2007. Dis/abling spaces of calculation: blindness and money in everyday life. *Environment and Planning D: Society and Space* 25(4), pp. 594–609.

Schillmeier, M. 2010. *Rethinking Disability: Bodies, Senses, and Things*. London: Routledge.

Scott, S. 2009. *Making Sense of Everyday Life*. Cambridge: Polity Press.

Serlin, D. 2010. Pissing without pity: disability, gender, and the public toilet. In: Molotch, H. and Norén, L. eds. *Toilet: Public Restrooms and the Politics of Sharing*. New York: New York University Press, pp. 167–185.

Slater, J., Jones, C. and Procter, L. 2016. School toilets: queer, disabled bodies and gendered lessons of embodiment. *Gender and Education* [Online First].

Thomas, C. 2010. Medical sociology and disability theory. In: Scambler, G. and Scambler, S. eds. *New Directions in the Sociology of Chronic and Disabling Conditions: Assaults on the Lifeworld*. Basingstoke: Palgrave Macmillan, pp. 37–56.

Thomas, G. M. 2014. Cooling the mother out: revisiting and revising Goffman's account. *Symbolic Interaction* 37(2), pp. 283–299.

Thomas, G. M. 2015. Un/inhabitable worlds: the curious case of Down's syndrome. *Somatosphere*. Weblog [Online]. Available at: http://somatosphere.net/2015/07/uninhabitable-worlds-the-curious-case-of-downs-syndrome.html [Accessed: 23 November 2017].

Thomas, G. M. 2017. *Down's Syndrome Screening and Reproductive Politics: Care, Choice, and Disability in the Prenatal Clinic*. London: Routledge.

Trnka, S. and Trundle, C. 2014. *Competing Responsibilities: The Ethics and Politics of Contemporary Life*. Durham, NC: Duke University Press.

Tronto, N. 1993. *Moral Boundaries: A Political Argument for an Ethic of Care*. London: Routledge.

Tyler, I. 2013. *Revolting Subjects: Social Abjection and Resistance in Great Britain*. London: Zed Books.

Warren, N. and Ayton, D. 2015. Loneliness as social suffering: social participation, quality of life, and chronic stroke. In: Anderson, R. E. ed. *World Suffering and Quality of Life*. Berlin: Springer, pp. 159–170.

Chapter 2

Keeping up appearances

Family carers and people with dementia negotiating normalcy through dress practice

Christina Buse and Julia Twigg

Introduction

Dress forms part of the tacit, taken-for-granted routines that constitute everyday life, but can be dys-rupted (Leder 1990) in the context of illness or disability – in this case, dementia.[1] This chapter situates dress practice as part of managing the rupture caused by dementia in the everyday lives of people with dementia and family carers, focusing on the renegotiation of ideas of *normality* and *ordinariness*. It begins by exploring interconnections between ageing, dementia, and disability studies in relation to concepts of embodiment, everyday life, and normalcy, before exploring the relevance of dress studies to these discussions. We then draw on ethnographic data from the *Dementia and Dress* study, an Economic and Social Research Council (ESRC)-funded project, described below (Buse and Twigg 2014, 2015, 2016). Within this data, dress is situated as part of renegotiating ordinariness and ontological security through daily routines and practices, and maintaining continuity in appearance. We go on to consider how dress also becomes incorporated into efforts to *pass* and manage the public presentation of self in ways that can normalise dementia, and some of the tensions embedded within this (Goffman 1963). The chapter concludes by arguing for the potential of dress as part of efforts to foreground embodiment and the everyday within disability studies, acting as a lens for tracing how corporeal norms are negotiated in everyday life. We further argue for the extension of a 'carnal politics of the everyday' (Paterson and Hughes 1999: 597) to dementia studies, with attention to dress as part of this.

Embodying ageing, dementia, and disability studies

The fields of disability studies and social gerontology have developed separately, so that discussions of later life are generally absent from collections on disability and vice versa (Oldman 2002). Yet it is argued that the social model of disability has much to contribute to the study of ageing, in terms of understanding the experiences of older people with disability, addressing issues of ageism, the physical environment, and offering a model for collective action (Putman

2002). Similar arguments have been made for the application of the social model of disability to the experiences of people living with dementia. In relation to dementia, this extension has proved significant in challenging the overreliance on biomedical/psychological models, allowing for a greater recognition of the socio-cultural context of the condition (Downs 2000). The *social model of dementia*, led by the work of Kitwood (1997), aims to focus on capabilities instead of losses, recognising the deleterious impact of social discrimination and marginalisation, and emphasising the importance of listening to the voices of people with dementia (Gilliard et al. 2005). The social model of disability also underpins recent thinking about collective action among people with dementia, resonating with the citizenship agenda in dementia studies (Bartlett and O'Connor 2007). This agenda aims to politicise dementia studies, drawing attention to the rights of people with dementia as equal citizens, and instances of discrimination. However, there are concerns that an emphasis on dementia activism may marginalise those who are not verbally fluent, visible, and confident (Bartlett 2012a).

In both ageing studies and disability studies, there has been a shift towards the recognition of the role of embodiment as part of understanding everyday lived experiences. Both the social model of disability and social gerontology in earlier stages tended to marginalise the role of the body, preferring to foreground the social and cultural determinants of old age and disability. More recent work, reflecting wider developments in body studies (Shilling 2013; Crossley 2001), has brought the body fully into view, emphasising the ways in which it is culturally constituted, and exploring the complex interplay of factors – social and physiological – in the constitution of age and disability (e.g. Davis 1995; Featherstone and Hepworth 1991; Gilleard and Higgs 2000; Gullette 1997; Hughes 2007; Paterson and Hughes 1999). For example, Kumar (2004: 31) describes embodiment as 'the site where ageing, disability and masculinity intersect'. Her work explores the disruption of ontological security following the onset of a disability in later life, and the embodied strategies older men deploy in order to maintain continuity of self. Other research has highlighted interconnections between ageing and disability in relation to changing experiences and awareness of the impaired body over the life-course (Deegan 2010; Williams and Barlow 1998).

Dementia studies is also beginning to incorporate concepts of embodiment as part of understanding the everyday experiences of *living with* dementia (Martin et al. 2013). A focus on embodiment is being used to extend arguments for the citizenship of people with dementia, critiquing notions of citizenship and personhood that rely heavily on language and cognitive ability (Boyle 2014). Kontos (2004) argues that people with advanced dementia can demonstrate intentionality and agency through embodied, habitual actions that reflect habitus and social location. Taylor (2008) challenges the focus on the capacity of the person with dementia to recognise and name family members, arguing that interpersonal connections continue to be enacted at an emotional and embodied level. Research by Phinney and Chesla (2003) has also highlighted the significance of the *lived body* for understanding experiences of dementia, though their work by contrast emphasises the way that dementia disrupts everyday embodied practices and relations to objects.

Through attending to lived experiences of bodily impairment, this body of work draws attention to how dynamics of normalcy are negotiated in everyday life. In disability studies, research has explored how people maintain a sense of ordinariness (Coleman-Fountain 2017) or *feeling normal* in the face of bodily impairment (Deegan 2010). This includes the day-to-day management of the impaired body, and creating new ways of *doing daily living* (Hansen and Philo 2007). This research parallels literature in the sociology of health and illness, which highlights efforts to retain a sense of ordinariness and continuity (Gregory 2005; Prout et al. 1999) in the face of the 'biographical disruption' caused by chronic illness (Bury 1982: 167). However, disability studies literature also demonstrates how a sense of *feeling normal* fluctuates across different contexts (Deegan 2010), as disabling spaces and social interactions remind the person of bodily impairment, reflecting Leder's idea of bodily dys-appearance (Paterson and Hughes 1999). This includes the pressures to normalise the impaired body in everyday spaces in response to the non-disabled gaze, managing bodily appearance and movements in order to pass and perform as normal (Hansen and Philo 2007). As argued by Paterson and Hughes (1999: 608), oppression is not simply produced at a structural level, but 'is made manifest in corporeal and intercorporeal norms and conventions' which are enacted within 'everyday encounters'.

Such concepts of normalcy also hold significance for dementia, which Schillmeier (2014: 44) argues 'troubles the normal, the given and expected personal and social life', disrupting affective and embodied relations to objects and people. In this way, he suggests, experiences of dementia can draw attention to normalcy as a mode of social ordering and an ongoing collective achievement. Dementia also raises particular issues concerning pressures to *normalise* the body, including dress and appearance, to which we now turn.

Dress practice, normalcy, and normalisation

Dress is central to the social experience of embodiment, providing a direct interface between the body and the public realm. Entwistle (2000: 11) describes dressing as a 'situated bodily practice', involving 'both an intimate experience of the body and a public presentation of it'. In the context of disability, everyday dress practices can become disrupted, providing challenges both in terms of the physicality of dressing and the symbolic transgression that assistance with dressing entails (Hayman 2009). Research on disability has highlighted people's capacity to identify strategies and creative individual solutions for managing dress, thus retaining possibilities for a continuity of identity and self-expression (Hayman 2009; Linthicum 2006). For instance, Hayman (2009: 630) gives the example of a male participant 'casually slinging' an expensive suit jacket on the back of his power-chair when he was in the workplace, creating the image of smart, masculine dress, while avoiding the difficulties of putting the jacket directly on his body.

Dress is also entangled with issues of normalcy and normalisation. Historical research on dress and learning disability has highlighted the stigmatising nature of institutional dress, with unfashionable and ill-fitting garments signifying difference/disempowerment and constructing disabled people as asexual (Linthicum 2006). In contrast, the normalisation movement called for the integration of people with learning disabilities into *normal* social life, emphasising the importance of maintaining positive social roles for devalued groups (Wolfensberger 1972, 1983). Dress and appearance were emphasised as part of maintaining a positive social image, and avoiding an appearance that would mark the person out as deviant. More recently, though, the movement has been subject to critique for presenting an over-normalised model of behaviour that imposes standards of conformity as a 'condition of acceptance' (Yates et al. 2008: 249). Research on learning disability and embodiment has also highlighted tensions around choice and control in an institutional context, with a tendency of staff to interfere with the person's decisions around dress (McCarthy 1998).

Dynamics of normalcy and efforts to pass (Hansen and Philo 2007) are also played out in relation to everyday dress practice in disability. Fashion and dress, as Simmel (1904) argued, embody a fundamental tension between a desire to fit in, and a desire to emphasise uniqueness and self-expression. Dress can thus be used to reveal, as well as to conceal, aspects of identity, including ones in relation to class, gender, sexuality, and disability (Banim et al. 2001; Woodward 2007). These dynamics have been explored in the context of disability and illness with Van Wersch (2001), for instance, examining how women negotiate decisions around revealing, versus concealing, the impaired body through dress and prosthetics. Linthicum (2006) has shown that there is a different relationship to dress and visibility among individuals with a lifelong disability compared with those who are more recently disabled. She found a stronger emphasis on dress as a way of camouflaging impairment among the more recently disabled, and a greater focus on self-expression through dress among those with a long-term disability.

Like intellectual disability, dementia raises issues around choice and control in relation to dress and the normalisation of bodies in both institutional and home contexts (Buse and Twigg 2014, 2015; Twigg 2010). Dress practices can be disrupted in dementia, with difficulties relating to sequencing, recognition, and concentration, as well as managing fastenings and difficult garments (Feyereisen et al. 1999). This can create challenges in living up to social norms of acceptable dress which can extend beyond the domestic context, disrupting attempts to pass in the wider community. In an article John Keady co-authored with his father who has dementia (Keady and Keady 2005: 36), his father recounts the embarrassment caused by incorrect dress in public spaces, realising he had been 'wearing the wrong shoes for several months' and 'having a panic attack in a department store's public toilet when I put my underpants on back-to-front and realised what I had done'. Bartlett's (2012b) work on dementia activism shows the power of correct dress – in her case, the wearing of a suit by a man – in affecting how the person is seen, allowing them to continue to draw on the embodied status that suits convey (Breward 2016) and to counter preconceptions of people with dementia. It is these issues around constructions of *normalcy* and *ordinariness* through everyday embodied practice that we will now focus on, turning to the findings of the Dementia and Dress study.

Introducing the study

Dementia and Dress was a two-year ESRC-funded study conducted between 2012 and 2014, exploring the role of clothing and dress in the everyday lives of people with dementia, family carers, and care-workers. The research was conducted across three care homes and fifteen domestic households in Kent, UK. The sample included thirty-two case studies of people with dementia: fifteen living in their own homes, and seventeen in care home settings. People with dementia were sampled purposively to explore differences relating to class, gender, and stage of dementia, and included nine men and twenty-three women from different occupational backgrounds and at different stages of dementia (from mild to severe). The study also included interviews and observations with twenty-nine family carers and relatives, and twenty-eight members of care home staff. This chapter focuses on the accounts of family carers and people with dementia, focusing in particular on the domestic context and the dynamics of everyday life.

   Data were gathered using ethnographic methods including observations, qualitative interviews, and visual and sensory methods such as *wardrobe interviews* (Banim and Guy 2001). This involves interviewing the person alongside their wardrobe, using clothes as material prompts for eliciting discussion. In domestic households, participants generally chose to conduct wardrobe interviews jointly with family carers, enabling the carer to provide support during the interview, and facilitating direct observation of interactions and negotiations around dress (Valentine 1999). Observations facilitated inclusion of people with more advanced dementia who were unable to participate in more formal interviews (Hubbard et al. 2003). The study received ethical approval from the Social Care Research Ethics committee. Every effort was made to involve the person with dementia in the consent process, explaining the study verbally as well as using adapted information sheets with visual images. For people unable to give informed consent, we sought the advice of a personal consultee, generally a family member. For all participants, consent was treated as ongoing and the respective researcher responded to verbal or non-verbal indicators of assent or dissent (Black et al. 2010).

Daily routines, dress, and negotiating ordinariness

Dress and dressing are part of the 'day-to-day activities' that underpin daily life, actively producing a sense of the 'normality of the ordinary and the everyday' (Gregory 2005: 374). Dementia can disrupt these taken-for-granted routines and *body techniques* (Mauss 1979). As one family carer, Cora, explains regarding her husband:

> I don't think he could do the . . . the bow [on shoelaces] now because he has a job with his dressing gown tie. . . . Some things I think would come automatic, like playing the organ but no, it's completely gone and yet he's played it for what? Thirty-five years and all the chords he knew off by heart, they've gone. You know, because it's immediate memory.

As Cora describes, the embodied tacit knowledge involved in dressing becomes disrupted in the context of dementia, and clothes as material objects are no longer ready-to-hand (Heidegger 1962). Dress can therefore bring the impaired body and a sense of 'feeling disabled' to the 'forefront of everyday life' (Deegan 2010: 25). For Joe, difficulties with dressing prompted reflection on his decreasing cognitive and physical abilities: 'Invariably now, well you see I can't do it. I used to, used to be no problem at all'. As found by Kabel and colleagues (2016), aspects of clothing such as shoelaces, socks, and fastenings can be particularly challenging in the context of disability, posing apparel related barriers which contribute to disablement.

Dementia also alters the temporality of dressing. Family carers described this in terms of 'slowing down', and altering taken-for-granted bodily movements. As one family carer, Jane, said: 'Everything takes so long because it's slow motion'. Another couple joked:

BARBARA: If we are going out, I should say it takes two hours to get both of us ready. . . . It takes an hour and half to get him ready, and ten minutes for me [laughs].
JOE: Used to be the other way round!

As Phinney and Chesla (2003) also found, the flow of taken-for-granted activities is disrupted by dementia, with bodily movements becoming halting and tentative. Research on physical disability similarly highlights concerns with timing and slowness, which signify bodily difference, with everyday activities like dressing perceived to take 'longer than is "normal" or acceptable' (Hansen and Philo 2007: 498). Paterson and Hughes (1999: 605, 607) argue that time 'is the primary criteria of exclusion and discrimination', with the status of social competence withdrawn from bodies that fail to live up to 'norms of speech, timing and movement'.

People with dementia and family carers deployed a range of practices to manage these temporal disruptions, engaging in the 'embodied art of managing the time, space and speed realities of "doing" daily living' (Hansen and Philo 2007: 497). Adjustments to daily routines included planning ahead and laying out clothing the night before as well as allowing additional time, particularly if going out. The potentially disrupted and fluid character of such activity is well captured by Davies' (1994) concept of *process time* which reflects the unpredictable, non-linear nature of care processes, and their interweaving with the body. As a result, the act of dressing was felt to be something which could not be rushed. This slower and more uncertain temporality of dressing seemed more accepted by retired couples, perhaps reflecting changing meanings of time in retirement, associated with a sense of freedom from fixed routines and *slowing down* (Roche 1989; Tsuji 2005). As retired family carer, Fred, claimed: 'Time doesn't matter'.

To a significant extent, ontological security rests on the familiarity of daily routines, repetition, and rituals (Giddens 1992). For people with dementia, maintaining these can be important to coping with the condition (Keady and Keady 2005), and retaining a sense of normality. In the face of the disruption of everyday temporality, spousal carers tried to embed dressing into new routines which were relational and embodied. Female carers in particular talked about washing and dressing alongside their husbands, as one woman, Barbara, said: 'It's quicker . . . than trying to wash in relays, because he keeps calling me. I wash my face and then go and run some hot water and wash the rest of him'. Spousal carers often re-embedded dressing within other household routines and activities that were associated with relaxation and security, such as reading or watching television, as Cora (family carer) describes:

> And then I usually help him undress in the evening. We go in there together, don't we, and I put my dressing gown on as well at about eight [PM] and then we come back and watch something on the telly [television].

These routines reconstitute a sense of familiarity and continuity with existing relationships. However, other carers felt that the unpredictable bodies of relatives with dementia were less amenable to being routinised, as family carer, Grant, explained: 'You try and keep them in a routine but it just doesn't work. You know, you have to go with the moods'. Temporal disorientation means that routines can be disrupted and difficult to maintain (Bartlett 2012a), with carers describing relatives with dementia who would go to bed in the afternoon or get up in the middle of the night and start dressing, often putting on clothing in the wrong order.

For some family carers and people with dementia, helping the person to continue dressing independently was described as an important part of keeping things *normal*. This was facilitated by the management and spatial ordering of the material environment, including the micro-space of the wardrobe. As argued by Woodward (2007), ordering our wardrobes can be a strategy for the ordering and management of our everyday lives. In the context of dementia, family carers took on the responsibility of this, placing frequently worn habitual clothes to the front of the wardrobe so they were accessible, but also circulating the order of clothing so that the person did not wear the same thing every day. Family carers also engaged in *aesthetic ordering* (Woodward 2007), placing items of clothing together co-ordinated in terms of colour and style. As family carer Greg said, he and his wife had ordered his mother-in-law Pearl's wardrobe 'to help her make choices and also in the drawers put colour-co-ordinated, if you like, sweaters and t-shirts that matched'. Pearl agreed this helped make dressing easier to manage: 'They've arranged all my . . . my clothes, you know, in colour co-ordinate. . . . All the colours that go with each other on the bottom so that I don't have to reach up'. Ordering the wardrobe aesthetically makes dressing easier, enabling the person to 'get it right' (Woodward 2007: 44). Such strategies of tailoring and adjusting the home environment to disability act as 'recipes which create and maintain situations for "feeling normal"' (Deegan 2010: 33). Yet such ordering can also mean that the family carer has taken over aesthetic decisions involved in self-presentation, limiting the agency of the person with dementia in terms of their dress and appearance.

What constitutes ordinariness or normality is differentiated, however, according to gender and generation. In relationships which involve a wife caring for her husband, assistance with dress was more in keeping with traditional gendered roles, which often continue into retirement (Loretto and Vickerstaff 2012; Szinovacz 2000). Men with dementia spoke more readily about being assisted with dress, at least by their wife, saying things like 'I couldn't manage without her' or she 'looks after me on that score'. In contrast, women with dementia tended to minimise or dismiss any difficulties; as one woman said, they are 'just part of life', emphasising the ordinariness of these experiences (Prout et al. 1999). Another woman, Diane, dismissed such concerns as reflecting her husband's inability to cope with illness: 'I don't let it spoil my life – I try not to. It affects my husband more than it does me but . . . his family doesn't do illnesses very well'.

In relation to laundry and shopping, the pattern of activity was affected by earlier gendered roles. As family carer Jane explained, she had 'always done the washing and ironing', while Cora described how her husband has 'always left [clothes shopping] to me really'. Therefore, such caring activities are subsumed within gendered family practices 'seen as just part of the "normal" task of running the home' (Gregory 2005: 374). In contrast, men taking on these roles was frequently viewed as a disruption of normal life for both parties. George stated that he had only taken on laundry activities 'since the illness' and 'I'm not doing it because I particularly want to, or enjoy it'. His wife Diane, by contrast, saw his taking on these tasks as unnecessary interference: 'He just gave up work early and he just took over'. Nonetheless, some men would get their wife or mother to help with laundry activities, as a way of maintaining normal gendered routines. Grant tries to involve his Mum in 'washing day' on a Thursday, although her twin tub no longer worked and he had to take the fuse out of her iron for safety: 'We just go through the pretence and I bring it all home and do it'. Housework had been important to his Mum, who even 'used to iron handkerchiefs', and he felt that involvement in these activities helped her to 'keep in a routine'.

In intergenerational and cross-gender caring relationships, assistance with dress that required intimate hands-on care and exposure to the unclothed body was experienced as a disruption of the ordinary, transgressing norms of family relations and body privacy (Isaksen 2002; Twigg 2000). One family carer, Grant, described the difficulties of assisting his Mum with dress:

> The main problem I have is getting her to change, and being . . . like her son I can't get too involved. . . . She doesn't change very often, and I was trying to get her to change her underclothes, and she ended up with her dirty clothes on and still two pairs of clean drawers on top of that. And I'm trying to do it all through a closed door.

Grant tried to reassert boundaries of bodily privacy through reconstructing material and spatial boundaries, as he says above: 'I'm trying to do it all through a closed door'. This was in contrast with couples, where assistance with dress was consistent with relations of intimacy. As family carer, Cora, said: 'We know each other so well. We've been together thirty-seven years and neither of us are embarrassed at all'. Her husband, Douglas, agreed: 'You can't be shy about it'.

The discomfort of assistance with dress could be confounded by the transgressive nature of dealing with gendered garments. Grant describes the embarrassment of 'bra shopping for the first time in my life'. Other male carers (including husbands) described the particular difficulties of tights and bras. This partly related to the physicality of manoeuvring them onto the body, involving gendered practices and body techniques, but it also related to the way handling such garments was transgressive for men. As one family carer, Frank, said: 'I mean all these are things I never even thought of: gussets'. Taking on a caring role could be discontinuous with men's earlier histories and gendered identities. As family carer, Grant, who had originally worked as a labourer, explained: '[This] isn't my game at all, nursing . . . You know, it isn't my history'.

Male carers engaged in different strategies for managing role reversals and transgressions, in order to re-establish a sense of ordinariness (Gregory 2005). Some male carers resigned themselves to new roles. As Grant said, regarding his experience of bra shopping: 'That was quite embarrassing, but I got over it in the end'. He resituated his new role within normal family relationships of caring, saying 'this is the family, mate! You know, there isn't anyone else' and there was 'no choice' in terms of his 'conscience'. In other cases, carers made material adjustments to the dress of the person with dementia. A number of male carers, for example, switched to dressing their wife or mother in trousers to save 'messing about with tights'. Such material adjustments, however, raise questions regarding continuity of embodied identity, to which we now turn.

Maintaining familiarity and continuity through dress

Maintaining a sense of normality and ordinariness was not only a matter of temporal routines and practices, but also of maintaining continuity in the person's appearance and personal aesthetic (Woodward 2007). Dress practice therefore becomes significant as part of everyday 'acts of construction and reconstruction' which 'create a continuous sense of ontological security; meaning a desire for continuity of self-identity and the reliability of social life over the life-course' (Gregory 2005: 374). Family carers generally described this continuity as the most important thing for them. As family carer, George, stated: 'She's always dressed smartly so what matters to me, I suppose, is that she continues to do so'. Similarly, family carer Jane stated that what was most important to her was 'making him look as smart as possible, because he has always been a very smart man'. As we have discussed elsewhere, dress and appearance are significant in terms of maintaining continuity of self at an embodied level, entangled with attributes of personal and social identity (Buse and Twigg 2015) and embodied biographies (Buse and Twigg 2016).

People with dementia frequently described the continuing importance of their personal style or aesthetic (Woodward 2007) or their 'appearance signature' (Ward et al. 2014). They often retained a strong sense of the styles, colours and textures that were – or were not – *them*. These notions of personal aesthetic also related to dimensions of social identity. For women, whether they were a skirt or a trouser person could be important, affecting the wearer's ability to enact a particular form of gendered identity, shaping the potential of the body to move in particular ways (Twigg 2013). As one woman said: 'I could never feel comfortable going out in trousers', while another described herself as 'more of a trouser person'. For many men in the sample, it was a sense of smartness that was most important, for instance, one man described how he had 'just felt right' wearing a suit tie and jacket. This sense of what feels right relates to the 'notion of aesthetic fit: the wearing of clothes which are "you" ' (Woodward 2007: 73). Clothing can therefore retain a sense of familiarity and feeling normal (Deegan 2010) at an embodied, tactile level; as one woman with dementia said: 'I think it's what you get used to and what you like . . . what you feel comfortable in'.

When people with dementia could no longer maintain their dress and clothing choices independently, family carers became involved in 'curating identity' on their behalf (Kricton and Coch 2007). Such practices illustrate embodied identity as mutually constituted and intercorporeal, as a 'becoming-in-the-world-with-others' (Hughes et al. 2005: 268), challenging notions of the *normal* body as autonomous and bounded (Weiss 2009). Dress practice is always relational and intersubjective, shaped by the anticipated responses and feedback of others (Banim et al. 2001). In the case of dementia, this becomes more pronounced, with decisions about dress becoming a negotiation between family carers and the person with dementia, blurring their personal histories and aesthetics, locating dress choices in the space between *one* and *one another* (Jackson 2012). Making decisions about dress on someone's behalf involves drawing on tacit, biographical knowledge that is embedded in shared histories, as Ellie (family carer) suggests:

> I think it's important to me because I know, I understand, it's important to her. . . . I understand she's a proud lady and, you know, I've grown up with

her always having certain routines and she would always explain to me as a little girl, you know, she always had her lipstick on and the way she did her hair and the way she dressed. It was always important to her. So I've just, you know, I've taken that on board, I think, and I just do it instinctively, to be honest.

Maintaining embodied routines of dress and appearance management can become instinctive through the depth of connection to the person. As the extract relates, the little aspects of someone's dress could be most significant – the fact she 'always had her lipstick on', or 'mum always has tights', or a partner 'always likes to have his wallet', or always wears a watch. This extract also illustrates how maintaining continuity of dress reaffirms a version of the person long-established in the mind of the carer, associated with their recognition of the person (Taylor 2008).

Maintaining continuity in appearance was also important for family carers because of the way in which dress stands for the person (Ash 1996), and their relationship to them. In the face of rupture caused by dementia, clothing can be a way of holding onto the person, and managing biographical disruption (Bury 1982). As family carer, Mark, explained: 'because their personality's changing anyway and if you change the way they look . . . I think you'd be coping with losing another part of them'. For him and for others in the study, dress could come to symbolise a continuing sense of normality and ordinary life:

> You're thinking 'if mum looks normal, if we're keeping it normal we're keeping life normal and it's not as bad as it is'. It's slightly denial but it's also . . . it makes you feel I suppose better with them that you're not . . . it's not as – I don't know – hopeless a situation as it could be where you just give up.

As Mark describes, maintaining his Mum's appearance became a way of keeping life normal and retaining a sense that things were 'not as bad' as they might seem, staving off fears of a situation that was 'hopeless'. Maintaining her dress was also a way of not giving up on his Mum and his relationship to her. On the other hand, some carers recognised that clothes no longer mattered to their relatives, or indeed to them, but that they remained significant to the wider family. As family carer, Annette, explained: 'Once they get to the stage that Mum's at, it's almost what's more important to the family rather than what's more important to the person'.

Clothing could disrupt as well as sustain a sense of continuity and familiar-ity. People with dementia sometimes ceased to recognise clothes belonging to them and refused to wear them, illustrating how the familiar and everyday can become 'uncomfortable and unwelcome' (Longhurst 1994: 219). One woman, Diane, had amassed a pile of seventeen pairs of jeans in her bedroom, explain-ing to the researcher 'I don't think they're mine' and 'I don't know when I last wore jeans', whereas her husband insisted 'they are hers'. This was particularly the case with clothes that were bought more recently and held less emotional salience – Diane provided detailed accounts of clothes worn for holidays, graduations, and family weddings, while forgetting the jeans bought more recently.

Changes in the person's clothing and appearance could be viewed by family carers as marking the progression of dementia. Sometimes families reported that the person's clothing choices changed following the onset of dementia, for instance, wearing more 'garish' colours and styles. Often family carers reported a loss of interest in or ability to maintain appearance, as Ellie said regarding her Nan (grandmother): 'She was very proud of how . . . how she appeared . . . Not anymore at all'. Embodied changes associated with the progression of dementia could also lead to family carers making adaptations to dress. Some family carers introduced jogging bottoms for men rather than smart trousers, because they supported ease of dress. Jane had started buying jogging bottoms for her husband instead of his usual jeans or smart trousers because he had incontinence and struggled with zips and buttons. She recalled that 'when he was younger he wouldn't have worn jogging bottoms – he wouldn't have been seen dead in them!' but now 'I've got used to seeing him with his trainers and his joggers'. Fred had switched to dressing his wife Alice in trousers because 'it's easier for me to dress her', though he would still help her dress up and wear skirts for special occasions: 'It's nice to see her when we go out when she is dressed up, if you know what I mean?' These changes were made for practical reasons but undermined a continuity of identity and family relationships and signalled further stages in the decline of the person with dementia.

The disruption of continuity in appearance and dress could be particularly stark following transitions to care, and family carers would sometimes remark that the person looked 'completely different' when they visited them in a care home. Some family carers would try to pass on detailed information to enable care-workers to continue to curate person's identity, and we observed a number of examples of good practice in this (Buse and Twigg 2015, 2016). However, families also described instances where the person was dressed in crumpled clothes or in someone else's clothes. These instances were hurtful because they were seen as a betrayal of the person's embodied identity, a 'curtailment of self' (Goffman 1968: 24) through the failure to maintain personalised clothing which is a fundamental part of the person's 'identity kit' (p. 29). As family carer, Melissa, describes:

> I've never seen my dad scruffy. Never. Until that day I turned up in the home and he's sitting there in screwed up clothes which really hurt me because I'm not used to that – not at all.

Here, Melissa's Dad's standards of smart, well-ironed clothes were disrupted in the context of care. Such judgements about acceptable and normal dress are read in the context of embodied biographies and standards of dress which are generational, gendered, and classed, as discussed below. The laundry regime in care homes also limited the range of fabrics which could be brought into care, with fabrics like tweeds, silks, and proper woollens being particularly discouraged. Such fabrics can convey comfort and familiarity at a tactile level, as well as ideas about quality fabrics being embedded with the habitus and identity of middle-class participants. Therefore, possibilities for maintaining continuity of self associated with *normal life* and ontological security at a tactile, embodied level can become limited following transitions to care and the progression of dementia.

Passing, stigma, normalisation

There was a tension in the interviews between the desire to respond to the wishes of the person with dementia, and what were seen as traditional performance norms in relation to dress. Dress is part of the micro-order of social life and dressing inappropriately can incur moral judgements (Entwistle 2000). In the context of later life, these judgments can take on a new meaning, with slippages of dress such as tears, stains, or drooping hems becoming interpreted as signs of wider mental or moral failure, pointing to the dereliction of age (Twigg 2013). Dressing as one gets older, therefore, can become a process of staving off such dereliction. But this can be increasingly challenging in the context of dementia where odd, discordant, or bizarre dress can signal a reduced, and potentially stigmatised, social status. Stigma here can also be associative (Goffman 1963). One woman described how when she takes her friend Deirdre out shopping, who tends to wear the 'same old tatty clothing', she was concerned that 'people seemed to look' and might think 'poor old lady', although Deirdre herself 'doesn't care'. Mark discussed how 'little slips' in appearance – incorrectly applied make-up, incorrect or uncoordinated dress – become read as signs of dementia and the progression of the condition. In contrast, Mark suggests that a 'normalised' appearance can be a way to avoid the stigma associated with the condition: 'I think it normalises in a strange way and makes dementia more acceptable, because I still don't think it's acceptable by a lot of people'.

Dress, therefore, becomes part of the hidden labour involved in achieving the appearance of normalcy (Deegan 2010) and maintaining a public 'front' (Goffman 1959). For some people with dementia, maintaining an appropriate presence in the wider public world remained important. Pearl described how this still mattered to her, saying 'well I wouldn't like to go out looking, you know, a mess' and that if 'you didn't think that you looked very nice you would feel people were saying, "oh look at her"'. Similarly, Kathy described how she was 'very particular' about her appearance 'even if you're going up the shops' or 'going to the doctor's'. Kathy described her appearance as 'the thing that I am most particular with . . . and my housework'. Her linking of the two spheres of dress and housework, and her close association of herself with both, reflected classed standards of neatness and cleanliness, which have traditionally been important for working-class women in achieving 'respectability' (Skeggs 1997). Twigg's (2013) study of women, dress, and age similarly found that working-class women in their seventies and eighties emphasised the importance of neatness and cleanliness in dress above considerations of fashion or style.

Avoiding the dereliction of age was also linked to the stigma associated with leaky bodies and incontinence (Lawton 1998), which disrupt the normative body as clean and proper (Paterson and Hughes 1999). Family carers often emphasised the importance of clothes being 'clean' and 'fresh'. This not only related to appearance, but to anxieties about smell, that most pervasive and insidious of presences, with its capacity to cross boundaries and evoke hidden transgressions (Classen et al. 1994). As Barbara said: 'My main concern is that he is clean and fresh smelling, because that can be offensive'. Smell epitomised the dereliction of age. As Cora explained: 'I can't bear an old man to smell an old man smell, so I never ever let him get to that stage'. This was partly about maintaining the person's earlier standards of dress and laundry, but it was also about protecting them from the exposure of bodily betrayals (Isaksen 2002).

Adaptive clothing was sometimes described as a solution to help avoid bodily betrayals. Jane had encouraged her husband to wear tracksuit bottoms which were easier to manage, because she said: 'I would hate for him to wear trousers with zips and buttons and have an accident' in public. On the other hand, some people with dementia avoided simplified clothing because it held associations with frail and disabled bodies. Joe refused to wear the Velcro shoes someone had passed on to him because he felt they were 'old people's shoes': 'I don't want people to think "oh there's the old boy"'. Velcro has been argued to signal disability and mark the person as different (Linthicum 2006). Joe also resisted his wife's suggestion of tracksuit bottoms because 'I feel an idiot wearing a tracksuit now when I can't even walk across the room!' Other participants resisted the idea of adaptive clothing, concerned that it might convey a uniform or standardised appearance which conveyed the 'look' of dementia, creating rather than avoiding a stigmatised appearance.

The intersection of the physical environment with dress practice provided further barriers to the maintenance of a *normal* appearance and bodily performance. As described in the example by Keady and Keady (2005), clothes shopping could become difficult and embarrassing in the context of dementia. Gender-coded dressing rooms made assistance with dress difficult when out shopping, as family carer Greg recounted:

> She went back into the changing room and . . . she hadn't come out and I said to the girl, I said, 'There isn't anybody . . . Can I go in because I'm not sure what on earth she's doing?' and I went in and she was wandering around because she couldn't find where she'd left her original trousers. . . . I think it did knock her confidence that, you know, she . . . she was embarrassed to come out and say, 'I can't find my trousers'.

This reflects the findings of previous research on shopping, in which fitting rooms were a major barrier for people with disabilities (Macdonald et al. 1994). Such incidents disrupt efforts to 'pass' (Goffman 1963), bringing awareness of impairment to the fore (Paterson and Hughes 1999). Other family carers talked about a lack of available gender-neutral toilets when out shopping or in public. Tom 'used to love shopping', but his wife Jane tends to go shopping for him now because, as she explains, 'I can't go in the gents with him, it's difficult'.

The reach of the public gaze and judgements about dress was not limited to public space but extended to practices in the home. Home is classically regarded as private space, though its privacy is structured spatially and temporally (Twigg 1999). This structuring is reflected in dress practices, with different forms of dress and undress being thought appropriate for different times of day and different social circumstances. The coming of disability can disrupt this ordered privacy, exposing patterns of behaviour previously hidden. Barbara recounted how her husband's tendency to walk 'around in underpants in the house is a bit embarrassing' when visitors come to the house. Her efforts to encourage him to dress sometimes sparked off an argument: 'I'll say "go and shut yourself in the room or put your trousers on"'. Mark describes how the coming of carers to help with his mother meant that dress in the home came to conform closer to public standards: 'You do set to conform, even within the house' when 'other people are coming through'.

Dress was not only viewed as something which incurred moral judgements on the person with dementia, but was also experienced by family carers as a comment on their own care practices. As family carer Frank said, maintaining his wife's appearance was important to him because 'it's a reflection on me as well, you see'. This response appeared more significant for male carers, perhaps reflecting the contrast with their earlier gendered roles and a greater need to prove they were able to care adequately. Frank describes other women at the day centre whose appearance was not so well-maintained and were 'always in the same outfits', reflecting that 'some men haven't got any idea of how to dress a woman'. Family carer Mark similarly described appearance as a sign that the person was well cared for and stated 'there was always that element of, you know, nothing's going to slip'.

Clashes and tensions sometimes emerged in efforts to maintain a normalised appearance. Mark described disagreements when his father had put on clothing which was 'muddled' and he would encourage him to change. He reflected 'I don't know whether it's the right thing to do', accepting that his father being incorrectly dressed was embarrassing for him and not his father. A focus on maintaining a normalised appearance can also undermine the special meanings that certain items of dress can have. Torn and old clothing, for example, can seem to signify dereliction or neglect, but they may also have personal and biographical significance for the person with dementia. Jane had a number of disagreements with her husband Tom over his old work clothing, which he used to wear on site as a builder. Jane regarded these clothes – torn and marked with plaster – as acceptable for 'pottering round the garage' or garden, but not for more public spaces. Often she would help him to dress in what she saw as suitable clothing, and then he would undress and put on his work clothes:

> I've got sort of certain clothes which I say are okay for indoors, but not when he goes to the day centre . . . some days he'll get up and he'll . . . he'll put his working clothes on and . . . in the summer that's okay because he'll do his gardening in his working clothes. But usually when he gets up and puts his working clothes [on], I know trouble's in store!

Within disability studies, the argument has been made for challenging the necessity to normalise appearance. Disability theorists have sought to *queer* the normative body, and through doing so, to validate and make politically visible the range of human experience (Samuels 2003; Sherry 2004). As a result, disabled people should not be required or encouraged to hide their conditions. This aspiration becomes more complex, however, in the case of dementia where there is a past history of identity to reflect and respect, and where the person with dementia may not be aware of the ways in which their current expression of choice could undermine this, exposing them in ways that they would have found undignified in their earlier lives. As one family carer Mark reflected, these processes of normalisation, though they may protect the person by making their dementia less visible, can act to hide the condition socially:

> We're all being driven to do or conform to all these too many things and, you know, people don't know what goes on in the day-to-day if we appear to be normal. I mean we don't want to go around with a badge, you know, I'm la-loo, or whatever, but we do not deal with it. We do not deal with it at all.

Helping someone with dementia pass as normal protects the individual, but leaves the wider stigma unchallenged. Mark reflects on conformity as the 'condition of acceptance' that normalisation imposes (Yates et al. 2008: 249). However, he recognised how failure to conform can lead to exclusion, talking about friends who 'stopped coming' as his Mum's condition, and appearance, increasingly fell short of normative standards. As argued by Paterson and Hughes (1999: 608): 'The price of integration is normalisation'. These issues and tensions between normality, passing, and inclusion/exclusion are complex and not easily resolved, entangled with everyday dress practices in the lives of people with dementia and their families.

Conclusion

This chapter has explored dynamics of normalcy, ordinariness, and normalisation through an analysis of dress practice. A detailed analysis of dress as 'situated bodily practice' (Entwistle 2000: 11) can contribute to efforts to *reincorporate the body* into disability studies (Linthicum 2006). We have used dress as a lens to 'trace patterns of embodiment as they are lived', and explore the negotiation of 'corporeal and intercorporeal norms' in everyday encounters (Paterson and Hughes 1999: 598, 608). An analysis of dress brings into focus patterns of bodily dys-appearance in relation to physical difficulties with dressing, but also dynamics of normality, passing and stigma which fluctuate across different spatial contexts (Deegan 2010). Dress can make visible – as well as conceal – dementia as a form of impairment, with small slips in the maintenance of a normal appearance and dress becoming read as signs of the condition. However, dress can also support a sense of *feeling normal* through the maintenance of clothing and routines which sustain biographical continuity at an embodied and tactile level.

This chapter highlights how difficulties with dress can disrupt the flow of day-to-day life, and betray efforts to maintain a *normal* appearance. As has been argued in relation to the physical environment, one possible answer is adaptive design solutions. However, our research also suggests problems with adaptive clothing, which can be viewed as stigmatising or as inconsistent with the person's embodied biography and identity. A focus on difficulties with dress and adaptive solutions can also reflect a limited, medicalised focus, which ignores the wider social contexts, relationships, and meanings within which dress is embedded. Such solutions tend to focus on the functionality of dress at the expense of any discussion of what is viewed as *fun* or *stylish* (Linthicum 2006). Design solutions cannot be understood in isolation from the contexts and relationships within which they are embedded, although there is now research that is beginning to take such dynamics into account (Kabel et al. 2016).

Focusing on dementia also brings these debates on normalcy, normalisation, and dress into new terrain, opening up new questions and challenges. Arguments for a *politics of difference* (Coleman-Fountain 2017) which resists the normalisation of disabled bodies become more complex in the context of cognitive impairment, such as dementia, since it raises issues of choice, agency, and control. Nonetheless, a focus on dress highlights the importance of an embodied approach in thinking about the dialogue between the social model of disability and dementia. Restricting discussions to dementia activism, which relies on cognitive and verbal ability, can exclude people with dementia who are less verbally fluent or visible. Instead, perhaps the best way forward is to extend a 'carnal politics of the everyday' to dementia (Paterson and Hughes 1999: 597), focusing on everyday encounters, and how agency, normalcy, and oppression are enacted and negotiated at an embodied level, recognising dress as part of this.

Note

1 Dementia is not generally included under the rubric of disability in popular understandings. However, the social model of disability has now been broadened to include cognitive or sensory impairment. Like other aspects of disability, the diagnosis, experience, and

response to dementia is shaped by the socio-cultural context, and physical and social barriers shape experiences of dementia as disabling (Downs 2000; Kitwood 1997).

References

Ash, J. 1996. Memory and objects. In: Kirkham, P. ed. *The Gendered Object*. Manchester: Manchester University Press, pp. 219–224.

Banim, M., Green, E. and Guy, A. 2001. Introduction. In: Guy, A., Green, E. and Banim, M. eds. *Through the Wardrobe: Women's Relationships With Their Clothes*. Oxford: Berg, pp. 1–17.

Banim, M. and Guy, A. 2001. Discontinued selves: why do women keep clothes they no longer wear? In: Guy, A., Green, E. and Banim, M. eds. *Through the Wardrobe: Women's Relationships With Their Clothes*. Oxford: Berg, pp. 203–219.

Bartlett, R. 2012a. The emergent modes of dementia activism. *Ageing and Society* 34(4), pp. 623–644.

Bartlett, R. 2012b. Taxing work: visualising and reflecting upon the impact of 'user involvement policies' on men and women with dementia. *Paper presented at the British Sociological Association Annual Conference*, University of Leeds, UK, 11–13 April 2012.

Bartlett, R. and O'Connor, D. 2007. From personhood to citizenship: broadening the lens for dementia practice and research. *Journal of Aging Studies* 21(2), pp. 107–118.

Black, B. S., Rabins, P. V., Sugarman, J. and Karlawish, J.H. 2010. Seeking assent and respecting dissent in dementia research. *American Journal of Geriatric Psychiatry* 18(1), pp. 77–85.

Boyle, G. 2014. Recognising the agency of people with dementia. *Disability and Society* 29(7), pp. 1130–1144.

Breward, C. 2016. *The Suit: Form, Function and Style*. London: Reaktion Books.

Bury, M. 1982. Chronic illness as biographical disruption. *Sociology of Health and Illness* 4(2), pp. 167–182.

Buse, C. and Twigg, J. 2014. Looking 'out of place': analysing the spatial and symbolic meanings of dementia care settings through dress. *International Journal of Ageing and Later Life* 9(1), pp. 69–95.

Buse, C. and Twigg, J. 2015. Clothing, embodied identity and dementia: maintaining the self through dress. *Age, Culture, Humanities* 2, pp. 71–96.

Buse, C. and Twigg, J. 2016. Materializing memories: exploring the stories of people with dementia through dress. *Ageing and Society* 36(6), pp. 1115–1135.

Classen, C., Howes, D. and Synott, A. 1994. *Aroma: The Cultural History of Smell*. London: Routledge.

Coleman-Fountain, E. 2017. Youthful stories of normality and difference. *Sociology* 51(4), pp. 766–782.

Crossley, N. 2001. *The Social Body: Habit, Identity and Desire*. London: Sage.

Davies, K. 1994. The tensions between process time and clock time in care-work: the example of day nurseries. *Time and Society* 3(3), pp. 277–303.

Davis, L. 1995. *Enforcing Normalcy: Disability, Deafness, and the Body*. New York: Verso.

Deegan, M. J. 2010. 'Feeling normal' and 'feeling disabled'. In: Barnett, S. N. ed. *Disability as a Fluid State*. Bingley: Emerald, pp. 25–48.

Downs, M. 2000. Dementia in a socio-cultural context: an idea whose time has come. *Ageing and Society* 20(3), pp. 369–375.

Entwistle, J. 2000. *The Fashioned Body: Fashion, Dress and Modern Social Theory*. Cambridge: Polity Press.

Featherstone, M. and Hepworth, M. 1991. The mask of ageing and the postmodern life-course. In: Featherstone, M., Hepworth, M. and Turner, B. S. eds. *The Body*. London: Sage, pp. 371–389.

Feyereisen, P., Gendron, M. and Seron, X. 1999. Disorders of everyday actions in subjects suffering from senile dementia of Alzheimer's type: an analysis of dressing performance. *Neuropsychological Rehabilitation* 9(2), pp. 169–188.

Giddens, A. 1992. *Modernity and Self-Identity*. Cambridge: Polity Press.

Gilleard, C. and Higgs, P. 2000. *Cultures of Ageing: Self, Citizen and the Body*. Edinburgh: Pearson.

Gilliard, J., Means, R., Beattie, A. and Daker-White, G. 2005. Dementia care in England and the social model of disability. *Dementia* 4(4), pp. 571–586.

Goffman, E. 1959. *The Presentation of Self in Everyday Life*. London: Lane.

Goffman, E. 1963. *Stigma: Notes on the Management of Spoiled Identity*. Englewood Cliffs, NJ: Prentice Hall.

Goffman, E. 1968. *Asylums: Essays on the Social Situation of Mental Patients and Other Inmates*. Harmondsworth: Penguin.

Gregory, S. 2005. Living with chronic illness in the family setting. *Sociology of Health and Illness* 27(3), pp. 372–392.

Gullette, M. 1997. *Declining to Decline: Cultural Combat and the Politics of the Midlife*. Charlottesville: University Press of Virginia.

Hansen, N. and Philo, C. 2007. The normality of doing things differently: bodies, spaces and disability geography. *Tijdschrift Voor Economische En Sociale Geografie* 98(4), pp. 493–506.

Hayman, E. 2009. Dressing made tangible: disability perspectives. In: Rouse, E. ed. *Conference Proceedings 2009 Fashion and Well-Being? International Foundation of Fashion Technology Institutes*. London: Centre for Learning and Teaching in Art and Design, pp. 627–638. Available at: https://opus.lib.uts.edu.au/handle/10453/11285 [Accessed: 23 November 2017].

Heidegger, M. 1962. *Being and Time*. Oxford: Blackwell.

Hubbard, G., Downs, M. and Tester, S. 2003. Including older people with dementia in research: challenges and strategies. *Aging and Mental Health* 7(5), pp. 351–362.

Hughes, B. 2007. Being disabled: toward a critical social ontology for disability studies. *Disability and Society* 22(7), pp. 673–684.

Hughes, B., McKie, L., Hopkins, D. and Watson, N. 2005. Love's labours lost? Feminism, the disabled people's movement and an ethic of care. *Sociology* 39(2), pp. 259–275.

Isaksen, L. W. 2002. Toward a sociology of (gendered) disgust: images of bodily decay and the social organization of care work. *Journal of Family Issues* 23(7), pp. 791–811.

Jackson, M. 2012. *Between One and One Another*. Berkeley: University of California Press.

Kabel, R., McBee-Black, K. and Dimka, J. 2016. Apparel-related participation barriers: ability, adaptation and engagement. *Disability and Rehabilitation* 38(22), pp. 2184–2192.

Keady, J. and Keady, J. 2005. The wrong shoes: living with memory loss. *Nursing Older People* 17(9), pp. 36–37.

Kitwood, T. 1997. *Dementia Reconsidered: The Person Comes First*. Berkshire: Open University Press.

Kontos, P. 2004. Ethnographic reflections on selfhood, embodiment and Alzheimer's disease. *Ageing and Society* 24(6), pp. 829–849.

Kricton, J. and Coch, T. 2007. Living with dementia: curating self-identity. *Dementia* 6(3), pp. 365–381.

Kumar, A. 2004. *The Lived Experience of Aging and Disability.* New York: Lulu Press.

Lawton, J. 1998. Contemporary hospice care: the sequestration of the unbounded body and 'dirty dying'. *Sociology of Health and Illness* 20(2), pp. 121–143.

Leder, D. 1990. *The Absent Body.* Chicago: University of Chicago Press.

Linthicum, L. 2006. Integrative practice: oral history, dress and disability studies. *Journal of Design History* 19(4), pp. 309–318.

Longhurst, R. 1994. The geography closest in – the body . . . the politics of pregnability. *Australian Geographical Studies* 32(2), pp. 214–223.

Loretto, W. and Vickerstaff, S. 2012. The domestic and gendered context for retirement. *Human Relations* 66(1), pp. 65–86.

MacDonald, N. M., Majumder, R. K. and Bua-Iam, P. 1994. Apparel acquisition for consumers with disabilities: purchasing practices and barriers to shopping. *Clothing Textiles Research Journal* 12(2), pp. 38–45.

Martin, W., Kontos, P. and Ward, R. 2013. Embodiment and dementia. *Dementia* 12(3), pp. 283–287.

Mauss, M. 1979. *Sociology and Psychology: Essays.* London: Routledge.

McCarthy, M. 1998. Whose body is it anyway? Pressures and control for women with learning disabilities. *Disability and Society* 13(4), pp. 557–574.

Oldman, C. 2002. Later life and the social model of disability: a comfortable partnership? *Ageing and Society* 22(6), pp. 791–806.

Paterson, K. and Hughes, B. 1999. Disability studies and phenomenology: the carnal politics of everyday life. *Disability and Society* 14(5), pp. 597–610.

Phinney, A. and Chesla, C. A. 2003. The lived body in dementia. *Journal of Aging Studies* 17(3), pp. 283–299.

Prout, A., Hayes, L. and Gelder, L. 1999. Medicines and the maintenance of ordinariness in the household management of childhood asthma. *Sociology of Health and Illness* 21(2), pp. 137–162.

Putman, M. 2002. Linking aging theory and disability models: increasing the potential to explore aging with physical impairment. *The Gerontologist* 42(6), pp. 799–806.

Roche, M. 1989. Lived time, leisure and retirement. In: Barrett, T. and Winnifrith, C. eds. *The Philosophy of Leisure.* London: Macmillan, pp. 54–79.

Samuels, E. 2003. My body, my closet: invisible disability and the limits of coming-out discourse. *Gay and Lesbian Quarterly* 9(1–2), pp. 233–255.

Schillmeier, M. 2014. *Eventful Bodies: The Cosmopolitics of Illness.* Surrey: Ashgate.

Sherry, M. 2004. Overlaps and contradictions between queer theory and disability studies. *Disability and Society* 19(7), pp. 769–783.

Shilling, C. 2013. *The Body and Social Theory.* London: Sage.

Simmel, G. 1904. Fashion. In: Levine, D. C. ed. *On Individuality and Social Forms: Selected Writings.* Chicago: University of Chicago Press, pp. 294–323.

Skeggs, B. 1997. *Formations of Class and Gender: Becoming Respectable.* London: Sage.

Szinovacz, M. 2000. Changes in housework after retirement: a panel analysis. *Journal of Marriage and the Family* 62(1), pp. 78–92.

Taylor, J. 2008. On recognition, caring, and dementia. *Medical Anthropology Quarterly* 22(4), pp. 313–335.

Tsuji, K. 2005. Time is not up: temporal complexity of older Americans' lives. *Journal of Cross Cultural Gerontology* 20(1), pp. 3–26.

Twigg, J. 1999. The spatial ordering of care: public and private in bathing support at home. *Sociology of Health and Illness* 21(4), pp. 381–400.

Twigg, J. 2000. Carework as a form of bodywork. *Ageing and Society* 20(4), pp. 389–411.

Twigg, J. 2010. Clothing and dementia: a neglected dimension? *Journal of Aging Studies* 24(4), pp. 223–230.

Twigg, J. 2013. *Fashion and Age: Dress, the Body and Later Life.* Oxford: Berg.

Valentine, G. 1999. Doing household research: interviewing couples together and apart. *Area* 31(1), pp. 67–74.

Van Wersch, A. 2001. Cancer, breast reconstruction and clothes. In: Guy, A., Green, E. and Banim, M. eds. *Through the Wardrobe: Women's Relationships With Their Clothes.* Oxford: Berg, pp. 189–202.

Ward, R., Campbell, S. and Keady, J. 2014. 'Once I had money in my pocket, I was every colour under the sun': using 'appearance biographies' to explore the meanings of appearance for people with dementia. *Journal of Ageing Studies* 30, pp. 64–72.

Weiss, G. 2009. Intertwined identities: challenges to bodily autonomy. *Perspectives: International Postgraduate Journal of Philosophy* 2(1), pp. 22–37.

Williams, B. and Barlow, J. H. 1998. Falling out with my shadow: lay perceptions of the body in the context of arthritis. In: Nettleton, S. and Watson, J. eds. *The Body in Everyday Life.* London: Routledge, pp. 124–141.

Wolfensberger, W. 1972. *The Principle of Normalization in Human Services.* Toronto: National Institute of Mental Retardation.

Wolfensberger, W. 1983. Social role valorization: a proposed new term for the principle of normalisation. *Mental Retardation* 21(6), pp. 234–239.

Woodward, S. 2007. *Why Women Wear What They Wear.* Oxford: Berg.

Yates, S., Dyson, S. and Hiles, D. 2008. Beyond normalisation and impairment: theorising subjectivity for learning difficulties theory and practice. *Disability and Society* 23(3), pp. 247–258.

Part II

Youth, normalcy, and disability futures

Chapter 3

The everyday worlds
of disabled children

*Tillie Curran, Kirsty Liddiard, and
Katherine Runswick-Cole*

Introduction

The everyday worlds of disabled children and young people (hereby disabled children) often fall under the spotlight of adult attention. Indeed, disabled children's lives are surveilled by adults more than any other group of children; a host of professionals including doctors and allied health professionals, teachers, and social workers are involved in monitoring their lives (Goodley and Runswick-Cole 2012b). However, when disabled children are included in academic theory and research (and it is still the case that they are often excluded), the focus of the inquiry is frequently targeted at the impact of a particular condition on *normal* development and/or the exploration and evaluation of the associated services disabled children receive. Increasingly, though, attention is paid to children's everyday interests and *their* concerns (Connors and Stalker 2007; Curran and Runswick-Cole 2013, 2014; McLaughlin et al. 2008; Shakespeare et al. 1999). This chapter aims to challenge the negative practices and stereotypes that persist in the lives of disabled children and, in doing so, aims to celebrate their lives and to focus on the hopes, dreams, and aspirations of disabled children, young people, and their families and allies.

We begin with a discussion of how theories of disability and childhood in the Global North (a term used to indicate the unequal socio-economic relations between countries) have produced a deficit view of disabled children as in need of professional intervention. Though more social and active constructions of childhood and campaigns around children's rights have gained momentum, a rights discourse also tends to be normative. Disabled children continue to be portrayed as passive and their rights are often assumed, remain absent, or are discussed as an add-on; as illustrated in the studies discussed below, a rights approach that is relevant entails listening to and learning from their experiences. The emergence of disabled children's childhood studies draws upon both disability studies and childhood studies, but develops an approach that challenges the ideas and practices of exclusion and opens with a positive view of disabled children's childhood. By presenting a range of disabled children's childhood studies produced with disabled children, young people, and their family members and allies, we seek to re-orientate research inquiry, moving away from professionals' concerns about children's and young people's *deficits* and *lack* to focus, instead, on their hopes, dreams, and aspirations. Disabled children's childhood studies is a developing field and we end the chapter with future directions. In particular, we explore intimacy and intersectionality, linking the societal context and debates with the personal, social, and everyday lives of disabled children and their families.

Understandings of disability and of childhood

Approaches to the study of disabled children's lives in the Global North are generally premised upon what has been described as a medical, or individual, model of disability. This medical model approach conceptualises disability as a *medical problem* for *individuals* (Oliver 1991); notably, it has been widely critiqued (Goodley 2011; Mallett and Runswick-Cole 2014; Oliver 1991). More than thirty years ago, the emergence of social oppression models of disability began to shift the focus away from the *problems* of individuals' bodies and minds to look instead at the ways in which disabled people are subjected to everyday exclusion and discrimination because of disablism (Mallett and Runswick-Cole 2014). Disablism is described as 'a form of social oppression involving the social imposition of restrictions of activity on people with impairments and the socially engendered undermining of their psycho-emotional wellbeing' (Thomas 2006: 73). Oliver (1991) made a powerful case when he argued that disabled people are not disabled by their bodily impairments, but by the attitudes of a disabling society. Oliver (1991) urged researchers to work as allies to disabled people in research and to focus their attention to the systemic, cultural, and attitudinal barriers that exclude disabled people, and to consider how these might be exposed and removed.

In the intervening thirty years, disability studies has gained far-reaching recognition across networks of disabled people and their allies, and continues to develop as an action-orientated praxis. The emergence of critical disability studies has seen a shift within disability studies towards embracing the intersections of class, gender, race, ethnicity, *and* disability in order to expose and to challenge disablism (Goodley 2014). Academics working within British disability studies identify, almost exclusively, with the social model of disability, which is concerned with disability as social oppression. This approach contrasts with North American and Nordic approaches that draw on a range of resources beyond the social model. For example, North American approaches to disability studies have often drawn on cultural theory and minority group models to theorise disability (McRuer 2006). In the Nordic countries, approaches to disability have focused on relational and *normalisation* approaches in which the aim has been for disabled people to live culturally normative lives (Mallett and Runswick-Cole 2014; Traustadóttir 2004; Tøssebro 2004).

The application of social models and critical theories of disability has progressed slowly and sporadically in relation to disabled children. Medical, individualised, and psychologised models have continued to dominate, with the deficit constructions of any child who is not assessed as *typically developing*, in turn, narrowing attention to professional intervention, service provision, and its adequacy. In the 1990s, research exposing the lived realities of institutional and segregated services highlighted the need for inclusion and an attention to the voices of disabled children (Morris 2003). The focus on disabled children as people with childhoods in a social context is clear in the Economic and Social Research Council (ESRC) funded research project *Life as a Disabled Child: A Qualitative Study of Young People's Experiences and Perspectives* (Shakespeare et al. 1999). This research set out to challenge traditional medicalised approaches to the study of disabled children's lives in the UK, drawing instead upon social oppression models of disability and seeking to challenge the focus of research about disabled children's lives on service use and delivery. In their final report, the authors foregrounded children's perspectives and experiences:

> Much research into disabled childhood has been preoccupied with impair-ment, vulnerability and service use; this has compounded a view of dis-abled children as passive and dependent. The voices of disabled children themselves have frequently been excluded as research has focused on the perspectives of parents, professionals and other adults. This project aimed to explore the perspectives of disabled children themselves, their own roles in negotiating their daily lives, and to investigate the relationships, environ-ments and structures, which shaped their experiences.
>
> (Shakespeare et al. 1999: 2)

In 2007, Connors and Stalker (2007: 19) were still able to make the claim that:

> The social model of disability has paid little attention to disabled children, with few attempts to explore how far it provides an adequate explanatory framework for their experiences.

While others have followed Connors and Stalker in bringing social oppression approaches to the exploration of the lives of disabled children (Goodley and Runswick-Cole 2010, 2011, 2012a; Greenstein 2015; McLaughlin et al. 2008; Read et al. 2006; Slater 2014), it remains the case that British disability studies is often an adult-centric area of study which has under-theorised the lives of disabled children.

At the same time, as Wells (2017) points out, disabled children's lives have been marginalised within childhood studies. Searching the journal *Childhood*, Wells discovers that there are only seventy-one mentions of disability since 1993 and that in the majority of papers where disabled children are mentioned, this is only in passing. It seems that the presence of disabled children within childhood studies troubles some of the foundational principles of the new sociology of childhood (James et al. 1998) which characterise children as active social agents interacting with and shaping the world around them. Children's agency is constructed as bounded within the individual child, that is, as free, independent, and rational. This means children who cannot conform to this account of agency are then a problem for childhood studies and, all too often, the response to the challenge presented by the presence of disabled children in childhood studies has simply been to exclude them from the inquiry (Wells 2017). Childhood studies has included discussions about how childhood is socially constructed in its historical and temporal locations. In the Global North, concepts of childhood have continued to define disabled children against the *norms* of child development (Burman 2008). The desire to maintain and preserve the boundaries of these norms has provided the rationale for segregated or special welfare and education provision in the lives of disabled children (Burman 2008). Paradoxically, research shows that the focus on medical diagnosis has contributed to a lack of attention to the wider social worlds of disabled children and the levels of inequality that they and their families are likely to experience in all areas of their lives (Read et al. 2006).

In contrast to the negative images of disabled children promoted within some traditional approaches to research with children, disabled children's childhood studies seek to do something different. The focus is on the positive contributions of disabled children in their everyday worlds. We recognise that the presence of disabled children in the social world often provokes a moment of disruption, as an accommodation is made or an adaptation required. However, in disabled children's childhood studies, these moments of disruption are seen as desirable and always potentially productive. Disability offers exciting opportunities to re-shape, re-fashion, and revise accepted practices, assumptions, and norms that dominate children's lives and, so, to promote *all* children's potential (Goodley and Runswick-Cole 2014; Goodley et al. 2015). Disabled children's childhood studies offer, therefore, more than a critique of services, and more than a combination of disability studies and childhood studies, as they seek out the positive contributions that disabled children make to their communities (Curran and Runswick-Cole 2013).

We reaffirm disabled children's childhood studies as a distinct area of inquiry as we outline the emergence of this new area of study. Next, we explain the principles upon which disabled children's childhood studies is based and how these principles may re-orientate childhood research, including how we understand ethical research. In what follows, we discuss a number of studies focused on the lives of disabled children and young people, influenced by a disabled children's childhood studies approach. We go on to identify some further shifts emerging as disabled children's childhood studies continues to grow as a field of inquiry. These developing ideas include a requirement to focus on global perspectives, intersectionality, and emotion in children's lives. Many of the studies discussed employ qualitative research approaches to explore everyday life, but we also ask how quantitative research and big data questions might strengthen their impact and avoid repeated stories being told to no avail. We end with a discussion of recent developments to disabled children's childhood studies emerging through a new ESRC-funded research project – *Life, Death, Disability and the Human: Living Life to the Fullest* – as an example of how disabled children's childhood studies might be enacted in research.

The emergence of disabled children's childhood studies

Disabled children's childhood studies have emerged from a number of research and community networks in the UK and internationally. Disabled children, young people, parents, family members, activists, and academics came together at a series of annual conferences – *Child, Youth, Family and Disability* – which began in 2008 (initially hosted at Manchester Metropolitan University, but now hosted around the UK). Contributors from these conferences, who have produced the studies that we discuss, have developed the approach together. In addition to these conferences, some contributors' engagement with the UK-based *Disabled Children's Research Network* has strengthened disabled children's childhood studies as an area of study. The use of social media and international networks has generated momentum and action orientation, with many authors bringing their own experience and involvement in making change through projects and campaigns and, importantly, through everyday life. In 2013, we saw the publication of an edited collection *Disabled Children's Childhood Studies: Critical Approaches in a Global Context* (Curran and Runswick-Cole 2013) and, in 2017, the book *The Palgrave Handbook of Disabled Children's Childhood Studies* (Runswick-Cole et al. 2017). Those involved in promoting the area of disabled children's childhood studies value the contributions of disability studies and childhood studies to disabled children and young people's lives. Disabled children's childhood studies are an attempt to re-invigorate debates and to challenge the persistent professionalisation, medicalisation, and pathologisation which continue to dominate accounts of disabled children's everyday worlds.

With these concerns in mind, disabled children's childhood studies is premised on three principles:

1   The starting point for inquiry should be on the experiences of disabled children and young people that are beyond discussion of impairment, and abuse, so that disabled children can step out from under the shadow of the normative expectations that have clouded their lives.
2   Disabled children's childhood studies demand an ethical research design that seeks to position the voice and experiences of disabled children at the centre of the inquiry.
3   Disabled children's childhood studies seek to trouble normalising practices in their local, historical, and global locations.

(Curran and Runswick-Cole 2013)

These principles have led us to argue for a reorientation of research with disabled children. Re-orientating research to the voices of disabled children and their aspirations can only come after critical conversations have taken place. We need to move research inquiry away from professionals' concerns that have too often focused on issues of impairment and service evaluation in the lives of disabled children. We challenge generic claims related to children made in research which do not clarify whether, or not, disabled children and young people's experience is included, as highlighted by Wells (2017). We also question how research seeking to make generic claims about the lives of all children, and yet excludes disabled children, can be justified as ethical.

Ethics

We are not the first to note that for research to be considered ethical, it is necessary to go beyond the act of getting ethical approval as a one-off act (Cocks 2006). We agree that there is a need to apply ethics to the topic definition and whole research process, from initial research design right through to dissemination of the findings and generating impact. For example, how do research-funding bodies justify proposals limited to non-disabled children? How are selection practices that settle for mainstream schools justified when we know many children and young people are not in school or are in segregated schools and secure institutions? *Who* identified the *problem* and *whom* is it a problem for? Do the topics of research reflect disabled children's concerns, or do they repeat the mistake of asking *what is wrong with you?* rather than *what is wrong with society?* and *what needs to change?* (Oliver 1991). These questions are fundamentally ethical questions. Crucially, re-orientating inquiry is not only a matter of involving disabled children in research, but questioning what is constructed as the *problem* to be researched.

Contributors to the field of disabled children's childhood studies have continued to push what the boundaries of ethical research with children could and should be. For example, Naseem (2017), in her auto-ethnographic study, details how research with ethical approval can actually be used to objectify disabled children. She describes the use and re-use of images of body parts in genetic research as dehumanising and objectifying. In the use of such images, children and families are denied their expertise and insights. Naseem argues that the promises of anonymity or confidentiality are not enough to protect participants, and she describes how research can become an exercise in exploitation. Participants are commonly encouraged to participate in research for the benefit of others *like them* or for future generations. However, in some cases, when medical research is carried out with children to find out the cause of an impairment, the future benefit being offered to the child participant is the possibility that there will be no children *like them* in a future world. Children and families are invited to participate in a process that conspires to invalidate their existence. As academics and activists, we believe that we need to continue to build and maintain strong relationships with disability activists to question the purpose of proposed research, the inclusion of disabled children, the nature of that inclusion, and its impact regarding benefit for disabled children, young people, and their families now and in the future.

The development of links between ethics, topic, and methods is a critical, spiral, and continuing process. For example, Pickering (2017) began her research with an interest in how disabled children's cycling impacts on motor function from her perspective as a physiotherapist and educator. However, what she observed was the impact of cycling on children's social participation and recreation. At that point, her research interest developed around accessible recreation, the provision of play space, and access to cycling. Slater and Chapman (2017) reflect on the centrality of disabled children's voices in disability studies, demanding us to think again about what this might tell us about what it means to be *adult* and *able*. Studies of disabled children's childhoods have generated a focus on their experiences, but Slater and Chapman point out that learning needs to be about ableism and how to challenge ableism. If we invite young people to tell their stories and take no action, we risk exploiting their experience and repeating indifference. It follows that professionals and academics need to be encouraged to learn about how to undertake social action, how to network with community activists, and how to recognise, investigate, and change ableism. Studies explore pedagogy, learning approaches, and discuss experiential opportunities in professional education for skills in critical analysis and social action (Curran et al. 2017; Greenstein 2017). Curran et al. (2017) explore the leadership of experts by experience in professional education using an activist learning approach. Leadership defined from this perspective is more than service user and carer involvement. Experts by experience in a leadership role highlight the need for professionals to recognise and support their networks, to really listen, and to know how to make the changes that they want. Educators who are not experts by experience need to, for instance, find ways to tackle their own ableism and share their own experiences of stress if *othering* practices are to end in professional education.

Regarding methods, the research tools we use need to be accessible, and researchers should be open to revisiting their initial approaches – for example, changing from an interview to multi-method approaches. And yet making such tools accessible does not transform or re-orientate research by itself. For instance, Hambly (2017) develops her use of play activities to gain perspectives of children's experiences of speech and language needs and the views of their family, peers, and school staff. The social context is clearly significant to children; speech and language is discussed as a relational experience and one that demands professionals' listening skills and development of a positive school culture, rather than a problem focus that can reproduce individualised bullying and low staff confidence to identify and change a negative culture. Dowling et al. (2017) also explain how when their planned interview methods did not prove to encourage young people to share their experiences, the approach was rethought for young people to produce their account through a collage developed over time. Again, an intention to develop methodology to maximise participation and benefit in such responsive and flexible ways needs to be viewed positively in funding and ethics scrutiny.

Working with disabled children, families, and activists also raises important ethical questions about voice. We have argued that the voice and concerns of the child are at the heart of disabled children's childhood studies if we are to work in ethical ways in research. We also suggest that the voice of family members, and others who care for disabled children, is significant in disabled children's childhood studies. At the same time, we recognise that this focus raises further ethical issues. For example, when parents are the researchers writing auto-ethnographic studies about their children, ethical issues come to the fore about whose story is being told and about anonymity and confidentiality. Thackray (2017) and Watson (2017), both mother-researchers, reflect in their studies on the decision-making processes and steps taken in writing about their experience without compromising their child's privacy into the future. As editors of *The Palgrave Handbook of Disabled Children's Childhood Studies*, we had discussions with some parent/carer researchers who were worried about sharing their critical perspectives on their lives for fear that this would offend practitioners working with their children, or, worse still, negatively affect the services their children receive.

These ethical and practical issues are very carefully considered in auto-ethnographic studies, yet authors have reported continuous questioning of the value of auto-ethnography in terms of its status as research. From such positivist critique, emotions are seen as problematic regarding *objectivity* and researcher *rigour* (Dickson-Swift et al. 2009). Of course, any research methodology might be undertaken without rigour and have poor accountability, but emotion is valued here as a source of knowing and understanding. We have found auto-ethnographic research studies to be steeped in emotion and, in the case of disabled children's childhood studies, this is how further insights into the ethics of the research process have been made possible, thereby strengthening both rigour and accountability. Coles (2017) discusses the distress that engaging in research as a parent-researcher can provoke. From these studies, we suggest that ethical guidelines need to consider the risks to disabled children and also to parent/carer researchers in order to plan and resource support. Ethics committees need to consider how they can promote equality of opportunity and, at the same time, take clear steps to avoid the exploitation of researcher and child. The standard for high quality research is often thought to be its originality and criticality and, so, if researchers are simply conforming to formal 'tick box' ethics which are routinely signed off, the quality of research conduct, outcome, and impact is put into jeopardy.

The shift that disabled children's childhood studies encourage is the re-positioning of emotion in research. Traditionally, the place of emotion in research is problematised in the scientific, modern discourse in opposition to *reason* and as something which compromises objectivity and thereby validity, although we acknowledge that the place of emotions in research has been more explicit in recent years (see Coffey 1999; Doucet and Mauthner 2012). However, as shown above, the historic preoccupation with normalisation is clearly not emotion or value-free. Rather, it is generated within a paradigm that constructs and relies upon the emotions of sympathy, such as the tragedy discourse of disability (which denotes disability as a tragic fate, worse than death), and colonial global relations of *othering*. Transformation of this imperial paradigm of emotion begins by making the dominant emotions visible. It involves constructing alternatives to sanitised claims in research by drawing from activism which calls for aspiration for disabled children and young people, and rages against normalcy.

In their research with adults with the label of learning disability, Runswick-Cole and Goodley (2017) draw upon the notion of the 'disability commons' – campaigns, activism, and other interventions produced through recognising common humanity and interdependence. Transformative research that invokes open emotion draws on the disability commons, a sense of reciprocity of loving bonds and intimacy in the lives of disabled children, which, in turn, drive up expectations and offer the possibility to reimagine possible futures for disabled children and young people. For example, Jones and Liddiard (2017) emphasise the need to centre emotion in reflexive research, rather than attempting to write it out. In this sentiment, feelings are not barriers to inquiry, but become necessary forms of affective labour for reflexivity itself (Burkitt 2012). Emotions emerge, then, as forms of knowledge in their own right that are vital to draw upon for inquiry, analysis, and theory. Applying Mills' (2014) work on private troubles as public issues, the disability commons at once de-individualises and politicises experiences of disablism for disabled children and young people and their families.

Research approaches in which parents include their child in decisions about the topic, ethics, and methods together, and which they then co-author, are very powerful. Manns and Manns (2017) decide upon the use of a text conversation as a familiar mode of conversation to maximise both independent and relational authorship. Merchant and Merchant (2017) made a cartoon film about summer play aspirations and a drama depicting the realities of accessing play opportunities. Co-production has many different forms and in these two studies, it is the time taken to tailor and create it that makes the accounts poignant and memorable – many, many miles away from the deficit accounts that we began the chapter with. As authors and readers of research, we need to examine our own ethical stance in relation to the stories we tell and hear about disabled children. If we are telling or reading stories of bullying in our writing or hearing accounts of distress presented at conferences, and do nothing, we are drawn into a passive vicarious role. Too often the *lived experience* of disabled children and parents is harvested by researchers and professionals from children and families as a story of inspiration which only serves to shore up the notion of the norm and to endorse the tragedy dynamic of disablism.

A developing field

As the field of disabled children's childhood studies develops, we are witnessing further shifts in inquiry. For the remainder of this chapter, we describe these under three broad themes: (1) de-centring inquiry from the Global North; (2) quantitative research and big data; and (3) intersectionality and intimacy. We end with some considerations of future research directions.

De-centring from the Global North

The first shift away from what might be described as the *view from the centre* (represented by medicalised and psychologised accounts of disabled children's lives) involves re-orientating research to recognise and engage with the global context and post-colonial relations. Meekosha (2011: 670) explains that the 'claim of universals', like 'normative' child development, usually stems from the Global North, but this knowledge is often de-contextualised. The absence of any reference to geopolitical locations in research with children renders the experiences of children in the Global South invisible. The impact of Global North practices – in terms of inequalities, war, violent exploitation and environmental degradation – are ignored. 'Reading from the centre', Meekosha (2011: 670) argues, positions those excluded as beneficiaries of 'development' or as being outside of forms of Northern welfare, with the priority on survival erasing the connection between impoverishment, colonial systems, and their continuing effects.

In response to Global North–centric accounts, disabled children's childhood studies includes research studies coming from the Global South that have illustrated the contributions of disabled children to family and community life. In Guatemala (Grech 2013: 95), disabled children are part of and contribute to their community, and he suggests that we begin by being open about those goals and the futility of seeking universal concepts of childhood and disability:

> It is perhaps more important for any analysis to start off by understanding what surrounds the child, what it means to be a 'full' child and a 'full' person, because this is what disability is positioned along/against and how it is defined and interpreted by both disabled people and those around.

Community and a full family concept of reciprocal care in African cultures is presented as well as the poverty and alienating practices introduced by colonial governance (Chataika and McKenzie 2013). Clearly, individualistic research or policy approaches are not going to be of relevant value if the context is not explored as the basis for developing focus and co-production. The value of engaging with the issues of geopolitical relations is also the feedback and challenge that such studies provide in *writing back* to the Global North. Why, when we have strong social model theories in Britain, are we not seeing more co-production and family, community participatory research that sees disabled children as contributors to communities?

Others, such as Mills (2014) and Wells (2009), have made visible the export of normalising and segregating practices of the Global North, the continuing exploitation of the Global South, and the profit reaped. We need to be cautious as studies concerned with the childhoods of disabled children in the Global South are currently limited and we do not wish to overgeneralise or further *other*, but we want to support the innovations in academia which are promoting opportunities for voices from around the world (such as the journal *Disability and the Global South*). As editors of *The Palgrave Handbook of Disabled Children's Childhood Studies*, we invited contributors to locate the geopolitical context of their studies, but also to discuss the significance of those relations. This can be especially challenging for authors in the Global North privileged by the weight of de-contextualised literature, and needing to learn to see our own contexts critically.

Quantitative research and big data

While much research in disabled children's childhood studies has been drawn from qualitative inquiry, we propose a re-orientation of quantitative research and the use of big data that is often premised on narrow constructs of normative child development or are focused on gathering information about the prevalence of childhood impairment, mapping milestones reached, and service cost implications – see McLaughlin et al. (2017) for a discussion of such monitoring research and its impact. As such, we need to orientate quantitative questions to take account of the concerns of disabled children and their families, and to dig deep into the existing qualitative studies in the field to generate those questions. In the following examples, we can see how concerns and opportunities raised in personal accounts or small qualitative studies can be the impetus for generating big data or using existing data to track or to extend impact from the studies.

An auto-ethnographic account of the experience of maternity services for disabled women (Skitteral 2017) – which found inaccessible parking, buildings, and barriers to supportive services – might be followed up with an audit to map the accessibility of maternity services for policy development with disabled consultants and service providers. We could draw on Merchant and Merchant's (2017) difficult experience of finding a school holiday period play scheme and set out to measure the annual take-up of play schemes by disabled children as a right to community participation. However, quantitative research interested in correlations in order to ascertain significant factors on outcomes, and regarding outcomes in terms of *typical* development, would ask how outcomes for a population are different when an intervention occurs; it would look at outcomes as a measure of the play scheme, not just whether a child can or does attend, but what impact it has on their development. This type of research might at first be attractive to a funder interested to know if an intervention has any value. However, quantitative researchers would not claim to know about the experience of the child or assume any factor outside of the study is not important. If, for example, attending a play scheme led to an improvement of communication skills, it might be because the parent/carers were able to take up employment and spend more time with the child, or have more income to arrange other supports. For the child, it also might or might not be an enjoyable experience or one of bullying. So, how might quantitative research ask questions about experience?

In Savage's (2017) account of her experience as a young person at school with a long-term health condition, she describes the teacher and peer hostility she encountered, with a teacher shouting at her when she had a nose bleed and her peers stealing her things when she was away from school. She developed a joy of reading in response. She now views her school experience as central to her identity and to her current contributions as a mentor to other young people with long-term and life-threatening conditions at school. Quantitative research can ascertain the number of schools with policies for flexible attendance, policies to address bullying, staff training in disability equality, and identify the data needed to track and analyse the impact of those policies. Quantitative research could be used to gather data about family and community contributions that disabled young people make to everyday civic society and to find out how many disabled young people are in the paid and unpaid workforce. In their *Tree of Participation* study, McElwee et al. (2017) illustrate the ways that disabled young people's participation can stem from small and service-led beginnings and then, when nurtured, gain momentum with young people beginning to develop the purpose from their own agenda. At a big data level, we can ask how many small-scale projects there are in public services and provide larger dissemination platforms to maximise impact. There may also be potential in the value of utilising existing databases, such as the European Union Statistics on Income and Living Conditions (EU-SILC), and others around the world.

In their qualitative study of disabled young people's care, Dowling et al. (2017) illustrate how local authorities have resourced distant services when no specialist service is available locally. Their account allows us to ask why specialist services are sought when the young person and their family had been expected to manage everyday life without that level of resource in their home or community. Quantitative and qualitative research could be used to map disabled children's journeys against the provision of local services in order to track and compare the level of resources put in place after a family has raised an urgent lack of home-based support, and after a child has been placed in a service away from the family. This scenario suggests we should think outside an oppositional quantitative/qualitative box to ask how both approaches can be used in concert to attend to disabled children and young people's experiences, and to the action for changes needed. We can ask how disabled children's rights might be defined and indicators of those rights be composed and tracked towards their enhancement. Participation, in the United Nations statement (OHCHR 2016), is key to any data collection – participation of children and other stakeholders should include free opportunity and capacity strengthening, and use a wide variety of opportunities. Furthermore, 'human rights indicators are a learning-by-doing instrument' (de Beco 2013: 396) and how rights are realised – not just how they are violated – is an important focus to encourage improvement to be used not to judge, but to motivate (Ennew 1998, in Op de Beeck 2015).

Intersectionality and intimacy

Without doubt, re-orientating research ensures that disabled children's childhood studies capture the intersectional lives of disabled children and their families. Too often, disabled children and young people are considered the sum of their impairments, or are subject only to a unitary disability identity. This is to the exclusion of all other categories of identity such as gender, class, race, sexual orientation, and nationality (Slater and Chapman 2017). Such a perspective objectifies disabled children and young people at the same time as stripping them of identities which are important to them and their families. For example, viewing disabled children and young people as gendered subjects challenges the degendering and desexualisation of disabled people, and the ways in which they are excluded from normative categories of sex and gender (Liddiard 2014; Shakespeare 1999).

This intersectional approach is important to further locate the relative differences in social and sexual power between men/boys and women/girls (and people of other genders) within disability, childhood, and youth, recognising that, in adulthood, disabled women are relatively more disadvantaged than disabled men (Thomas 2006). For example, Skitteral's (2017) auto-ethnographic account reminds us of the complex intersections of disability and gender through the paradox of being expected, as a girl, to undertake childcare responsibilities for siblings, while at the same time actively being written off as future-woman and mother because of disability. So too does Watermayer's (2017) account, in which he draws upon the presence of masculinity and reminds us of the sensitivity required to draw in and upon one's own childhood. In her study of fathers of children with the label of autism, Heeney (2017) contests assumptions around gender and disability, appealing for change to enable fathers' and young people's participation in personal and community life. Such discussion offers a rich appreciation of diversity, fluidity, and stresses the importance of recognising intersectionality with further dimensions of multiplicity, and its transformative potential for a better understood and better enjoyed life.

Disabled children's childhood studies make visible, then, the heterogeneity of both disability and childhood, acknowledging disabled childhoods as that which may be shaped by a number of experiences, privileges, and oppressions. Multiple oppressions are not seen as additive, but as presenting particular acute forms of experience across identities. For example, an intersectional approach enables an understanding of the relative power between disabled children and young people across a number of axes: a trans boy of colour will markedly experience both disability and childhood/youth differently to a white cisgendered, middle-class girl. Thus, disabled children are theorised in disabled children's childhood studies as having rich, vital, and complex intersections. According to Kafer (2013: 3), and crucially for disabled children and young people and their families, this complex, expansive disabled subject 'makes it possible to imagine disability and disability futures differently'.

Future directions: living life to the fullest

As we near the end of our contribution, we wanted to highlight recent developments to disabled children's childhood studies emerging through a new ESRC-funded research project titled *Living Life to the Fullest*. These developments embody the principles of disabled children's childhood studies and emphasise (1) new approaches to research bidding and co-authoring of funding proposals; (2) engagement with the arts and arts-making; and (3) active co-production, welcoming disabled children and young people into research collaborations as researchers. In short, through co-production with disabled children and young people with what are categorised as life-limiting and life-threatening impairments (LL/LTIs) and their families, allies, and organisations, *Living Life to the Fullest* seeks to forge new understandings of the lives, hopes, desires, and contributions of disabled children and young people with short lives. To counter the tragedy discourse of disability endemic to cultural and symbolic understandings of impairments of this kind – the dying child, the end of future – we centre affirmative politics to assert the vibrant offerings of these disabled children and young people to their families, schools, intimacies, and communities. In the last section in this chapter, we outline such developments in order to emphasise the many future re-orienting possibilities of disabled children's childhood studies.

Co-authoring the shape of inquiry

In *Living Life to the Fullest*, we use a transdisciplinary co-production methodology to work in partnership with disabled children and young people and their parents/carers and allies to explore their lives as they experience and understand them. We understand co-production as academics working together with a range of partners to produce research and outcomes not possible in isolation. At the foundations of co-productive research is a shared responsibility and collectivity, echoing the disability commons. Moreover, the research questions, methods, strategies of analysis, and plans for impact and public engagement reflect the ambitions of children, young people, their families, and community partners. Thus, co-production becomes a necessary part of shaping inquiry at the very early stages. Our funding bid was co-written with disabled children and young people, their parents/allies, and key representative non-governmental organisations (NGOs). For us, co-writing involved the discussion of ideas and research and impact planning through a number of writing workshops and meetings. We asked children and young people many questions, such as: What should we be asking questions about in the research? Whom should we be asking? What aspects of your life often goes unnoticed that you would like to see explored in our project? What would enable you to participate in our research if you wanted to? How can we make it easier/appealing for you and other young disabled people to take part? What do we need to get right in our project? What could we get wrong? For accessibility, and to reach more young people, we made a short narrated film (Liddiard 2015). To sum up, the emphasis is upon making the inception of research accessible and enacting a shared distribution of responsibility from the outset by expanding the typically ableist and elitist ways in which bids for research funding get produced.

Arts and arts-making

Exploring disability through art offers a different point of entry, a chance to see disability from the inside out. *Living Life to the Fullest* purposefully draws upon and makes use of the arts and art-making due to the myriad ways they open up alternative ways of knowing and communicating – crucial in the context of disability research with children and young people (Rice et al. 2015). We centre transformative narrative and arts-informed methods precisely because they push the rigid boundaries of traditional social scientific research methodologies, gaining new insights and understandings about the liminal or the ambiguous in-between spaces of people's lives. They also advance social inclusion and justice by making space to challenge stereotypes and speak back to dominant discourses (Rice et al. 2015, 2017). They draw research and art out of 'the elitist institutions of academe and art museums' and relocate inquiry within 'local, personal, everyday places and events' (Finley 2008: 72). They are also accessible to people with a range of abilities and support and enable multiple ways of thinking and knowing, often far removed from academic/research discourse in its conventional sense. Engaging with the arts also offers the tools to resist the well-known *single story* of disability (Liddiard 2014; Rice et al. 2015) by creating and centring, without normalising, representations of disability that have previously been relegated to the margins, namely the lives of disabled children and young people (Curran and Runswick-Cole 2013, 2014).

Children and young people as co-researchers

In *Living Life to the Fullest*, children and young people – as active co-researchers – have opportunities to both learn from and bring to inquiry a multitude of skills to participate in the research process. Rather than a space of no future (Kafer 2013), disability becomes valued, vibrant, and future facing through opportunities to participate in collaborative inquiry and scholar activism (Runswick-Cole 2017) which aims to engender social change. Past this, we have seen in our previous research the affective and psychic impact made possible when disabled people become leaders of research that is about their lives (Liddiard 2014; Rice et al. 2015). For example, learning new skills, working in a team, being valued for your lived experience, and having opportunities to offer expert contributions serves to build confidence, esteem, and self-worth (Graham and Fitzgerald 2008). In this way, *Living Life to the Fullest* serves to speak back to disabled children and young people as passive subjects, along with acknowledging and affirming their agency and capacity to support and collaborate with others.

Conclusion

In this chapter, we have drawn upon work in the burgeoning field of disabled children's childhood studies. We began by outlining the multiple oppressions in the lives of disabled children – pathologisation, professional surveillance, and routinisation of the everyday – lives so often overshadowed by the tyranny of the norm and mundane disablism. In what followed, we demarcated where multiple fields of study – new sociologies of childhood and disability studies – have written out or left unattended the lives, concerns, and experiences of disabled children and their families. Such fields have omitted both disability and childhood from their agendas respectively. Importantly, we have shown the difference that disabled children's childhood studies make to researching and theorising disabled childhoods, and to imagining the lives of disabled children, young people, and their parents and families differently. We have articulated the importance of re-orientating research inquiry away from *professional concerns*, which routinely focus on issues of impairment and service evaluation in the lives of disabled children. At the same time, we have focused on locating the politics of researching with disabled children and young people, exploring their location, participation, and voice in inquiry, as well as issues of consent, anonymity, risk, institutional ethics demands, researching bidding and funding, and parents' stories and privacy. We have also considered the need to welcome emotion as part of the process of research, and engage with the global context and postcolonial relations. Lastly, we have imagined the use and application of big data and reified the benefits of researching disabled childhoods as rich and intersectional. Centring these ethical, political, emotional, and institutional factors within all disabled children's childhood studies avows a commitment to the hopes, dreams, and aspirations of disabled children and young people.

Acknowledgements

We would like to acknowledge and express our gratitude to the Economic and Social Research Council for funding our project 'Life, Death, Disability and the Human: Living Life to the Fullest' (ES/P001041/1).

References

Burkitt, I. 2012. Emotional reflexivity: feeling, emotion and imagination in reflexive dialogues. *Sociology* 46(3), pp. 458–472.
Burman, E. 2008. *Deconstructing Developmental Psychology*. London: Routledge.

Chataika, T. and McKenzie, J. 2013. Considerations of an African childhood disability studies. In: Curran, T. and Runswick-Cole, K. eds. *Disabled Children's Childhood Studies: Critical Approaches in a Global Context.* Basingstoke: Palgrave Macmillan, pp. 89–104.

Cocks, A. J. 2006. The ethical maze: finding an inclusive path toward gaining children's agreement to research participation. *Childhood* 13(2), pp. 247–266.

Coffey, A. 1999. *The Ethnographic Self: Fieldwork and the Representation of Identity.* London: Sage.

Coles, B. 2017. Personalisation and parents: the formalisation of family care for adult children with learning disabilities in England. In: Runswick-Cole, K., Curran, T. and Liddiard, K. eds. *The Palgrave Handbook of Disabled Children's Childhood Studies.* Basingstoke: Palgrave, in press.

Connors, C. and Stalker, K. 2007. Children's experiences of disability: pointers to a social model of childhood disability. *Disability and Society* 22(1), pp. 19–33.

Curran, T. and Runswick-Cole, K. 2013. *Disabled Children's Childhood Studies: Critical Approaches in a Global Context.* Basingstoke: Palgrave Macmillan.

Curran, T. and Runswick-Cole, K. 2014. Disabled children's childhood studies: a distinct approach? *Disability and Society* 29(10), pp. 1617–1630.

Curran, T., Sayers, R. and Percy-Smith, B. 2017. Disabled children's childhood studies and leadership as experts by experience: the case for learning activism in health and social care. In: Runswick-Cole, K., Curran, T. and Liddiard, K. eds. *The Palgrave Handbook of Disabled Children's Childhood Studies.* Basingstoke: Palgrave, in press.

De Beco, G. 2013. Human rights indicators: from theoretical debate to practical application. *Journal of Human Rights Practice* 5(2), pp. 380–397.

Dickson-Swift, V., James, E. L., Kippen, S. and Liamputtong, P. 2009. Researching sensitive topics: qualitative research as emotion work. *Qualitative Research* 9(1), pp. 61–79.

Doucet, A. and Mauthner, N. S. 2012. Emotions in/and knowing. In: Spencer, D., Walby, K. and Hunt, A. eds. *Emotions Matter: A Relational Approach to Emotions.* Toronto: University of Toronto Press, pp. 161–176.

Dowling, S., Kelly, B. and Winter, K. 2017. Disabled children in out-of-home care: issues and challenges for practice. In: Runswick-Cole, K., Curran, T. and Liddiard, K. eds. *The Palgrave Handbook of Disabled Children's Childhood Studies.* Basingstoke: Palgrave, in press.

Ennew, J. 1998. *Monitoring Children's Rights: Indicators for Children' Rights Project.* Newmarket: Global Gutter Press.

Finley, S. 2008. Arts-based research. In: Knowles, G. and Cole, A. eds. *Handbook of the Arts in Qualitative Research: Perspectives, Methodologies, Examples and Issues.* Los Angeles: Sage, pp. 71–82.

Goodley, D. 2011. *Disability Studies: An Inter-Disciplinary Introduction.* London: Sage.

Goodley, D. 2014. *Dis/ability Studies: Theorising Disablism and Ableism.* London: Routledge.

Goodley, D. and Runswick-Cole, K. 2010. Emancipating play: dis/abled children, development and deconstruction. *Disability and Society* 25(4), pp. 499–512.

Goodley, D. and Runswick-Cole, K. 2011. The violence of disablism. *Sociology of Health and Illness* 33(4), pp. 602–617.

Goodley, D. and Runswick-Cole, K. 2012a. Decolonizing methodologies: disabled children as research managers and participant ethnographers. In: Grech, S. and Azzopardi, A. eds. *Inclusive Communities: A Reader.* Rotterdam: Sense, pp. 215–231.

Goodley, D. and Runswick-Cole, K. 2012b. Reading Rosie: the postmodern disabled child. *Journal of Educational and Child Psychology* 29(2), pp. 53–66.

Goodley, D. and Runswick-Cole, K. 2014. Becoming dishuman: thinking about the human through dis/ability. *Discourse: Cultural Politics of Education* 37(1), pp. 1–15.

Goodley, D., Runswick-Cole, K. and Liddiard, K. 2015. The DisHuman child. *Discourse: Studies in the Cultural Politics of Education* 37(5), pp. 770–784.

Graham, S. and Fitzgerald, J. 2008. *Handbook of Writing Research.* New York: Guilford Press.

Grech, S. 2013. Disability, childhood and poverty: critical perspectives on Guatemala. In: Curran, T. and Runswick-Cole, K. eds. *Disabled Children's Childhood Studies: Critical Approaches in a Global Context.* Basingstoke: Palgrave Macmillan, pp. 89–104.

Greenstein, A. 2015. *Radical Inclusive Education: Disability, Teaching and Struggles for Liberation.* London: Routledge.

Greenstein, A. 2017. Being a speech and language therapist: between support and oppression. In: Runswick-Cole, K., Curran, T. and Liddiard, K. eds. *The Palgrave Handbook of Disabled Children's Childhood Studies.* Basingstoke: Palgrave, in press.

Hambly, H. 2017. A relational understanding of language impairment: children's experiences in the context of their social worlds. In: Runswick-Cole, K., Curran, T. and Liddiard, K. eds. *The Palgrave Handbook of Disabled Children's Childhood Studies.* Basingstoke: Palgrave, in press.

Heeney, J. 2017. Intersectionality theory in research with the fathers of children with the label of autism. In: Runswick-Cole, K., Curran, T. and Liddiard, K. eds. *The Palgrave Handbook of Disabled Children's Childhood Studies.* Basingstoke: Palgrave, in press.

James, A., Jenks, C. and Prout, A. 1998. *Theorising Childhood.* Cambridge: Polity Press.

Jones, L. and Liddiard, K. 2017. A diversity of crip childhoods? Considering the looked after childhood. In: Runswick-Cole, K., Curran, T. and Liddiard, K. eds. *The Palgrave Handbook of Disabled Children's Childhood Studies.* Basingstoke: Palgrave, in press.

Kafer, A. 2013. *Feminist, Queer, Crip.* Bloomington: Indiana University Press.

Liddiard, K. 2014. The work of disabled identities in intimate relationships. *Disability and Society* 29(1), pp. 115–128.

Liddiard, K. 2015. Living life to the fullest. *YouTube* [Online]. Available at: www.youtube.com/watch?v=OqlERha3yMQ [Accessed: 23 November 2017].

Mallett, R. and Runswick-Cole, K. 2014. *Approaching Disability: Critical Issues and Perspectives.* London: Routledge.

Manns, B. and Manns, S. 2017. The texting project. In: Runswick-Cole, K., Curran, T. and Liddiard, K. eds. *The Palgrave Handbook of Disabled Children's Childhood Studies.* Basingstoke: Palgrave, in press.

McElwee, J., Cox, D., Cox, T., Holland, R., Holland, T., Mason, T., Pearce, C., Sobey, C., Bugler, J., James, A. and Pearce, B. 2017. The tree of participation: our thoughts about growing a culture of participation between young people, parents and health team staff. In: Runswick-Cole, K., Curran, T. and Liddiard, K. eds. *The Palgrave Handbook of Disabled Children's Childhood Studies.* Basingstoke: Palgrave, in press.

McLaughlin, J., Goodley, D. Clavering, E. and Fisher, P. 2008. *Families Raising Disabled Children: Enabling Care.* London: Sage.

McLaughlin, J., Coleman-Fountain, E. and Clavering, E. 2017. *Disabled Childhoods: Monitoring Differences and Emerging Identities.* London: Routledge.

McRuer, M. 2006. *Crip Theory: Cultural Signs of Queerness and Disability.* New York: New York University Press.

Meekosha, H. 2011. Decolonising disability: thinking and acting globally. *Disability and Society* 26(6), pp. 667–682.

Merchant, J. and Merchant, W. 2017. 'What can I say?'. In: Runswick-Cole, K., Curran, T. and Liddiard, K. eds. *The Palgrave Handbook of Disabled Children's Childhood Studies.* Basingstoke: Palgrave, in press.

Mills, C. 2014. *Decolonizing Global Mental Health: The Psychiatrization of the Majority World.* London: Routledge.

Morris, J. 2003. Including all children: finding out about the experiences of children with communication and/or cognitive impairments. *Children and Society* 17(5), pp. 337–348.

Naseem, S. 2017. 'Just Sumaira: Not her, them or it'. In: Runswick-Cole, K., Curran, T. and Liddiard, K. eds. *The Palgrave Handbook of Disabled Children's Childhood Studies.* Basingstoke: Palgrave, in press.

OHCHR. 2016. A *Human Rights-Based Approach to Data.* United Nations: Human Rights Office of the High Commissioner Guidance Note.

Oliver, M. 1991. *The Politics of Disablement.* Basingstoke: Macmillan.

Op de Beeck, H. 2015. Children's rights indicators from theory to implementation: the Flemish case. *Child Indicators Research* 8(2), pp. 243–264.

Pickering, D. 2017. Shared perspectives: the embodiment of disabled children and young people's voices about participating in recreational activities. In: Runswick-Cole, K., Curran, T. and Liddiard, K. eds. *The Palgrave Handbook of Disabled Children's Childhood Studies.* Basingstoke: Palgrave, in press.

Read, J., Clements, L. J. and Ruebain, D. 2006. *Disabled Children and the Law: Research and Good Practice.* London: Jessica Kingsley.

Rice, C., Chandler, E., Harrison, E. Liddiard, K. and Ferrari, M. 2015. Project Re-Vision: disability at the edges of representation. *Disability and Society* 30(4), pp. 513–527.

Rice, C., Chandler, E., Rinaldi, J., Liddiard, K., Changfoot, N., Mykitiuk, R., and Mundel, I. 2017. Imagining disability futurities. *Hypatia* (Early View).

Runswick-Cole, K. 2017. *(Re)Imagining the Research Assemblage: Toward Scholar Activism.* Inaugural Lecture, Manchester Metropolitan University, 10 January 2017.

Runswick-Cole, K., Curran, T. and Liddiard, K. eds. 2017. *The Palgrave Handbook of Disabled Children's Childhood Studies.* Basingstoke: Palgrave.

Savage, S. 2017. The heaviest burdens and life's most intense fulfilment: a retrospective and re-understanding of my experiences with childhood liver disease and transplantation. In: Runswick-Cole, K., Curran, T. and Liddiard, K. eds. *The Palgrave Handbook of Disabled Children's Childhood Studies.* Basingstoke: Palgrave, in press.

Shakespeare, T. 1999. The sexual politics of disabled masculinity. *Sex and Disability* 17(1), pp. 53–64.

Shakespeare, T., Priestley, M. and Barnes, C. 1999. Life as a disabled child: a qualitative study of young people's experiences and perspectives. *Centre for Disability Studies* [Online]. Available at: http://disability-studies.leeds.ac.uk/research/life-as-a-disabled-child/ [Accessed: 23 November 2017].

Skitteral, J. 2017. Being a disabled woman and mum: my journey from childhood. In: Runswick-Cole, K., Curran, T. and Liddiard, K. eds. *The Palgrave Handbook of Disabled Children's Childhood Studies.* Basingstoke: Palgrave, in press.

Slater, J. 2014. *Youth and Dis/ability: A Challenge to Mr. Reasonable.* Farnham: Ashgate.

Slater, J. and Chapman, E. 2017. Normalcy, intersectionality and ableism: teaching about and around 'inclusion' to future educators. In: Runswick-Cole, K., Curran, T. and Liddiard, K. eds. *The Palgrave Handbook of Disabled Children's Childhood Studies.* Basingstoke: Palgrave, in press.

Thackray, L. 2017. Anonymity, confidentiality and informed consent: exploring ethical quandaries and dilemmas in research with and about disabled children's childhoods. In: Runswick-Cole, K., Curran, T. and Liddiard, K. eds. *The Palgrave Handbook of Disabled Children's Childhood Studies.* Basingstoke: Palgrave, in press.

Thomas, C. 2006. Disability and gender: reflections on theory and research. *Scandinavian Journal of Disability Research* 8(2–3), pp. 177–185.

Tøssebro, J. 2004. Understanding disability. *Scandinavian Journal of Disability Studies* 6(1), pp. 3–7.

Traustadóttir, R. 2004. Disability studies: A Nordic perspective. *Paper presented at the British Disability Studies Association Conference*, Lancaster, UK, 26–28 July 2004.

Watermayer, B. 2017. Growing up disabled: impairment, familial relationships and identity. In: Runswick-Cole, K., Curran, T. and Liddiard, K. eds. *The Palgrave Handbook of Disabled Children's Childhood Studies*. Basingstoke: Palgrave, in press.

Watson, T. 2017. The construction of life trajectories: reflections, research and resolutions for young people with behavioural disabilities. In: Runswick-Cole, K., Curran, T. and Liddiard, K. eds. *The Palgrave Handbook of Disabled Children's Childhood Studies*. Basingstoke: Palgrave, in press.

Wells, K. 2009. *Childhood in a Global Perspective*. Cambridge: Polity Press.

Wells, K. 2017. *Childhood Studies: Making Young Subjects*. Cambridge: Polity Press.

Chapter 4

Pursuit of ordinariness

Dynamics of conforming and resisting in disabled young people's embodied practices

Janice McLaughlin and Edmund Coleman-Fountain

Introduction

Young people's everyday cultural practices are a major theme of youth studies (Blatterer 2010; Bucholtz 2002; Bynner 2005; Epstein et al. 2001). This work provides insights into dynamics of social negotiation, identity making, and body work, which are seen as defining adolescence (Furlong and Cartmel 2007; Geldens et al. 2011). One argument made within youth studies is that opportunities are increasing in contemporary society (in the Global North)[1] for young people's identity practices to be expansive and fluid, partly due to the decline of old certainties around class, alongside new material and consumption imaginaries (Bynner 2005; Furlong et al. 2011; Mørch and Andersen 2006; Nayak 2006). These practices are associated with new ways of expressing identity and fashioning the body, producing an image of youthful agency and resistance. In contrast, others argue that while some old pathways may have fallen by the wayside, others remain, ones which generate particular boundaries and limitations for young people in specific material and cultural locations (Bradley and Devadason 2008; Irwin 1995; MacDonald 2011). Such boundaries lead to dynamics of judgement and stigma in the lives of young people, manifesting in the regulation of the body; for example, the policing dynamics around gender and young women's sexuality are well documented (Nayak and Kehily 2008).

The focus on the body in youth studies has frequently neglected the difference disability makes to the scope for identity negotiation for young people and how this speaks to possibilities and limitations to young lives. This chapter addresses this gap by seeing the relationship between disability and identity as shaped by practices that entail both creative expression and normative constraint (Pink 2012). Turning to practice, we argue, means seeing disability as embodied due to the way impairment and associated technologies matter for the enactment of practices, a concept we derive from symbolic interactionism that links social *knowing* to everyday doings (Denzin 1992). By this, we mean that what people do with their body matters to their social position and identity, but how such doings come to matter is also shaped by the surrounding values that ascribe meanings to them. Such an understanding does complicate social model under-standings of disability. This is because the greater inclusion of impairment into the interactional production of disability means that it is important to acknowl-edge that, while there are shared challenges – including to interaction – disabled people face due to discriminatory social environments and structures, there will also be variations in both challenge and possibility (Coleman-Fountain and McLaughlin 2013). These flow from how particular embodied disabled practices form in the interaction between specific impairment effects, the possi-bilities allowed in specific contexts via technologies, other social actors, material constraints, and the norms and values available to make sense of that particular body and its presence in the world (Scully 2010). We still deploy the language of disability to reflect both the renewed importance of disability politics and the commonalities that remain. The specific social position and identity that emerges in interaction for a disabled person will vary, but we can use disability to refer to all those who face the challenges of managing the greater enforced complexity of their interaction with the world.

Our particular focus here is on linking the production of disability to judgements or *valuations* (Edwards and Imrie 2003) – informed by notions of *normality* – which are made in the social evaluation of bodies as correct, appropriate, and something to aspire to. The demonstration of competence in mundane social activities, we argue, occurs through practices (Rock 1979); the recognition of competence in others (and oneself) speaks to the narrowness or expansiveness of what is contained within the category. What we are interested in is whether, in the contexts of changing attitudes around disability and the broader identity landscapes of youth, disabled young people are participating in embodied identity negotiations that imply an expansive and welcoming space for them. Or, we may ask, do their approaches to social participation imply perhaps changing, but nevertheless persistent, flaws in society's willingness to embrace difference and diversity? We use the term *pursuit of ordinariness* to ask whether wanting to be ordinary suggests that high costs remain for not being so, or that ordinariness has broadened in meaning to encompass new possibili-ties and practices.

We begin by discussing how critical disability studies (CDS) argues that discourses of normality continue to be important to the marginalisation of disabled people. We then broaden this approach by adding a focus on how dis-courses influence (and are influenced by) everyday interactions and practices. The rest of the chapter uses those ideas to discuss a recent research project we undertook in the North-East of England with disabled young people focusing on transitions to adulthood via a focus on narratives and practices of the dis-abled body. After introducing the study, we show how the young people spoke of their lives as normal and ordinary, what meaning they gave to those terms, and how that influenced the way they embodied and spoke of themselves as disabled.

Normality as ordinariness

The discursive production of normality

There are several pointers to how the lives of disabled young people growing up now in the Global North are different from those of previous generations of disabled young people (Runswick-Cole and Curran 2013). They are more likely to be educated in mainstream schooling, rather than confined to residential institutions; they are protected by anti-discrimination legislation in many countries, which has transformed their local material and social environments; people's attitudes show many signs of being more welcoming to disabled people, and; disabled role models have greater visibility through public events such as the Paralympics and other cultural representations. The important achievements of the disability movement have helped shift understandings of disability away from tales of tragedy, pity, and fear, towards recognition, pride, and assertive demands for citizenship rights (Shakespeare 2006). Technological possibilities, such as those generated by principles of universal design (Ferri 2015) and the availability of communication technologies (Söderström 2009), blur the line between assistive and everyday technology and ease interaction in both the *virtual* and *real* world (Moser 2006). All of this suggests new possibilities for a life like others lead; normal – in the context of the current adult transition imaginaries (Furlong and Cartmel 2007) – aspirations of education, career, an intimate life, and independence are now viable and meaningful options.

While these developments are important and hard-won by disability activists and organisations, contemporary researchers, particularly in CDS, argue that we need to maintain at least a scepticism about how far that movement towards inclusion and the welcoming of disabled people has travelled (Holt 2004). CDS argues that disabled people continue to experience marginalisation due to the way notions of normality sustain a policing of social relations and processes of othering (Goodley 2007; Goodley and Runswick-Cole 2011; Goodley and Runswick-Cole 2013). To make this argument, CDS moves away from institutional rules and legislative protection to focus on the importance of cultural and discursive meanings to constructing disabled people as the other – a switch in focus that some have criticised for not giving enough emphasis to the material struggles of disabled people (Vehmas and Watson 2014). The argument is that we cannot understand why disabled people continue to be marginalised in society without understanding how discursive processes still situate disability outside normality. Discourse is the key means of defining and embedding what is considered normal. Institutions, whether medicine (Canguilhem 1989; Thomas 2017), education (Holt et al. 2012), or welfare (McLaughlin and Goodley 2008), are powerful in shaping disability through meanings they generate and secure in the production of policies, rules, and practices: 'Through a priori standards that are situated within culturally and historically contingent values and practice, that which counts as *abnormal, disabled*, or *pathological* is constituted and continues to be re-constituted discursively' (Lester and Paulus 2012: 260). As Garland-Thomson (1997: 6) suggests, disability is 'a product of cultural rules about what bodies should be or do'. This clearly echoes Foucault's (1975, 1990) ideas about the productive capacity of institutions – such as medicine – to create categories of people, as well as conditions, which help shape social order and the position of individuals within it.

CDS writers argue that for those with embodied differences that are categorised as disabled, definitions of normality matter (Goodley 2011). To be *different* opens up a question about whether one fits in or belongs; stepping away from established normal ways of being positions the person as other. Shildrick (1999: 79) emphasises that 'the standard is not normal but normative'. Through the privileging of the normative, the disabled body is positioned as 'corporeal deviance' (Garland-Thomson 1997: 6). As Braidotti (1996: 146) explains: 'We all have bodies, but not all bodies are equal: some matter more than others; some are, quite frankly, disposable. . . . The monstrous body, which makes a living spectacle of itself, is eminently disposable'. Looking out to the discursive privileging of 'normality', CDS writers see a social world uneasy with difference, a world where '[t]o be perceived as differently embodied . . . is still to occupy a place defined as exceptional, rather than to simply be part of a multiplicity of possibilities' (Shildrick 2012: 31). Shildrick speaks of contemporary society as displaying 'minimal hospitality' to embodied difference. This is because we operate in the context of the fiction that some bodies are normal and others are not, rather than acknowledging that we all live in bodies that are fragile and only (for some) temporarily able. Garland-Thomson (2007: 114) speaks of this in a similar way, arguing that those who see themselves within the category of normality are uncomfortable around those 'whose way of being and appearing in the world offer evidence against the myth of certainty and compliancy in regard to human bodies'. The implication is that while some life possibilities are being opened up for disabled people, the imaginaries for what kind of lives equate to good lives remain narrow. What is on offer is to be accepted if disabled people can do the normal things that other people do. For those disabled people who appear unable to be normal and do normal things, exclusion through social rejection is the dominant social response. It is tolerance that is on offer, tolerance of those who can achieve against existing markers of acceptable humanness.

Ordinary practices

Much of the CDS work focuses on cultural processes through which discourses of normality circulate. While this is important, it is necessary to understand how those circulations are replicated, maintained, and changed in their presence in social interaction, particularly in the enactment of practices which become a focus of social judgement. In short, it is important to attend to how people engage practically with concepts of normality. The power of discourse, we argue, operates through the engagement with symbols and meanings in everyday practices, which embed those meanings in everyday life. Discursive effects require their reproduction within social life and in this reproduction, they are translated and altered. Our use of the notion of practice derives from our turn to symbolic interactionism and its focus on joint action and interaction (Blumer 1986). Symbolic interactionism proposes that meaning and selfhood are constructed through people's combined practical engagement with social worlds, including the objects, technologies, people, and physical spaces that comprise them (Monaghan 2006). While allowing for creativity, this engagement can also entail a fitting in with others who are powerful sources of expectation and valuation (Azarian 2015). Thus, the power of other people's behaviours and representations remains central. In addition, the body is not framed as inert matter, which becomes meaningful through discourse. Rather, it is lived, mobilised, and enacted, and, through this process, it becomes meaningful (Crossley 2001; Vannini 2006), but also regulated and constrained.

Taking this back into questions of normality, we can see how normal ways of doing things, as well as normal ways of speaking of such things, regulate social life. Fitting in is an embodied dynamic of displaying bodies that appear able to do normal things and look normal. Discursively produced meanings about what is normal are secured in their articulation, their embodied interaction. This helps highlight the inclusion of individuals in their own regulation, not just by how they come to understand themselves to be (their self-hood), but also how they come to move and shape their bodies according to available norms. Such norms are presented as socially valued in opposition to a stigmatised, demeaned, or derided difference. While situated agency, desire, and pleasure also shape embodied practice, it is important to acknowledge that for socially marginalised groups, the experienced need to avoid stigma to some degree compels particular relationships to the body (Moffatt and Noble 2015); '[i]ndividuals regulate *themselves* in relation to the norms that circulate social spaces' (Holt et al. 2012: 2194, emphasis in the original).

Our focus on *ordinary practices* is therefore to think about what people do as they engage with concepts of normality, both to their bodies and within their embodied interactions with others. This means holding onto the body in its material and representative forms – including differences in the ways different bodies look and move. Bodily form and function are significant in informing social interactions and fundamental in deciding how bodies and persons fit within normative frameworks of understanding (Garland-Thomson 2009). One individual mode of regulation is the efforts people make to pass, to fit in via minimising the presence of that which signals a difference. In relation to disability, this means working on the body to appear normal. Doing so, including by doing things normally, facilitates social interaction and 'repair[s] the fabric of the relation so that it can continue' (Garland-Thomson 1997: 13). Being able to replicate normality can enable the 'material anonymity' (Garland-Thomson

2011: 596) that allows for inclusion, but doing so requires that the labour, the work involved in that replication, be invisible (Scully 2010).

Drawing all of this back to disabled young people, the question is to what degree do they care about, and/or try to minimise, their differences from other young people? In considering this, it is helpful to also acknowledge debates in youth studies about identity formation and negotiation in adolescence. We began the chapter by noting that many scholars working within youth studies argue that adolescence remains a contested period of life, where dynamics of acceptance, exclusion, and hierarchies between different modes of identity and embodiment have to be worked through by young people. We also spoke of contemporary adolescence as being a period where there *may be* scope for experimentation and fluidity in identity (Traver and Duran 2014). One argument in youth studies is that young people live in an increasingly individualised context of transitions to adulthood where new possibilities are now available, but also new challenges exist to find one's way in the world without material support or clear pathways to independence and security. Gill et al. (2005: 7) refer to this as a 'grammar of individualism'. This reflects both the scope for experimentation and diversity, and the presence of inequalities reshaped for the contemporary era between those with the capital which enables experimentation and those without and struggling towards a precarious transition to adulthood (Prout 2000).

What we want to do now is consider these questions, around the regulatory potential of normality and the role of individuals themselves in shaping their social position in response, by considering how some disabled young people we worked with pursued ordinariness in their everyday cultural practices.

The study

Our qualitative study[2] involved working with disabled young people on the production of narratives and representations of the socially situated disabled young body as they planned for, and moved towards, their transitions to adulthood. Recruitment to the study was from a cohort of young people (aged 14 to 20) with a diagnosis of cerebral palsy who were resident in the North-East of England. This cohort were participants in an earlier study on childhood cerebral palsy and pain (recruitment from the cohort also gave us access to qualitative data derived from interviews carried out with some members of this group from five years earlier). Thirteen young people were recruited from the cohort, with another four recruited from a local school for disabled pupils. Seven young women and ten young men were involved. The diagnosis of cerebral palsy which each had affected them in varied ways relating to speech, mobility, dexterity, body shape, and other issues such as epilepsy and learning disabilities. The primary access route to recruitment was via a National Health Service (NHS) held patient database. Ethical approval for the project was granted via the NHS. While the focus on cerebral palsy was due to the cohort of young people with the condition that we (and other researchers at Newcastle University) have been working with over time, the forms of embodied difference associated with it are particularly useful to what we are examining here. Cerebral palsy is a diagnostic category used to refer to people whose muscle tone, movement, and motor skills are effected by a brain injury, which occurs either prior to or during birth. This means it is a category where there is a range of impairment effects which lead to varied types and levels of embodied difference. Examining the management of social interaction by young people who have had that diagnosis, therefore, is a useful way to examine the relationship between stigma, interaction, and the social production of disability.

We wanted to work with the disabled young people through a variety of routes that could provide both choice in what they wanted to engage with and opportunities for them to reflect on their lives (Bagnoli 2011; Brannen and O'Brien 1996). The specifics of what we did was also influenced by the input of a research panel of disabled young people who offered their thoughts and ideas regarding the design and focus of the research, including our use of cameras and notebooks. The work with each participant began with an open-ended interview to introduce the project's themes, including what disability meant to participants and how their body was changing as they were ageing. This interview also included discussion of the childhood interviews that had been undertaken. They were then invited to create a photo journal that captured their identities as disabled young people. This was done using the young people's existing photographic practices, including letting them use cameras they already owned (often on their phones) and allowing them to source old images of themselves or images found elsewhere (like stock-images found on the internet). They were given a paper journal to display the photographs and invited to put any thoughts they had about the photos and why they had chosen them alongside. Cameras and printers were provided for those who did not have them. Participants had several months to complete this task. The researcher maintained contact over that time to provide them with prompts, ideas, and to discuss things that may have prevented their participation.

After all materials were gathered, the images and journals were discussed with the participants in a second interview, so that we did not jump to our interpretation without exploring what they sought to capture via the images they took. The completed journals were digitally scanned and returned to each participant to keep. Finally, two creative workshops were held in the final stages of the fieldwork, during which jewellery-making was used to gather additional stories and generate representative artefacts that represented the participants' embodied experiences in non-narrative form (Wallace and Press 2004). Seventeen young people took part in the first interviews; eight engaged in photo journal work, six of whom participated in the second interview; and three of those took part in the workshops. The reduction in numbers can be attributed to a number of factors. Common explanations were time available to commit long-term activity (for instance, owing to schoolwork or hospital appointments), difficulties travelling to research events, and interest (for instance, it is notable that only girls took part in the workshops).[3]

An ordinary life

Practices of ordinariness

Before discussing the participants' approaches to ordinariness, it is worth acknowledging that across the interviews (and the childhood interviews as well), dynamics of stigma were spoken of at length. A range of social responses across their young lives had made them realise that others did not treat them as belonging in their social words; name-calling, being the subject of jokes and left out of social activities, people speaking to their parents rather than to them, physical bullying, and other forms of social harassment were all catalogued. We would argue that these everyday social realities are an important context to the approach to ordinariness the participants spoke of.

The importance of ordinariness was a common theme in the discussions with our participants. This was prominent in their discussion about their cultural practices, which tended to be commonplace rather than expressive or stylistic (Bennett 1999; Roberts and MacDonald 2013). A sense of ordinariness filtered both into the types of things that they wanted for themselves now and in the future (e.g. to drive a car, to have a relationship, to live on their own, to go out with their mates), and also into the close work and oversight they maintained over the bodies in the production of those practices.

Our participants took great pride in being able to do ordinary things, even if it was more difficult for them due to difficulties they had with dexterity, mobility of joints, and muscle strength. In interviews with us, participants spoke in close up detail of the daily activities they could do for themselves – as well as the dedicated training they had undergone to enable them to do so:

> I can work a phone, I can work a laptop, I can work an oven, I can do all kinds of stuff, I can do stuff for myself.
>
> (Lauren, mother present, Interview 1)

> I can tie my shoelaces normally.
>
> (Jenny, Interview 1)

There was a strong preference for doing things themselves, rather than having to be dependent on someone else helping them. Mark, who was heavily involved in disability sport and regularly worked on building up the strength and dexterity of his body, emphasised the connection between doing daily activities himself and feeling positive about what he could do:

> To do it yourself, it's a little buzz inside you it's like, you know, I can do this myself but I don't need anyone to do it for me. I can make a cup of tea. I

don't need anyone to watch me pour the hot water 'cos my stick could go at any moment, and I can sit down and pour. I don't know. It just gives you a little sense of achievement.

(Mark, Interview 1)

There was a palpable discomfort, which appeared to have become more of an issue as they reached adolescence, with symbols of help such as technologies like sticks or wheelchairs, or people, whether family or care assistants. This led to rejections of help, whether this was asking for a classroom assistant not to help them anymore, or a refusal to use a stick or wheelchair in social settings, or asking family not to assist them in public. It was clear from how the participants spoke of removing visible signs of requiring help, that what they sought was to avoid a stigma they associated with dependency. Doing everyday activities themselves was not just important to them because they were useful things to be able to do, but because they also had significant symbolic value; these are the ordinary things out of which an independent life is created. For example, making a cup of tea on their own was described by several of the participants. This was something that could prove their ability to live independently. Thus, they worked very hard to build up their dexterity and strength in order to succeed:

I was making a cup of tea this morning. If you're not gonna make a cup of tea, you're probably not gonna be able to drink while you're in your own house. It wouldn't be what I'd be thinking about for a while, I don't think I'd be able to live without my mum there. So I don't think moving out will be on my agenda any time soon. But yeah, it's something to be thought of, and obviously you need to be able to do things for yourself – cook, make drinks, just look after yourself in general really.

(Mark, Interview 1)

While Mark acknowledged the social reality that he did require help from others (in particular his mum), his clear preference was to be able to do everyday things himself. In his hope that he could continue to build his body into a vehicle for independence, he articulated a version of independence that equated it to individual activity, rather than achieved in the company of others. There was a gulf between his articulation of doing things by yourself as a central aspiration and other approaches to living interdependently (Morris 2001; Paulsen and Berg 2016). His account of independence as individual capacity fit with his broader gendered embodied narrative as a fit, strong, masculine (wheelchair rugby was his sport) embodied subject, which others could see as valuable (McLaughlin 2017).

The accomplishment of such practices represented the marking and making of an ordinary life and highlighted the potential for practices to regulate through specific codification or constitution. Aspiring to conform provided an impetus for self-control as the young people sought not to deviate in their practices. Those practices, therefore, were not just an organised set of behaviours, but were 'entangled', as Pink (2012: 56) puts it, with an imaginary of ordinariness through which a sense of value was derived. A negotiation of social normativity and a desire for the usual and mundane marked the reproduction of everyday life through the enactment of normative practices.

'Normal' personhood and the managed body

Such attempts to do ordinary things *right* also emphasised how normal embodiment is something that involves placing disability into the background by re-training the body to do things the way others do them. Kate was keen to become a medical doctor. In preparation for that, and to prove to others it might be possible even with a body which was different, she had spent hours training herself to be able to suture like a non-disabled person. She reflected on both her ability to do the sutures and – as above – to make a cup of tea as proof of her similarity to others:

> There is a set of things that you have to be able to do to become a doctor, but my GP is also a good friend of mine so he's taken me through each one of those things. So, the first one is suturing, and the first few, you know, while I got used to it, were not great, but then the last few I got it off to a T and I could do it. It is just all about perseverance and that kind of thing. So, I mean, by no means are they hugely effective, it's just things like if I was writing a long piece of writing in class, my hand would get tired and then someone would have to come and scribe for me. Or things like pouring something from one container into another is difficult. But if I really do concentrate I can do it, I can make cups of tea and stuff, so I can pour the kettle in to the cup, so it's just it's just very, very little effect really.
>
> (Kate, Interview 1)

The micro-management and commitment involved in making a body, such as Mark's or Kate's, that can do something as commonplace as make a cup of tea shows the deeply embedded nature of norms of independence as self-reliance in people's understandings of who is the valued subject. The body, thus, becomes a tool in the enactment of not just independence but in proving a version of self-worth that is tied to achievement and self-realisation:

> It's still the same with able bodied people, because all they'll ever do is do stuff to the best of their ability. So then, not that you weren't originally, but from the outside world you can do stuff to the same level.
>
> (Kate, Interview 1)

There is, therefore, a form of personhood being enacted, as well as a task being done, in these activities, a normal subject capable of being read as such by others through the things they do and want. This seems evident with how Mark explained he wanted others to see him, which he enacted through his participation in disability sport and social interaction with friends:[4]

MARK: A normal lad who's up for a laugh, really you know. I'm just a normal lad up for a laugh really. I wouldn't really describe anything about my disability 'cos I don't think that should, that should matter if people are interested in me, you know, a lad and out for a laugh.

EDMUND: *What do you mean by normal lad, what would you?*

MARK: Well just up for a laugh, likes a bit of sport, likes a bit of tele [television], likes a bit of his Xbox, chill out yeah pretty much I'd say.

(Mark, Interview 1)

Implicit in Mark's description of a normal lad is a young man who others treat the same as everyone else, someone whose embodied difference is considered as irrelevant to who they are as a person and, crucially, a friend. This was a common theme: the wish for others to see their disability as irrelevant, not as the source of who they are. When asked to define disability, Jenny said 'a slight difference to someone's life' (Interview 1). Seeing disability as only a 'slight difference' is only feasible when the body does not block the achievement of ordinary things, done in ordinary ways.

Where this was less possible due to the level of impairment effects, participants responded in a variety of ways. First was to try to hide or disguise the ways in which their bodies were not ordinary or could not do ordinary things. Craig, for example, volunteered at an amateur radio station and was keen to pursue this as a career. A key reason was that people could not see him and, because of that, would not see him through his disability:

CRAIG: [It] makes me feel like I'm able bodied when I'm on the radio 'cos nobody can see you, people can only hear you. So it makes me feel more normal. I can talk, so they can't see any physical problem with me, as far as they are concerned.

EDMUND: *Is that an important thing, to feel normal?*

CRAIG: Oh aye, it gives me more confidence, yeah. I just want to live life as normal as I can, really. I try not to encounter any problems if I can help it.

EDMUND: *In what way?*

CRAIG: Just physical things that might hold me back.

(Craig, Interview 1)

This desire for the anonymity of invisibility clearly resonates with the dynamics of passing that have been discussed in different ways across the stigma literatures, to identify the work people do for others to see them as credible subjects (Davis 1961; Garthwaite 2015; Goffman 1968). Being able to hide so completely as

Craig does is rare. For the most part, instead, what participants focused on to pass was disguising their limitations and differences as much as they could:

HANNAH: Cos to me when I'm out places I tend to hide my disability, try to hide it.

EDMUND: *How would you do that? What does that mean? . . .*

HANNAH: Walking like this with my right hand – my bad hand – so you can't really see, and trying to minimise my limp, 'cos I've got a limp and I've got a calliper, I can't get. . . . I tend to try and hide it by putting my calliper under my trousers, but some of them I can't, some of them need to go over and I don't like that huh. . . . So yeah, I do try to hide my disability, 'cos I just feel better if I try to hide it.

(Hannah, Interview 1)

Discussions of people hiding or disguising their disability, in terms of both appearance and action, were common in the interviews. Participants spoke of wearing long sleeves or trousers rather than skirts or shorts to hide scars, or the different shape of their limbs. The female participants spoke of wearing flesh coloured tights, which also could hide scars. One participant had moved schools and the information about her needs and disability had not been transferred over. For the two years she was at the school, no one knew that she had a diagnosis of cerebral palsy or a range of physical impairments. Her perspective was that this was a good thing because they treated her like everyone else.

There was, however, a fragility to the disguise; their body sometimes let them down and brought their embodied difference back into the foreground, most frequently in the process of accomplishing a practice: 'Just don't like that arm. I just think its flimsy and gives me away' (Andrew, Interview 1). The body's capacity to be disruptive meant it was an unreliable resource in the enactments they aimed for. Therefore, retaining the capacity to do ordinary things, and in ordinary ways, took close vigilance over the body to maintain:

SARA: I try to be like everybody else [laughs], although I'm not, I just sort of.

EDMUND: *And what do you mean by that, although you're not?*

SARA: Well I can't do as many things as anybody else, but I try. It might not work, but I try.

(Sara, Interview 1)

The capacity of the body to *give them away* led to close observation of it, and to high levels of participation in medical interventions, which could help maintain the levels of capacity their bodies had. The majority of participants were actively focused on keeping their bodies fit and healthy; diet was monitored and regular physical activity was the norm. People regularly swam and used the gym, while everyday activities were also seen as opportunities to work on the body, either by stretching while watching the TV or using going up and down their staircases as an opportunity to work on body strength. If these activities were not enough, then surgery was also turned to as something that could help repair the additional damage they experienced as their bodies aged. Above all, there was a desire to appear *ordinary* and to avoid the stigmatising effect of being judged as extraordinary (Talley 2014):

> I looked really disabled when my legs were like they were, 'cos they were really bent. I could hardly do anything and that kind of thing, whereas now I look a lot less disabled because I'm a lot taller, my legs are, I don't like using the word normal, let's say ordinary, ordinary shape. So that in itself just makes me look less [disabled].
>
> (Kate, Interview 1)

The managed body of these accounts indicated a desire for the attainment of a version of personhood associated with a language of normality and ability. Having a body that could do certain things, and look a certain way in the process, exemplified the operation of a discourse of normality.

Monitoring disabled bodies

What do such careful and worked at attempts to claim ordinariness say about the young people's social status and how they felt others' reading of them as disabled affected their lives? First, like other young people, questions of being like others and belonging to the right social groups were important to them. Assistive technology, or additional help, or the distinctiveness of their own bodies, could get in the way of them being read as similar to other people. They enacted a self-consciousness about their bodies that is a familiar aspect of adolescence:

> I used to wear shorts, like I was saying, for PE [physical education], and now when in year ten I go in tracksuit bottoms and, and I'm not letting anyone, I don't like my legs, don't want people looking at my legs. So I'd like cover them up. . . . Obviously personal preference as well, but because of that reason as well, yeah, that, you know, people would stare at your legs anyway, your walking. So I'd try and cover them up, sort of make it a bit less obvious which is probably not the case, but you'd like to think it was.
>
> (Mark, Interview 1)

In such contexts, participants chose not to use things or people that could help them, due to the way that highlighted how they were different in the process of carrying out this or that practice. However, they also acknowledged that endeavouring to do things by themselves was more difficult without making use of such forms of support. They were caught in a balance between help enabling them to do ordinary things, while also symbolising the difference they wished to minimise by doing such ordinary things. Second, the varied ways they worked on their bodies was influenced by the way they were shaping their adolescent identities and working towards their adult aspirations. This work included the physical efforts to minimise disability and to reshape their bodies as proximate to normality.

There is a tendency to see the willingness of disabled children and young people to agree to medical intervention as a product of medicine's power (Parens 2006). Without rejecting the ability of medicine to shape people's choices, the choices young people in the project made to work on the body, to stay fit, to maintain participation in physiotherapy, to undertake new surgeries, were as much a product of the ongoing work they were undertaking to pursue a *normal* body, an ordinary body. The medical and social work come together to validate the norms young people aspire to. This does imply self-disciplining and self-monitoring; the young people measured themselves against other body norms and worked towards what, and who, they wanted to be. However, there are productive forms of agency also present in the pleasure they took in remaking their bodies, in imagining adult futures, and in their participation in choices about whether to have another surgery or whether to swim another lap. They did not passively go along with what medicine said. Instead, they were embedded in ongoing processes of forming and doing their relational identity through their situated pursuit of everyday ordinariness as normality.

Finally, all this work to produce ordinary bodies speaks to how previous experiences of being treated as different led them to expect that people would continue to see them as different from others, and treat them in ways which undermined their social status. There was much talk of how, even when people said they were fine with their disability, this did not mean they felt comfortable displaying it. Instead, they continued to feel discomfort in making use of assistive technology, of moving in unusual ways, and of having a different body:

> I do try to hide it even though everyone around me says there's nothing wrong with you being disabled, you can't, yeah, but you don't get the stares and the name-calling do you?
>
> (Sean, Interview 1)

Managing an expectation that others will treat them differently, as well as responding to the very visible ways in which people did treat them differently, was evident in both what the participants did and why, sometimes spoken of as the difference between 'felt' and 'enacted' stigma (Scambler and Hopkins 1986).

Bodies, practices, and displays

We will finish this section with a detailed account of one participant, Paul, and the key theme of his work with us: the wish that people could see him as an 'ordinary lad' like his brother. This is an account which has strong resonance with the social dynamics of staring that Garland-Thomson (2009) has documented so well. Paul spoke of how he was often, and had long been, stared at, particularly when he used his stick or wheelchair:

PAUL: You don't get all the people staring at you as much [referring to the non-disabled interviewer]. It's kind of really irritating. I find if I just walk, sometimes people will just stare and [this] really irritates us sometimes.

EDMUND: *So they stare when you walk, why would they do that?*

PAUL: I don't know, it's just with, 'cos like when I go for me dinner [at college] I'll go into [the] town centre and people that don't know you, haven't seen you before and they just have a little glare at you. I just don't, I just think it's kind of rude, just irritates me sometimes.

EDMUND: *So do you use the wheelchair less for that reason?*

PAUL: Yeah.

EDMUND: *So do you take your stick to college?*

P: Well I don't, I just don't think, [pause] in a way I would like to take it with us. 'Cos like a lot of people they are more likely just to stare 'cos I've got a stick. Just think it'll be easier to just go without a stick.

(Paul, Interview 1)

Paul's body, due to the visibility of its impairment effects and the technology he used to support himself, was on display for others to see – at college, or as he walked the streets near his home. The way he moved, along with the devices he used, appeared to mark his body out as different, as something *stareable* (Garland-Thomson 2009). In some contexts, assistive technology or the symbol of the blue badge can be used to be recognised as disabled (usually within a medical categorisation) and gain, rather than lose, social credibility (Ryan 2005). For example, forms of embodied differences, which are associated with the medical category of autistic spectrum disorder (ASD) or attention deficit disorder, are often socially read as behaviours judged as naughty, disruptive, and out of control (including out of control *bad mothers*).

Here, the assistive technology or the symbol of the blue badge can be used to support a medical explanatory, which is productive of social validity (in the words of the T-shirt: 'I'm not naughty, I'm autistic').[5] In contrast for Paul, in the context of embodied difference that was already visible as physical impairment, his decision to limit the use of his stick derived from an attempt to minimise the visibility of that difference. What the contrast between Paul and categories such as ASD speak to is hierarchies of types, categories, and explanations of embodied difference and the social interactions they generate. Being read as disabled is sometimes better than being read as disruptive, naughty, or a bad parent – while being read as ordinary can be better than being read as disabled.

In particular, it was important to Paul that people did not make unnecessary (in his eyes) judgements about the range of things they assumed he could not do. He emphasised his wish to be seen as capable of doing things, in particular as capable as his twin brother – who was not disabled:

> I would just like to be treated as a person, just like how my brother's treated. I would like to be treated in that way. . . . Like when I went to college, I was the only one with a disability in the class, so when I started they were like 'Are you alright', or 'Can you go downstairs like that', I didn't really like that. . . . I know it's trying to make it easier for us, but sometimes I just want to get on with it myself. . . . Or even when me mam, saying like if she needs help, if she would still ask me sometime, if it's got to do with something heavy, instead of asking [my brother] like I would like to be asked, you know.
>
> (Paul, Interview 1)

Both Paul and his brother were part of the same football club. However, while the brother was often chosen to play, Paul found himself always on the substitute bench (during the course of the research, he decided to switch to a disabled football team, something he had resisted doing for some time). The different social interactions Paul could see his brother engage with, which others made difficult for him, were an important marker of how his embodied differences influenced his social position. Paul's brother provided an embodied representation of the *ordinary guy* he wanted to be recognised as: one able to move through the social world without stares or offers of help, indeed, someone seen as being able to provide help.

The different responses people had to Paul and his brother shaped his desire to be left to get on with things. His sense of being on display, and being seen as somewhat less able or weaker, troubled his feelings of and claims to ordinariness, which were undermined by the presence of his body in spaces where people are apparently not accustomed to seeing young men walk with a limp or walking stick. In his photo journal, he chose a photograph of himself in a football top – the mundane practice of supporting a team offering up such symbols of ordinary masculinity – and with little trace of his disability visible. The text he produced alongside the image acknowledged his cerebral palsy, but stressed his focus on getting on with things and doing stuff that young men of his age do, such as learning to drive. Being seen as a normal teenager was important to Paul and influenced how he displayed disability as a minor part of his life, yet it appears possible that he read narratives of disability-as-failure into his own body. In his second interview with us, Paul commented that he was not *a normal child*, implying a sense of personal failure in his inability to perform normality. As a result, he made a conscious effort to embody ordinariness. Paul's desire for normalcy echoes attitudes that Gibson et al. (2013: 397) found among the disabled young men that they worked with, where 'identities intersected through narratives of non-difference, which were strategized by participants to minimise their disabilities and claim putatively "normal" masculine and generational identities'.

Conclusion

One locus of regulation that this chapter demonstrates are mundane everyday practices associated with a sense of ordinariness and normal personhood. For the young adults we spoke with, those practices – geared to both doing ordinary things and also for looking ordinary – provided a way for them to demonstrate their own normality and how they could (sometimes) fit within normative social worlds. However, those practices were also a container and focus of social expectation, which the young people acknowledged as they sought to fit in or conform, both in how they enacted practices and in how their bodies appeared or were displayed to others as bodies engaged in practices. This was, for the young adults, the cost of ordinariness, a seemingly incontestable requirement to manage the body. While the young adults did not often report a systematic or institutional desire to conceal or exclude their bodies from society (in contrast, they did talk about bullying, name-calling, and stigma), they did speak about engaging with representations of normality which were revealed to them in the ordering and structuring of everyday life, an engagement which entailed a management of the body. In the work towards ordinary normality that the disabled young people enacted, there is, therefore, much evidence of the *minimal hospitality* which Shildrick (2012) argues remains present in society towards embodied difference. The emphasis remains on disabled young people to do the work of fitting in; whether this is rejecting help, or trying to make their bodies capable of normalcy, all of these practices are evidence of social disquiet with bodily limitation. In an era privileging independence and self-reliance (McLaughlin 2017; Moffatt and Noble 2015; Tyler 2013), there is little choice but to work on the body to be able to do that. While the institutional segregation of disabled young people may have been reduced – although there are indications of some re-institutionalisation of young adults with learning and other disabilities in the refusals of mainstream schools to accept disabled pupils and in talk of the bias towards inclusion within government policy (Department for Education 2011) – what appears now is a switch to self-governance over bodies that must be worked upon. There is space and agency within this work, but there is also inequality in the labour involved, in the illusion of choice, and in the reality that the body will still falter and *give them away*, however hard they work on it.

Notes

1 The terminology of the Global North is not without critique. We use it here to acknowledge that global disparities are more complex than West/non-West and encompass not just questions of economic inequality, but also the privileging of certain cultural values and norms held by those in dominant social locations.

2 ESRC grant 'Embodied Selves in Transition: Disabled Young Bodies'. The full team is Professor Janice McLaughlin, Dr Edmund-Coleman Fountain, Professor Allan Colver, and Professor Patrick Olivier (RES-062–23–2886).
3 For further information on the methodology, discussion of the place of visual and other creative methods in work with young people, and analysis based on the visual work, see McLaughlin and Coleman-Fountain (2014) and McLaughlin et al. (2016).
4 It was also explored in his photography work, which we discuss in McLaughlin and Coleman-Fountain (2014).
5 The T-shirts (and other things such as badges) with this phrase and variations are used by parents to clothe their children with a diagnosis of autism with the aim of providing a medically legitimate explanation for their children's behaviour in social space. The intention is that their child's behaviour and their management of it is less questioned by others.

References

Azarian, R. 2015. Joint actions, stories and symbolic structures: a contribution to Herbert Blumer's conceptual framework. *Sociology* 51(3), pp. 685–700.

Bagnoli, A. 2011. Making sense of mixed method narratives: young people's identities, life-plans and orientations. In: Heath, S. and Walker, C. eds. *Innovations in Youth Research*. Basingstoke: Palgrave, pp. 77–100.

Bennett, A. 1999. Subcultures or neo-tribes? Rethinking the relationship between youth, style and musical taste. *Sociology* 33(3), pp. 599–617.

Blatterer, H. 2010. The changing semantics of youth and adulthood. *Cultural Sociology* 4(1), pp. 63–79.

Blumer, H. 1986. *Symbolic Interactionism: Perspective and Method*. Berkeley: University of California Press.

Bradley, H. and Devadason, R. 2008. Fractured transitions: young adults' pathways into contemporary labour markets. *Sociology* 42(1), pp. 119–136.

Braidotti, R. 1996. Signs of wonder and traces of doubt: on teratology and embodied difference. In: Lykke, N. and Braidotti, R. eds. *Between Monsters, Goddesses and Cyborgs*. London: Zed Books, pp. 135–152.

Brannen, J. and O'Brien, M. 1996. *Children in Families: Research and Policy*. London: Falmer Press.

Bucholtz, M. 2002. Youth and cultural practice. *Annual Review of Anthropology* 31, pp. 525–552.

Bynner, J. M. 2005. Rethinking the youth phase of the life-course: the case for emerging adulthood? *Journal of Youth Studies* 8(4), pp. 367–384.

Canguilhem, G. 1989. *The Normal and the Pathological*. New York: Zone Books.

Coleman-Fountain, E. and McLaughlin, J. 2013. The interactions of disability and impairment. *Social Theory and Health* 11(2), pp. 133–150.

Crossley, N. 2001. *The Social Body: Habit, Identity and Desire*. London: Sage.

Davis, F. 1961. Deviance disavowal: the management of strained interaction by the visually handicapped. *Social Problems* 9(2), pp. 120–132.

Denzin, N. K. 1992. *Symbolic Interactionism and Cultural Studies: The Politics of Interpretation*. Oxford: Blackwell.

Department for Education. 2011. *Support and Aspiration: A New Approach to Special Educational Needs and Disability – A Consultation*. London: Stationery Office.

Edwards, C. and Imrie, R. 2003. Disability and bodies as bearers of value. *Sociology* 37(2), pp. 239–256.

Epstein, D., Kehily, M. and Mac an Ghaill, M. 2001. Boys and girls come out to play: making masculinities and femininities in school playgrounds. *Men and Masculinities* 4(2), pp. 158–172.

Ferri, D. 2015. 'Subsidising accessibility'. Using EU state aid law and policy to foster development and production of accessible technology. *European State Aid Law Quarterly* 14(1), pp. 51–67.

Foucault, M. 1975. *The Birth of the Clinic*. New York: Vintage Books.

Foucault, M. 1990. *The History of Sexuality Volume 1: An Introduction*. New York: Vintage Books.

Furlong, A. and Cartmel, F. 2007. *Young People and Social Change*. New York: Open University Press.

Furlong, A., Woodman, D. and Wyn, J. 2011. Changing times, changing perspectives: reconciling 'transition' and 'cultural' perspectives on youth and young adulthood. *Journal of Sociology* 47(4), pp. 355–370.

Garland-Thomson, R. 1997. *Extraordinary Bodies: Figuring Physical Disability in American Culture and Literature*. New York: New York University Press.

Garland-Thomson, R. 2007. Shape structures story: fresh and feisty stories about disability. *Narrative* 15(1), pp. 113–123.

Garland-Thomson, R. 2009. *Staring: How We Look*. Oxford: Oxford University Press.

Garland-Thomson, R. 2011. Misfits: a feminist materialist disability concept. *Hypatia* 26(3), pp. 591–609.

Garthwaite, K. 2015. Becoming incapacitated? Long-term sickness benefit recipients and the construction of stigma and identity narratives. *Sociology of Health and Illness* 37(1), pp. 1–13.

Geldens, P., Lincoln, S. and Hodkinson, P. 2011. Youth identities, transitions, cultures. *Journal of Sociology* 47(4), pp. 347–353.

Gibson, B. E., Bhavnita, M., Smith, B., Yoshida, K. K., Abbott, D. and Lindsay, S. 2013. The integrated use of audio diaries, photography, and interviews with research with disabled young men. *International Journal of Qualitative Methods* 12(1), pp. 383–402.

Gill, R., Henwood, K. and McLean, C. 2005. Body projects and the regulation of normative masculinity. *Body and Society* 11(1), pp. 37–62.

Goffman, E. 1968. *Stigma: Notes on the Management of Spoiled Identity*. London: Penguin Books.

Goodley, D. 2007. Towards socially just pedagogies: Deleuzoguattarian critical disability studies. *International Journal of Inclusive Education* 11(3), pp. 317–334.

Goodley, D. 2011. *Critical Disability Studies: Expanding Debates and Interdisciplinary Engagements*. London: Sage.

Goodley, D. and Runswick-Cole, K. 2011. The violence of disablism. *Sociology of Health and Illness* 33(4), pp. 602–617.

Goodley, D. and Runswick-Cole, K. 2013. The body as disability and possability: theorizing the 'leaking, lacking and excessive' bodies of disabled children. *Scandinavian Journal of Disability Research* 15(1), pp. 1–19.

Holt, L. 2004. Childhood disability and ability: (dis)ableist geographies of mainstream primary schools. *Disability Studies Quarterly* 24(3). Online. Available at: http://dsq-sds.org/article/view/506/683 [Accessed: 23 November 2017].

Holt, L., Lea, J. and Bowlby, S. 2012. Special units for young people on the autistic spectrum in mainstream schools: sites of normalisation, abnormalisation, inclusion, and exclusion. *Environment and Planning A* 44(9), pp. 2191–2206.

Irwin, S. 1995. *Rights of Passage: Social Change and the Transition From Youth to Adulthood*. London: UCL Press.

Lester, J. N. and Paulus, T. M. 2012. Performative acts of autism. *Discourse and Society* 23(3), pp. 259–273.

MacDonald, R. 2011. Youth transitions, unemployment and underemployment. *Journal of Sociology* 47(4), pp. 427–444.

McLaughlin, J. 2017. The medical reshaping of disabled bodies as a response to stigma and a route to normality. *Medical Humanities* [Online]. Available at: http://mh.bmj.com/content/medhum/early/2017/02/06/medhum-2016-011065.full.pdf [Accessed: 23 November 2017].

McLaughlin, J. and Coleman-Fountain, E. 2014. The unfinished body: the medical and social reshaping of disabled young bodies. *Social Science and Medicine* 120, pp. 76–84.

McLaughlin, J., Coleman-Fountain, E. and Clavering, E. C. 2016. *Disabled Childhoods: Monitoring Difference and Emerging Identities*. London: Routledge.

McLaughlin, J. and Goodley, D. 2008. Seeking and rejecting certainty: exposing the sophisticated lifeworlds of parents of disabled babies. *Sociology* 42(2), pp. 317–335.

Moffatt, S. and Noble, E. 2015. Work or welfare after cancer? Explorations of identity and stigma. *Sociology of Health and Illness* 37(8), pp. 1191–1205.

Monaghan, L. F. 2006. Corporeal indeterminacy: the value of embodied, interpretive sociology. In: Waskul, D. D. and Vannini, P. eds. *Body/Embodiment: Symbolic Interactionism and the Sociology of the Body*. Aldershot: Ashgate, pp. 125–140.

Mørch, S. and Andersen, H. 2006. Individualization and the changing youth life. In: Leccardi, C. and Ruspini, E. eds. *A New Youth? Young People, Generations and Family Life*. Aldershot: Ashgate, pp. 63–84.

Morris, J. 2001. Impairment and disability: constructing an ethics of care that promotes human rights. *Hypatia* 16(4), pp. 1–16.

Moser, I. 2006. Disability and the promises of technology: technology, subjectivity and embodiment within an order of the normal. *Information, Communication and Society* 9(3), pp. 373–395.

Nayak, A. 2006. Displaced masculinities: chavs, youth and class in the post-industrial city. *Sociology* 40(5), pp. 813–831.

Nayak, A. and Kehily, M. J. 2008. *Gender, Youth and Culture*. Basingstoke: Palgrave Macmillan.

Parens, E. 2006. *Surgically Shaping Children: Technology, Ethics and the Pursuit of Normality*. Baltimore, MD: Johns Hopkins University Press.

Paulsen, V. and Berg, B. 2016. Social support and interdependency in transition to adulthood from child welfare services. *Children and Youth Services Review* 68, pp. 125–131.

Pink, S. 2012. *Situating Everyday Life: Practices and Place*. London: Sage.

Prout, A. 2000. Children's participation: control and self-realisation in British late modernity. *Children and Society* 14(4), pp. 304–315.

Roberts, S. and MacDonald, R. 2013. The marginalised mainstream: making sense of the 'missing middle' of youth studies. *Sociological Research Online* 18(1), p. 21.

Rock, P. 1979. *The Making of Symbolic Interactionism*. Basingstoke: Macmillan Press.

Runswick-Cole, K. and Curran, T. 2013. *Disabled Children's Childhood Studies: Critical Approaches in a Global Context*. Basingstoke: Palgrave Macmillan.

Ryan, S. 2005. People don't do odd, do they? Mothers making sense of the reactions of others to their learning disabled children in public places. *Children's Geographies* 3(3), pp. 291–305.

Scambler, G. and Hopkins, A. 1986. Being epileptic: coming to terms with stigma. *Sociology of Health and Illness* 8(1), pp. 26–43.

Scully, J. L. 2010. Hidden labor: disabled/nondisabled encounters, agency and autonomy. *International Journal of Feminist Approaches to Bioethics* 3(2), pp. 25–42.

Shakespeare, T. 2006. *Disability Rights and Wrongs*. London: Routledge.

Shildrick, M. 1999. The body which is not one: dealing with differences. *Body and Society* 5(2–3), pp. 77–92.

Shildrick, M. 2012. Critical disability studies: rethinking the conventions for the age of postmodernity. In: Watson, N., Roulstone, A. and Thomas, C. eds. *Routledge Handbook of Disability Studies*. London: Routledge, pp. 30–41.

Söderström, S. 2009. The significance of ICT in disabled youth's identity negotiations. *Scandinavian Journal of Disability Research* 11(2), pp. 131–144.

Talley, H. L. 2014. *Saving Face: Disfigurement and the Politics of Appearance*. New York: New York University Press.

Thomas, G. M. 2017. *Down's Syndrome Screening and Reproductive Politics: Care, Choice, and Disability in the Prenatal Clinic*. London: Routledge.

Traver, A. E. and Duran, J. 2014. Dancing around (dis)ability: how nondisabled girls are affected by participation in a dance program for girls with disabilities. *Qualitative Inquiry* 20(10), pp. 1148–1156.

Tyler, I. 2013. *Revolting Subjects: Social Abjection and Resistance in Neoliberal Britain*. London: Zed Books.

Vannini, P. 2006. Symbolic interaction as music: the esthetic constitution of meaning, self, and society. *Symbolic Interaction* 29(1), pp. 5–18.

Vehmas, S. and Watson, N. 2014. Moral wrongs, disadvantages, and disability: a critique of critical disability studies. *Disability and Society* 29(4), pp. 638–650.

Wallace, J. and Press, M. 2004. All this useless beauty: the case for craft practice in design for a digital age. *The Design Journal* 7(2), pp. 42–53.

Chapter 5

Worlding the 'new normal' for young adults with disabilities

Faye Ginsburg and Rayna Rapp

College for all?

For those with learning disabilities (LD), the transition from educational institutions to life beyond high school is often experienced as a crisis. In contemporary America, attending college after high school is the unexamined aspirational norm for young adult personhood. It has displaced long-standing opportunities for vocational education that were a standard part of American education until the late twentieth century (Ravitch 1985; Samuelson 2012). Such training offered potential pathways toward secure skilled employment for many students, including those with disabilities, who have not until recently been candidates for post-secondary education. Now, however, almost any alternative direction other than college is conceived of as a failure, even when advanced academic education might not be the best route to adult success. Indeed, a lively public debate has emerged around the widespread notion of *college for all.* As one economist opined: 'College became the ticket to the middle class, the be-all-and-end-all of K–12 education.[1] If you didn't go to college, you'd failed' (Samuelson 2012: n.p.). By the early twenty-first century, this idea had transformed the dominant American kinship imaginary, shaping coming-of-age experiences for young adults with disabilities, despite their egregiously high dropout rates of almost 60 percent (Wall 2016).

This dilemma became central to our research on the transformation of disability's public presence in New York City (NYC) as we encountered the gap between lived experiences of young adults with disabilities transitioning out of high school, and the ideology of *college for all.* For example, Faye's daughter attended a high school for students with learning disabilities that, in its publicity, suggested a high college admission rate for all its graduates, a statistic that had influenced the family's choice of that school. When, by her daughter's junior year, it became apparent that she and many of her classmates were not necessarily on this normative and highly desired path, a little research revealed that there was no game plan for the 20 percent or more of the students whose needs were neglected in a school culture valorising only certain kinds of success. When Rayna's son Teo, who is dyslexic, was applying to colleges, a main concern was the fit between outstanding drama departments (to support his passion for theatre) and truly robust campus support services for students with disabilities. Although support programmes are mandated by federal law for colleges receiving federal funding, their quality is uneven at best. Many of the parents we interviewed in our research encountered similar barriers as their kids – with a variety of disabilities from attention deficit and hyperactivity disorder (ADHD) and LD to autism to Down syndrome and more – aged out of high school and struggled to locate a sense of personhood and community beyond the conventional coming-of-age narrative. They searched for appropriate services and programmes that best supported their child's transition and a chance to embrace an alternative imaginary against the barrage of comments implying that not achieving a standard college admission constitutes failure not only for their child, but for their capacity as parents.

In short, we began to see how fragile and fraught the nature of transition to life after secondary school is for so many young adults with disabilities and their families. Whatever a particular child's circumstances and accommodation needs, all of them faced the disturbing lack of models to replace the dominant college narrative. The ideological power of this framework obfuscated the reality of diverse life trajectories for students with intellectual disabilities as they seek to transition from secondary school. In short, the trajectory of their lives rarely matches the norms of young adult personhood that are hegemonic in America today.

Studying disability worlds

Over the last decade, we have been researching the public presence of disability in the socio-cultural life of NYC. In this chapter, we focus on the experience of families and their children, and the work of visionary educators who are creating alternative programmes, particularly for young adults facing transition beyond high school. In our larger study, we use long-standing ethnographic methods: participant observation fieldwork, in-depth qualitative interviews, life histories, and analysis of media and secondary documents. Initially, we began our research studying how families with younger children who have cognitive differences (known as LD) juggled diagnoses, services, placements, and stigma, gradually developing both advocacy skills and new understandings of familial life. We interviewed over fifty parents of children with learning disabilities across all five of NYC's boroughs, incorporating a broad range of research subjects, crossing socio-economic and cultural/ethnic and religious backgrounds. Whatever their differences, all families had a child with a federally mandated Individualised Education Plan (IEP), the school district–issued legal document negotiated with teachers, parents, and relevant others. It serves as a passport to the specific services to which a student with a diagnosed disability is entitled, the cornerstone of a quality education for a child with disabilities (Rapp and Ginsburg 2012). Our sample was recruited via several pathways: internet support groups for parents of children in special education in the NYC public schools, through snowball sampling that crossed into the private school sector, and through our personal networks as parents of children with disabilities. We stayed in touch with families as they passed through both the life-course and the educational system, while balancing the demands of complex diagnoses over their children's school careers.

Additionally, our fieldwork encompassed work with teachers and advocates who were introducing a variety of cultural innovations into special education. For example, we carried out participant observation in what was then a new programme that trained special education teachers in an innovative curriculum introduced to the NYC public schools to support the integration of cognitive diversity in their classrooms. We also interviewed thirty advocates for special education, ranging from school principals and teachers, to lawyers to public health professionals. We also became actively involved in the transition programmes discussed more fully in this chapter.

While negotiating appropriate schooling is difficult, having a child in an educational setting is nonetheless a normative part of the life cycle. It is also the only American public institution where entitlements are legally in place for the education of every child, including those with disabilities. Furthermore, once services are mandated on a child's IEP, they are supposed to be provided in a timely manner. In contrast, there are no legal protections for the delivery of support services once students are out of school. The task of organising a meaningful transition to adulthood for an individual with disabilities, then, falls jointly on individuals with disabilities, their families, and allies such as educators, social workers, and others, should a young adult be fortunate enough to even have such reliable backing. As we have learned as parents and ethnographers, this requires considerable work and necessitates understanding what viable support systems might be available for those moving into the next stage of life. Even when expertise is available, paperwork often presents a bureaucratic obstacle course, and there are few guarantees regarding the quality of programmes.

Thus, the transition to life after high school is frequently experienced as a cultural freefall. Advocates for interdependent living have long understood that planning an atypical life often extends beyond a kin network, especially as people with disabilities and their families age. These are the conditions that motivated many activist educators, families, and others to demand legislative attention to advocate for a more structured pathway to the transition process. By law, transition programmes should be available to students until they graduate or age out at 21. Education for any child with disabilities must reflect planning for their lives beyond secondary school, accounting for students' interests, preferences, accomplishments, and skills – and not simply their limitations or impairments – in order to help them forge a satisfying future (Wright 2004).

Whatever the legal requirements for transition, the reality in much of America, and especially in NYC, is grim. Adequate transition planning rarely occurs beyond the most cursory *check the box* compliance. Only 25 percent of NYC students with IEPs complete high school in the normative four years, and of those who graduate, fewer than 17 percent are prepared to pursue higher education or careers (Arise Coalition 2011: 2; Otterman 2011; Wall 2016). This bleak situation was made clear in an influential report quoted below, aptly titled *Transitioning to Nowhere*. It analysed the insufficient attention to serious transition planning, as well as the lack of services available to students with disabilities exiting high school in NYC. As the report concludes:

> The most vulnerable students, those who need the greatest assistance in preparing for life after high school, are instead being shuttled through inadequate programs where no real efforts are made to prepare them for their futures.
>
> (Silverman 2007: 4)

A second, similarly depressing report came to the same conclusions in 2011, as indicated by its graphic and dour title *Out of School and Unprepared: The Need to Improve Support for Students with Disabilities Transitioning to Adulthood* (Arise Coalition 2011). Clearly, NYC, along with much of America, continues to be wildly out of compliance with federal legislation mandating rigorous transition for young adults with disabilities as they prepare to leave high school. A staff member who helps adults with developmental disabilities find work explained to us that many high schools do not have staff members that understand transition planning, despite the mandates. Consequently, those who are not college-bound have been overwhelmingly left with few publicly articulated options to this crucial rite of passage to young adulthood in America, not to mention a viable future. Reflecting on the lack of post–high school support for her young adult son on the autism spectrum, one mother told us: 'It's an unlatched window out there'. Another of our interlocutors, who teaches at a small model college programme for young adults on the spectrum, aptly describes his work as 'transition by fire', capturing the sense of challenge, uncertainty, risk, and constant improvisation that characterises this process. Unlike most of their peers without disabilities, many find themselves facing adulthood 'on their own without a net', the all too appropriate title of a book on the transition to adulthood for vulnerable populations (Levine and Wagner 2005).

The problematic situation faced by many young adults with disabilities transects other forms of historically entrenched bias based on racial, ethnic, gender, class, and sexual identities that shadow the evolution of educational policy and practice. The discriminatory intersection of these categories has come to be known as disproportionality (Elementary and Middle School Technical Assistance 2016). An avalanche of research has revealed that minorities are over-represented in special education across the US, although there is considerable variation in the numbers primarily because of statewide differences in how data are collected. However the numbers are parsed, the social fact of disproportionality is undoubtedly a result of 'how the confluence of multiple policy initiatives can have unintended consequences for various groups, particularly when implementation takes place in a racially stratified society, in this case, special education placement practices for historically underserved groups' (Ferri and Connor 2005: 462; Jackson 2013; Noguera et al. 2015; Trainor 2017).

Despite the promise of transition services that might truly launch disabled young adults into an integrated life after high school, we were struck by the glacial pace of progress toward that goal, an impression confirmed by the dispiriting reports, meetings, and family stories we encountered. Indeed, just under 17 percent of students with disabilities in New York State graduate high school ready for college and career (Arise Coalition 2011).

The crisis in transition

Flesh-and-blood children and their families carry the burden of these long-standing inequities that numbers point out. They often experience transition as a crisis. The reverberations of this situation go far beyond the failure of the school bureaucracy. Even for most typically developing young Americans, the transition to adulthood is usually stressful and uncertain, a classic liminal period where the change from one social status to another entails instability until the new status is achieved. This passage is especially precarious for young adults with disabilities and their families, as there is no normalising public discourse articulating their future trajectories. As noted earlier, the hegemony of a current American life-course narrative privileges attending college as the appropriate route for late adolescents. The people straying from this path inevitably experience their situation as deeply problematic, especially if their families are unable to grasp the reality of their situation. Educators working with teens with learning disabilities told us stories about parents who could not imagine that their child – who was functioning far below grade level academically – was not college bound. As long-time special needs consultant and transition expert Gary Shulman commented on this common situation in an interview with us: 'We have to convince parents that there is nothing wrong about not going to college'. Additionally, there are far too many students represented disproportionately in special education who do not have parents or other allies who can help them navigate this choppy passage. It is these children, thus, who face particularly uncertain futures.

In speaking with families and teachers, we repeatedly encountered a sense of rupture of an anticipated life-course as children approached the end of their high school years. Many expressed dismay about the lack of support or direction for the next life-stage. As one parent expressed it:

> Transition is really difficult. . . . I talk to parents all the time who are complaining about their kid's classroom, and I think 'this is the good part, at least you have a roadmap'. There's nothing clear once they are out of school. If they didn't have parents like us, a lot of these kids would be homeless on

the street. . . . Most families are scrounging and desperate, they don't know where to look.

This is not an unusual story. Youth with disabilities often continue to live with family members at a time when many of their peers are establishing independent lives. Some get lost in this unmapped territory, absorbed into *hard to count* demographic categories that encompass homelessness, unemployment, institutionalisation, and incarceration (Carey et al. 2014); Neuhaus et al. 2014). African-American youth classified for special education, for example, enter the juvenile justice system at five times the rate of their similarly classified non–African American peers (Osher et al. 2002).

These disturbing quantitative findings are only one measure of the everyday experience of social inequality and diminished opportunity that too often characterises living with disability for both students and parents, a dissonance from standard life narratives that comes into sharp relief at this critical juncture (Rapp and Ginsburg 2011). We argue that this can create a profound existential gap between normative ideas of American personhood and the unknown realities for young adults with disabilities and their families. As this growing population comes of legal age, they and their families confront the question of imagining and designing a future when few models are in place. The American stress on independence poses deep challenges to people who have grown up under the shadow of an IEP.

Nonetheless, we have found that this perilous breach is sometimes productive. Some respond to it with activist innovation; families work with their young adults to create unanticipated pathways, and in the process, invent a new version of their life-course that may present possibilities, as well as dangers and disappointments. It is our argument that in this complex process, incipient worlds are emerging. Indeed, as noted in a review of research on transition; 'many young adults living with [disabilities] are like the first astronauts to explore space . . . going where no-one has gone before without any hint of what they may anticipate along the journey' (Blum 2005: 323). In short, the challenges of this critical moment in the life cycle can sometimes serve to catalyse the creation of alternative social formations where pockets of a *new normal* begin to take shape in various projects. We discuss these projects in the following section.

Worlding disabilities

Despite the grim circumstances described above, we discovered that NYC was also home to nascent, innovative transition experiments, offering utopian glimpses into what happens when students with disabilities are provided the support they need to *transition to somewhere*. While small in number and almost artisanal in their efforts to make transition as person-centred as possible, each represents a step toward the creation of possible *disability world-making*.

We borrow the concept of world-making from two different philosophical lineages. One derives from philosopher Nelson Goodman's 1978 book *Ways of Worldmaking*, which addresses the role of both representational and material structures in shaping the realities in which we live. Goodman's work has influenced a lineage of thinkers including psychologists, anthropologists, and literary scholars (Bruner 1987, 1991; Gursel 2016; Nünning et al. 2015). Like them, we often felt we were witnessing the kind of active world-making to which Goodman refers, as we encountered new formations. In our case, this is the world that emerged after the passage of the Americans with Disabilities Act (ADA) in 1990. Despite its bureaucratic framework, the law has served as a beacon for imagining an inclusive cultural future for the range of humanity hailed by the language of disability rights. But language and law can only go so far without the claims to recognition that counter-publics demand through world-making projects such as the 'Capitol Crawl', when sixty activists abandoned their wheelchairs to ascend the steps of the US Capitol (Davis 2015), helping secure the passage of the ADA in 1990. Less visible but equally significant to world-making are the myriad parental projects insuring that their children have access to inclusive education, including experiments in transition that support young adults with disabilities to follow their passions and dreams.

Another intellectual lineage also helps us make sense of these and other empirical projects as they constitute new formations. The concept of 'worlding' was first introduced by Martin Heidegger in *Being and Time* (1962), where he explores the experience of 'being in the world'. Since then, the idea of worlding has been taken up across many disciplines. As art historian David Trend (2012) notes on his website:

> Historically critiqued as a colonialising device, the term worlding now also is regarded as a utopian strategy . . . The desire for something not-yet-achieved.

Among anthropologists, the concept of worlding has been used in science studies, medical anthropology, critical urbanism, and beyond (e.g. Geurts 2015; Roy and Ong 2011; Zhan 2009). In the introduction to her co-edited book on *Worlding Cities*, for example, Aihwa Ong (2011: 1) explains:

> We [ethnographers] stay close to heterogeneous practices of worlding that do not fall tidily into opposite sides of class, political, or cultural divides. Rather, a non-ideological formulation of worlding as situated everyday practices identifies ambitious practices that creatively imagine and shape alternative social visions and configurations – that is, 'worlds' – than what already exists in a given context. Worlding in this sense is linked to the idea of emergence. . . . Worlding projects remap relationships of power at different scales and localities . . . the ongoing result and target of specific worldings.

Anthropologists Michele Friedner and Emily Cohen (2015), working at the convergence of anthropology and disability studies, explain their title for a special issue of the journal *Somatosphere* titled *Inhabitable Worlds: Troubling Disability, Debility, and Ability Narratives*:

> We see inhabitable worlds as worlds that people themselves inhabit and aspire towards . . . [P]eople also transform these discourses through political advocacy and personal tactics they develop to navigate the material realities of bodily differences and built environments.

In short, we view creative approaches to transition as part of a larger project of making inhabitable worlds – or what we call disability worlds – for young adults who aspire to create meaningful futures, sometimes requiring ongoing political struggle. As disability advocate Ari Ne'eman (2012), co-founder of the Autistic Self Advocacy Network, makes clear, world-making requires a profound commitment:

> The history of disability rights progress of the last several decades is not one of undisputed, unified steps forward or technocratic tinkering at the margins of the status quo. It is a history of attack, of struggle and disputes over the very meaning of disability and society's appropriate response to it. It is a history of struggle, and titanic contests where people with disabilities, our family members and the professionals who provide services to us found ourselves at odds just as often as we fought side by side. Most importantly, it is a history, which is ongoing – the disability civil rights movement is by no means over, and the status quo today is just as much in need of change as it was in decades past.

Ne'eman is describing how disability world-making is a constant political challenge, deeply embedded in everyday acts. It goes far beyond checking a transition planning box on an IEP form with the overused stock phrase discovered in documents studied by Arise Coalition in their *Out of School and Unprepared* report: 'Johnny will integrate into the community with supports as needed'. Clearly, this excuse for what should be careful individualised planning just will not cut it. Johnny – and the many young people facing inadequate transition planning – needs a *disability world* (Arise Coalition 2011).

Transitioning to somewhere

Throughout our fieldwork, world-making was everywhere in evidence. Many of the projects we encountered were strikingly new. We often entered offices where the paint was still wet and boxes were not yet unpacked. Indeed, we began to use the phrase 'the paint is always wet' as a shorthand when one of us encountered yet another recently launched undertaking intended to creatively deliver on the promissory notes of disability legislation. For example, the Partnership for Children's Rights, funded in part by the Robin Hood Foundation, mobilises retired and student lawyers to carry out lawsuits on behalf of low-income families to secure appropriate education for children with disabilities. Its founder, Warren Sinsheimer, a high-powered lawyer in retirement who created the Partnership, became involved in this work after his granddaughter was diagnosed with learning disabilities. We first met with him in a brand-new office space; the elevator did not yet stop at their floor. Lacking signage, we ended up navigating a construction-filled stairwell, locating Mr Sinsheimer in the midst of new office furniture not yet set up. Likewise, we were invited to attend the inauguration of a project at the NYC Jewish Community Centre to find 'Just One Job' for adults with disabilities expanding the 'network of employers . . . for our committed and ready-to-work [learning and developmentally disabled] young adults'. Their work joined other veteran organisations (described below) in hunting down possible employment. Recently, we interviewed the Executive Director of the then 8-month-old Felicity House, an elegant townhouse established as the first community centre dedicated to creating a safe and supportive social space for women on the autism spectrum who are over 18, an underserved and barely recognised population. Activities range from cooking to comic book clubs, to movie nights and lectures. The inviting décor is thoughtfully adapted to the sensory needs of the participants; baskets of fidget toys are conveniently located in every room, lighting is adjustable, and noise managed by having quiet rooms available. These are just a few among the many *wet-paint* NYC-based initiatives in formation that we discovered while tracking transition in the greater metropolitan area.

At the same time, we encountered robust legacy groups, some almost a half century old, often in the process of refashioning their approach to keep in step with emergent disability worlds. Many of these had been founded by parents of children with developmental disabilities who were told 'your child is not and will never be able to learn anything'; 'he/she will be a burden to you and your family'; 'institutionalise him/her now'. Instead, these resistant parents organised to provide their children with opportunities denied them that were routinely available to *normal* children. These grassroots parent-driven efforts grew into foundational organisations such as the Association for the Help of Retarded Children (AHRC; 1948), YAI (1957),[2] and Jobpath (1978). These all have highly respected transition projects that emerged prior to much of the civil rights legislation that shapes the contemporary landscape for people with disabilities. All continue to offer important models even as they are transforming in a changing landscape. Taken together, these old and new social formations are worlding disability to normalise the presence of young adults who are building alternative life trajectories.

In the early stages of our research, we collaborated with some of our interlocutors to organise a day-long workshop at New York University (NYU) called *Rethinking Transition in the 21st Century: The After-Life of Special Education*. Seated at the table were many professionals who had spent years designing innovative programmes that ran against the grain of neglect, as well as dedicated heads of several small independent schools for students with LD. They inaugurated an innovative educational experiment: an agreement between two private schools to build a model transition programme together. A year later, they launched a pilot programme that included academic study, internships, classes on current events as well as daily life activities, social skills and sexuality and participation in arts and culture around NYC. SKILLs, an acronym for Skills and Knowledge for Independent Living and Learning, is now considered the gold standard by professionals in the non-profit sector working with young adults with developmental disabilities. The innovative philosophy of person-centred planning has been central to the SKILLs curriculum. It is a process-oriented approach to empowering people with disabilities by focusing on their particular passions, interests, and capacities as they develop a life plan. This includes work, recreation, housing, and other goals appropriate to establishing an adult life, in tandem with a circle of support made up of teachers, family members, social workers, friends, and others who can help put the plan into action.

As is often the case in NYC, the question of space for incubating this nascent transition programme soon became an issue for the high schools with whom we were collaborating. Most importantly, they stressed the significance for students of being in a new and more adult location, to underscore the students' progress beyond high school. We found temporary space for two years at NYU to incubate this project. Many faculty from across the campus stepped up with enthusiasm to support this innovative effort. They volunteered to help in multiple ways, from classes in DNA sequencing labs, to curatorial tours of the changing exhibitions of the campus art gallery, to an ongoing class in digital media that resulted in video blogging projects, and workshops in acting for the camera in order to create public service announcements in the campaign against the *R word* (retard) that was in full swing during their first year.

After two years, SKILLs had outgrown the available space and moved to its own location, designed to meet their unique needs, expanding from the original eight students to sixty-four. Initially, its gender profile was skewed toward male students; now, they are almost at fifty-fifty, with a large presence of minority students. The programme hopes to accommodate up to seventy-five students in the near future, the maximum amount they can serve in their current space. Many parents, initially resistant to the idea that their children were not immediately college-bound, came on board with this opportunity for such a well-designed and supportive programme to help them establish an adult life. The staff is acutely aware of the pressing need for more places for students who need programmes like this. Nonetheless, they want to preserve their high staff/student ratio, essential to their success.

On a recent visit, we counted thirty-five full-time staff, including teachers, social workers, administrators, and CIAs (community inclusion assistants) who accompany students off-site. Students were trooping in and out, some with walkers and wheelchairs and all with teenage exuberance, back from field trips. The classrooms were busy and lively, replete with a computer lab, a 'Daily Life Lab' with a kitchen for cooking classes and a washer and dryer, a 3D printer, as well as a full-size shower-curtain map of the NYC subway system, signalling the effort that goes into the achievement of independent travelling as a first step toward a more autonomous life.

By 2016, thirty-four students had graduated from the SKILLs programme. According to the director: 'All our students except one are engaged in post-secondary programmes that meet their needs and fit with their goals'. She estimated that 80 percent of their students leave SKILLs with paid employment, internships, or volunteer work, full or part-time, as well as educational programmes including a handful that go to community college or trade school. Others are in programmes sponsored by social service agencies that combine vocational, recreational, volunteer, and social activities. When we asked how they measure success, she explained: 'It's hard to have a single standard of measurement given how diverse our students' profiles are and how their needs change as they mature. They stay in touch. The question we ask is "are they meaningfully engaged?" ' Given the discouraging statistics that frame so much of the literature intended to measure the progress of students with disabilities, this approach is quite different. We were struck by the intimate knowledge that staff had of each student and their ongoing commitment to help them sustain 'meaningful engagement' beyond graduation as they create their disability worlds on their own terms.

During their time at SKILLs, students participate in internships that may lead to possible employment appropriate to their capacities and interests. This is foundational to the programme. Internship and job development take considerable effort on the part of staff. They comb the city as well as the area around the school where the students are known, and reach out to businesses and the non-profit sector. One social worker explained: 'It's one by one and so much work needs to be done with each potential placement. You are starting over again and again. It's tough work but we think we have made a difference in the neighbourhood, since students are out and about all the time'. For example, staff members who are regulars at a nearby coffee bar decided to take advantage of their status as loyal customers and asked the owners if they might be willing to sponsor a student for an internship there, which they did. This approach to persuading businesses to try 'just one job' for a young adult with disabilities has become an expanding model. When we commented on the intensive individualised attention required to place a single student in a potentially successful position, the social worker remarked: 'You can't mass produce this kind of experience'.

SKILLs has spurred other schools in the area to develop their own transition programmes tailored to the distinctive needs of individual students. Winston Preparatory School, an independent school in lower Manhattan serving students with learning disabilities, initially sent a small number of students to participate in SKILLs until the school created Winston Transitions (WT).[3] At first, the programme was very small and housed in the basement of the high school. Since then, it has grown and moved to its own location in midtown. Like SKILLs, it made the desired break from the high school campus, supporting students' sense of their own progress, both spatially and existentially. When we visited again in the summer of 2016, we were impressed with how much it had grown. The new space itself is nothing short of cool, both aesthetically and pedagogically. Walls are painted a calm dark grey and doors are silvery-brushed steel; lime green sleek leather couches are in the waiting room. The popular *Situation Room* – next to the director's office – is filled with moveable beanbag chairs, games, and a general sense of much welcome serenity. The walls are peppered with motivational aphorisms and, along the hallway, success has become an acronym for:

> *See your goal*
> *Understand obstacles*
> *Create a positive mental picture*
> *Clear your mind of self-doubt*
> *Embrace the challenge*
> *Stay on track*
> *Show the world you can do it.*

In 2016, Winston Transitions (WT) enrolments had increased to twenty students; the director anticipates doubling in size. Most stay two to three years, coming from all over the New York area. Like SKILLs, WT has no grades and stresses individualised learning. It is based on the philosophy developed by Winston called QSIL (Qualities of a Sustainable and Independent Learner) which guides their overall approach. QSIL includes resilience, social responsibility, self-advocacy, self-regulation, self-reflection, social/communication skills, problem-solving, and management and organisation. These qualities are woven throughout internships, individualised learning, and life skills classes. Cognitive behavioural therapy is available along with other popular techniques of self-regulation; mindfulness, meditation, and reflection are integrated into everything in 'one big giant overlap'. As the director noted: 'Individualisation is crucial. We're running 20 different kinds of curricula. We're constantly busy. Vocational and life skills really marry one another. Communication skills are everywhere'. At the same time, community building is a central tenet of the programme. He proudly noted the success of their 'anti-prom. It was a red carpet event. Everyone was dancing'.

When we asked him how the programme develops internships, the director's reply was reminiscent of what we heard at SKILLs and other places:

> A lot of networking! I have become an education salesman. I just walk into a local store – they know our kids – and I ask them if they want to take an intern. I go around the neighbourhood and tap into family bases as well. I just do it everywhere I go. It's not a product. It's all about the people. Some come on board and get hooked. At the end of the year, I have an

internship mixer. Employers narrate stories. Parents come. It's an opportunity for families to engage. The parents say they want their children to get a phenomenal career opportunity but really they are obtaining soft skills to enter the workplace. . . . Will they have a sustainable and realistic life? This is the question. This is what happens here!

WT staff also understand how important it is to work with families:

When they first get here, sometimes they are desperate, confused and scared. It's a big deal to get the families. You plant; you build; you wait. I see how we have changed student lives. Parents worry about what will happen to my child when I'm not here. We see changes in family dynamics as students learn to advocate for themselves.

Given the academic interests of some of their students, WT has an online collaboration with Landmark College, the oldest American freestanding college programme for students with LD, founded in 1971. They use a recently introduced e-based learning programme that enables students to take advantage of Landmark's tailored college curriculum as distance learning in the context of their own transition programme. Students Skype with professors at Landmark as they move through the curriculum. This extension of Landmark's dedicated teaching efforts for students with disabilities is part of a nascent movement to design college opportunities for constituencies like these who have rarely had the chance to attend tertiary educational institutions, a point to which we return in our conclusion.

Whether or not they participate in the Landmark courses, all WT students produce a culminating project in which they reflect on their own learning profile, evaluating themselves on the QSIL characteristics. The diverse families with students in both of these programmes told us how grateful they were for the educational care and launch into life that their young adult children received through these pioneering efforts. Our ethnographic attachment to these burgeoning projects that we watched from their inception is no doubt apparent, fuelled by our growing recognition of how impoverished transition opportunities really are for so many young adults and their families who desperately need them. However, as their founders are the first to point out, while they hope they have created vibrant models that can be used by others, their success depends on the small scale and deeply personal engagement with each student. This is a hard model to scale up.

Thinking college?

Not all transition innovation comes from the top down, spurred by the commitments of visionary educators and parents. Sometimes, young adults with disabilities take matters into their own hands. In the late 1990s, a small group of college students at Brown University with *invisible* learning disabilities founded an organisation – originally called Project Eye to Eye (PE2E) – to support college students like themselves. They mobilised a cadre of college students who had grown up with ADHD and LD labels, diagnoses that most had attempted to hide in order to succeed academically. Owning this identity was a critical step toward their emerging activism. As one of the founders told us:

> Lots of people said, 'wow! You have an LD, you seem too smart'. In my book, that translates to: 'I didn't know you were stupid? Really! You're so successful'. I will hide this, I will fake this. The misconception is their own. I mastered hiding my LD, it wouldn't come up in life, I'd memorise the paragraph I had to read in public, but I'd have no idea what's in the first 4 pages. . . . It blew up in my face in sophomore year: I had to discuss my topic for a 20 page paper with the professor. 'You have an LD! That's so cool . . . you're gonna write the best paper ever!' She helped me to do research and taught me that my experience could become a positive example for someone else. I got an A, holy shit! I can do this! Maybe these accommodations can help me to do well in school. And my grades started to rise. . . . Every time you come out of the closet, you're changing LDs for someone else.

The students who founded PE2E (now Eye to Eye, or E2E) are part of a generation who grew up after the 1990 passage of the Americans with Disabilities Act. They had intimate experience with diagnoses of disability and came to expect inclusive educational environments. Most of the thirty student activists we interviewed felt empowered to create their own representations that challenge purely medical understandings of their circumstances. We learned that *coming out* as having a *special* education in their past was a critical part of forging their identity as young adults. It also enabled them, we found, to speak and act with conviction as they reached out to students like themselves at local middle schools around their colleges. As these students contacted their friends from high school, now on other campuses across the country, E2E took root and flowered. On sixty college campuses coast to coast, chapters of E2E have been founded by labelled students who succeeded in getting into college, and now mentor youngsters identified as having similar issues in middle schools near their universities.[4]

At NYU, we helped an E2E chapter come into existence, facilitating their entry to three different local public middle schools with strong programmes for *at-risk* children. Here, they worked to enhance children's self-esteem by demonstrating the skills, creativity, and humour that the young adult mentors have learned to deploy along their own slower route to success. E2E's innovations are built on a sense of connection to youngsters struggling with the same diagnoses the college students have carried throughout their own life-course. This is foundational to the project. They recognise that middle school is a critical time in the development of a self-conscious identity, in which being labelled as different can be damaging. At middle schools, the college activists highlight the positive features of being *wired differently*, often identified with creativity and imagination. The centrepiece of E2E's strategy is their afterschool programme in local middle schools: the Beyond Normal Art Club (BNAC). The arts curriculum they use enhances children's self-esteem by demonstrating the hard-won skills and humour that the young adult E2E mentors have learned to deploy. Every middle schooler gets a college student mentor; they work together on art projects such as building *dream machines*, fantasy creations that children imagine would make school-based learning easier.

We observed one BNAC class in a Harlem school where a lot of parents had not communicated the specific diagnosis to their child who was participating in the programme. The chapter organiser, sensitive to the problem of disclosure, called out to the class: 'Anyone know what ADHD is?' When no one answered directly, he said: 'Well I've got it, I was way noisier in school than even Scotty or Jamal, and just look at how much I talk now!' Immediately, a participating 10-year-old volunteered: 'Oh yeah, ADHD, that's when you can't sit still and you talk too much and you're always buzzing around and I've got it'. The others chuckled in appreciation and started to talk among themselves about 'having ants in my pants' and 'always running around', normalising what had mainly been until then an unspoken and private issue. At the end of the school year, BNAC hosts an art exhibition to which the entire middle school is invited. They show all the student projects created over the year. Participating middle schoolers proudly mingle with their peers and family members as they display their accomplishments.

E2E activists designed BNAC in recognition of the difference it would have made to their school lives if they had a 'cool' college mentor as a role model. Demedicalising their diagnoses and embracing a social model of disability based on the philosophy of one-on-one mentoring (or 'each one, reach one'), they valorised self-help across school generations. In individual interviews, virtually all gave credit to their parents – overwhelmingly, their mothers – for the combination of advocacy, discipline and love that they understood as the basis of their current college-centred success.

At their national Organising Institute, an annual four-day workshop where new leaders are trained and new college chapters are incubated, we experienced material accommodations designed by the people who use them: baskets of rubber fidget toys were available, as were frequent stair running breaks intended to keep people with ADHD on task and energetically comfortable during intense, lengthy meetings. Participants receive T-shirts when they complete their rigorous training programme. The aqua T-shirt we earned proclaimed: 'A Special Ed Revolution Coming to a School Near You'. Their firsthand expertise gave us greater appreciation of what it means to actually make a disability world. No longer confined to the Ivy League colleges where it began, the organisation has sixty chapters in twenty states in both public and private institutions, and is found on elite as well as community college campuses.[5] In each chapter, E2E leadership identifies a team of students with learning disabilities to work with local middle schools. While E2E works closely with medical researchers, parent groups and national service agencies, this is the first national organisation created for, about, and most importantly *by* young adults with LDs.

Recently, the group launched *Understood*, a national network of 15 non-profits dedicated to reaching out and offering supportive resources to parents whose children have been diagnosed with learning and attention issues. E2E staff have also worked with sympathetic corporations to create job opportunities for young adults transitioning from college to the workplace. As E2E envisions it, they are building a community that extends from middle schoolers and their parents through college students into working adults, many of whom already have life partners and children together with professional jobs. They have started a movement in which the differences indexed by their disabilities are foundational to building inhabitable worlds and perhaps expanding the way personhood is imagined. E2E's intergenerational coalitional work moves LD from beyond normal to an emergent new normal that have helped to incubate.

Conclusion

As the work of E2E makes clear, the rapidly expanding demographic of young adults with disabilities will be the participating citizens of tomorrow. Their aspirations for ongoing inclusion are the *new normal* that challenges restrictive notions of personhood from which they have long been excluded. However, pathways to this future require the kind of creative support that has proven so successful in the cases discussed above. Clearly, transition done well is intensive and only a minority of families can afford to pay for that directly, or understand how to navigate the complex bureaucracy entitling their young adult students to support for the kinds of programmes – such as the ones we examine here – that promote meaningful engagement. Compared to the growing numbers of young New Yorkers who are ageing out of special education, too often 'out of school and unprepared', the model programmes we have described are only able to reach a small minority of students relative to the escalating need. The public schools are the location where the greatest proportion – over 95 percent – of IEP-holding high school students are educated, yet in this context, effective transition programmes are few and far between, despite the fact that they are legally mandated. Such initiatives cannot be mass-produced. Yet, the approaches in these exemplary cases have the potential to be adapted across many contexts. This is what we mean by active disability *world-making* that can expand everyday understandings of the *new normal*.

Can such programmes make a difference in transforming the limits to the *college for all* narrative that opened this chapter? Without dedicated expertise to help scaffold the path to educational life beyond high school, attending college risks deferring broader questions of transition to adulthood and the kind of bespoke preparation often required to prepare young adults with disabilities for meaningful engagement. Indeed, in the course of our research, we have encountered the sobering descriptions of parents (usually mothers) who have supported children diagnosed with ADHD or Asperger's syndrome successfully through college, only to find themselves with depressed young adult boarders who stay at home without a job or a community life. However, the kind of disability activists and visionary educators whose transition work inspired us to write this chapter are also busy reshaping what *college for all* might actually mean.

In the course of the last decade, a small but growing number of alternative college programmes dedicated to the needs of students with a variety of learning disabilities have materialised. Their presence is evident on the *Think College* national website established in 2010, providing information on college options for people with intellectual disabilities. Such initiatives move beyond the requisite learning centres mandated on any campus that receives federal funds to support students with documented disabilities who choose to disclose their diagnoses. In our work in NYC, we have learned about programmes ranging from very small enterprises supporting those with LD and autism spectrum disorders inside private liberal arts colleges, to our City University public system, which enrols over 9,000 students with disabilities across 24 campuses. Recently, City University of New York (CUNY) established Project REACH, an acronym for *Resources and Education on Autism as CUNY's Hallmark*, an important step forward in incorporating this underserved community. The question of scale troubles all such endeavours, given the difficulties in mass-producing educational resources for those who think and learn differently. Nonetheless, each of these projects opens doors for young adults with disabilities, contributing to the expansion of habitable worlds and broadening their possibilities for everyday life.

Acknowledgements

We are grateful to The Spencer Foundation and the NYU Institute for Human Development and Social Change, the National Endowment for the Humanities Collaborative Research Program, the Guggenheim Foundation, and the NYU Humanities Center for generously supporting our research. Above all, we thank the many people who generously shared their stories with us. We thank Gareth Thomas and Dikaios Sakellariou for inviting this contribution, for their editing suggestions, and for their patience.

Notes

1 In the American context, K–12 indicates all grades prior to post-secondary education, from kindergarten to the completion of secondary school.
2 Historically, YAI was an acronym for Young Adult Institute. However, since the organisation now serves clients with disabilities of all ages, they no longer use the name, but nonetheless have maintained the acronym YAI.
3 Their website describes the programme as 'a community of diverse learners aged 18–21 with unique patterns of strengths and weaknesses, all of whom need additional work to be

prepared for post-secondary programmes or gain further academic, work, and/or life skills. This includes, but is not limited to, students with complexities that can be fully understood only by working with them on an individual basis' (Winston Preparatory School 2017).

4 Now calling itself 'a mentoring movement for different thinkers', their website says that 'Eye to Eye no longer considers itself a project but rather a full-fledged instrument for change. It is widely recognised as one of the leading national not-for-profit mentoring programmes changing the lives of thousands of kids and young adults across the US. Each day, Eye to Eye gives students with LD/ADHD – often labelled "at-risk" at school – a feeling of empowerment because they now belong to a community of understanding and compassion that celebrates the differences inherent in us all . . . Knowing how you learn and standing up for the support you need are two of the most important attributes anyone with LD/ADHD can have' (Eye to Eye 2017).

5 As they explain in their mission statement: 'It starts with a label: Learning Disabled. Attention Deficit Hyperactivity Disorder. Too often, it also ends there. That's where Project Eye to Eye comes in. As the only national mentoring programme pairing kids with LD/ADHD with similarly labelled college students, Project Eye to Eye encourages labelled children to become their own best advocates. These kids need a safe place. They need, like all children, to be heard. And most of all, they need self-confidence. With Project Eye to Eye, they find not just a safe place, but also a great place. And it's fun! "Regular" school reminds children with LD/ADHD of what they can't do. With Project Eye to Eye, it's all about can do' (Eye to Eye 2017).

References

Arise Coalition. 2011. Out of school and unprepared: the need to improve support for students with disabilities transitioning to adulthood. *Arise Coalition* [Online]. Available at: www.advocatesforchildren.org/sites/default/files/library/out_of_school_2011.pdf?pt=1 [Accessed: 23 November 2017].

Blum, R. W. 2005. Adolescents with disabilities in transition to adulthood. In: Osgood, W. D., Foster, M. E., Flanagan, C. and Gretchen, R. eds. *On Your Own Without a Net: The Transition to Adulthood for Vulnerable Populations*. Chicago: University of Chicago Press, pp. 323–348.

Bruner, J. 1987. *Actual Minds, Possible Worlds*. Cambridge, MA: Harvard University Press.

Bruner, J. 1991. Self-making and world-making. *Journal of Aesthetic Education* 25(1), pp. 67–78.

Carey, A. C., Ben-Moshe, L. and Chapman, C. 2014. *Disability Incarcerated: Imprisonment and Disability in the United States and Canada*. New York: Palgrave Macmillan.

Davis, L. 2015. *Enabling Acts: The Hidden Story of How the Americans With Disabilities Act Gave the Largest US Minority Its Rights*. Boston: Beacon Press.

Elementary and Middle School Technical Assistance. 2016. The disproportionate representation of racial and ethnic minorities in special education: frequently asked questions. *EMSTAC* [Online]. Available at: www.emstac.org/registered/topics/disproportionality/faqs.htm [Accessed: 23 November 2017].

Eye to Eye. 2017. Our story. *Eye to Eye* [Online]. Available at: www.eyetoeyenational.org/about/our_story.html [Accessed: 23 November 2017].

Ferri, B. A. and Connor, D. J. 2005. Tools of exclusion: race, disability, and (re)segregated education. *Teachers College Record* 107(3), pp. 453–474.

Friedner, M. and Cohen, E. 2015. Inhabitable worlds: troubling disability, debility, and ability narratives. *Somatosphere* [Online]. Available at: http://somatosphere.net/2015/04/inhabitable-worlds-troubling-disability-debility-and-ability-narratives.html [Accessed: 23 November 2017].

Geurts, K. L. 2015. On the worlding of Accra's rehabilitation training centre. *Somatosphere* [Online]. Available at: http://somatosphere.net/2015/04/on-the-worlding-of-accras-rehabilitation-training-centre.html [Accessed: 23 November 2017].

Goodman, N. 1978. *Ways of Worldmaking*. Indianapolis, IN: Hackett.

Gursel, Z. D. 2016. *Image Brokers: Visualizing World News in the Age of Digital Circulation*. Oakland: University of California Press.

Heidegger, M. 1962. *Being and Time*. New York: Harper.

Jackson, D. D. 2013. Teaching tomorrow's citizens: the law's role in educational disproportionality. *Alabama Civil Rights and Civil Liberties Law Review* 5, pp. 215–288.

Levine, P. and Wagner, M. 2005. Transition for young adults who received special education services as adolescents: a time of challenge and change. In: Osgood, Wayne, Foster, E. Michael, Flanagan, Constance and Ruth, Gretchen eds. *On Your Own Without a Net: The Transition to Adulthood for Vulnerable Populations*. Chicago: University of Chicago Press, pp. 202–258.

Ne'eman, A. 2012. What do we mean when we say 'community'? *YAI* [Online]. Available at: www.yai.org/blog/what-do-we-mean-when-we-say-community [Accessed: 23 November 2017].

Neuhaus, R., Smith, C. and Burgdorf, M. 2014. Equality for people with disabilities, then and now. *GPSOLO* 31(6). Online. Available at: www.americanbar.org/publications/gp_solo/2014/november_december/equality_people_disabilities_then_and_now.html [Accessed: 23 November 2017].

Noguera, P., Pierce, J. and Ahram, R. 2015. *Race, Equity, and Education: Sixty Years From Brown*. Cham: Springer.

Nünning, V., Nünning, A. and Neumann, B. 2015. *Cultural Ways of Worldmaking: Media and Narratives*. Berlin: De Gruyter.

Ong, A. 2011. Introduction: worlding cities, or the art of being global. In: Roy, A. and Ong, A. eds. *Worlding Cities: Asian Experiments and the Art of Being Global*. Malden, MA: Blackwell, pp. 1–28.

Osher, D., Woodruff, D. and Sims, A. 2002. Schools make a difference: the relationship between educational services for African-American children and youth and their overrepresentation in the juvenile justice system. In: Losen, D. ed. *Minority Issues in Special Education*. Cambridge, MA: Harvard Educational, pp. 93–116.

Otterman, S. 2011. Most New York graduates are ill prepared, data show. *New York Times* [Online]. Available at: www.nytimes.com/2011/02/08/nyregion/08regents.html [Accessed: 23 November 2017].

Rapp, R. and Ginsburg, F. 2011. Reverberations: disability and the new kinship imaginary. *Anthropological Quarterly* 84(2), pp. 379–410.

Rapp, R. and Ginsburg, F. 2012. Anthropology and the study of disability worlds. In: Inhorn, M. C. and Wentzell, E. A. eds. *Medical Anthropology at the Intersections: Histories, Activisms, and Futures*. Durham, NC: Duke University Press, pp. 163–182.

Ravitch, D. 1985. *The Troubled Crusade: American Education, 1945–1980*. New York: Basic Books.

Roy, A. and Ong, A. 2011. *Worlding Cities: Asian Experiments and the Art of Being Global*. Malden, MA: Blackwell.

Samuelson, R. J. 2012. It's time to drop the college-for-all crusade. *Washington Post* [Online]. Available at: www.washingtonpost.com/opinions/its-time-to-drop-the-college-for-all-crusade/2012/05/27/gJQAzcUGvU_story.html [Accessed: 23 November 2017].

Silverman, M. 2007. Transitioning to nowhere: an analysis of the planning and provision of transition services to students with disabilities in New York City. *Advocates for Children of New York, Inc.* [Online]. Available at: www.advocatesforchildren.org/tracker?utm_campaign=pdf&utm_medium=pdf&utm_source=internal&utm_content=sites/default/files/library/transitioning_to_nowhere_2007.pdf [Accessed 16 January 2018]

Trainor, A. A. 2017. *Transition by Design: Improving Equity and Outcomes for Adolescents With Disabilities.* New York: Teachers College Press.

Trend, D. 2012. Worlding.org. *Worlding.org* [Online]. Available at: http://davidtrend.com/?page_id=142 [Accessed: 23 November 2017).

Wall, P. 2016. New York City's graduation rate hits 70 percent for first time. *Chalkbeat* [Online]. Available at: www.chalkbeat.org/posts/ny/2016/01/11/new-york-citys-graduation-rate-hits-70-percent-for-first-time/ [Accessed: 23 November 2017].

Winston Preparatory School. 2017. Winston preparatory school: transitions program. *Winston Preparatory School* [Online]. Available at: www.teenlife.com/gap-year-program/winston-preparatory-school-transitions-program/ [Accessed: 23 November 2017].

Wright, P. 2004. The Individuals with Disabilities Education Improvement Act of 2004: overview, explanation and comparison: IDEA 2004 v. IDEA 1997. *Wright's Law* [Online]. Available at: www.wrightslaw.com/idea/idea.2004.all.pdf [Accessed: 23 November 2017].

Zhan, M. 2009. *Other-Worldly: Making Chinese Medicine Through Transnational Frames.* Durham, NC: Duke University Press.

Part III

Doing care, creating living

Chapter 6

Who's disabled, Babe?

Carving out a good life among the normal and everyday

Helen Errington, Karen Soldatic,
and Louisa Smith

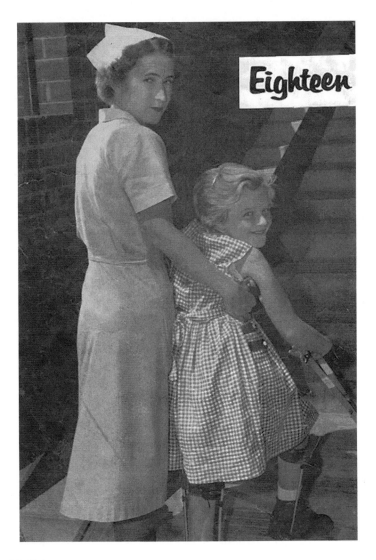

Figure 6.1 Helen

Introduction

The concept of *a good life* is an old philosophical question, the answers to which have most often ignored disability (Bickenbach et al. 2014). Today, this notion of a good life remains tied to certain kinds of ability and capability, and is one of the ways in which ideas of normalcy are produced in the everyday practices of being, doing, and acting. So, while disability studies aims to critically examine the ways in which cultural evaluations and material deprivations disenfranchise the lived experience of disability (Campbell 2009; Goodley 2014; Snyder and Mitchell 2006), disabled people themselves are engaged in everyday struggles to realise their personalised notions of the self and engage in processes which enable self-realisation (Hansen and Philo 2007). It is the daily lived struggle of navigating the tensions between normalcy and agency – of how our social worlds can elaborate or constrain our most intimate desires – that is the most troubling for disability scholarship (Shakespeare 2013). These social worlds entail a myriad of values which are often tied to humanity's constant striving for *the good life*, what it constitutes, and the costs that it entails (Pols and Limburg 2016; Skidelsky and Skidelsky 2013).

Disability studies has not often addressed the question of a good life. Instead, it has focused on refuting the idea that having a disability axiomatically undermines chances of living a good life (Bickenbach et al. 2014). People with disabilities have been excluded from the philosophical understandings of a good life, in part because they have not qualified as having the capacity to be human (Bickenbach et al. 2014). Johnson et al. (2010) have argued that philosophical descriptions of a good life usually make the rational and reasonable mind central to being able to live well. This requirement of reason excludes people with intellectual disability as unable to live good lives. In addition, philosophers have historically used impairments as metaphors for incapacity and, as such, emphasised disability as outside the world of good social and political life due to its innate vulnerability (Simplican 2015). Such a positioning of disability – as always outside the realm of living a good life – has led to some of the more extreme arguments from bioethics, like those of Peter Singer, that certain disabled lives are not worth living (Schaler 2009).

Other disability scholars, however, have taken up the very strong history of a good life in the history of philosophy and have brought new life to it through reworking it from the perspective of disability (Goggin 2008). This re-visioning of philosophy through a disability studies lens and experiences of disability allows us to understand and stretch our definitions of what it is to live well. For example, Simplican (2015) reframes Locke's positioning of impairment by suggesting that instead of it focusing on the impaired body's incapacity, it actually recognises the vulnerability of all human experience. For Simplican, then, Locke's capacity contract becomes a solidarity contract; we cannot have capacity without solidarity. Similarly, Kittay (2011, 2015) has spent the later part of her academic life as a feminist philosopher trying to stretch the limits of philosophy's rational definition of what it means to live well, finding that the individuality of this definition fails to recognise the goodness (and inevitability) of interdependence and care. So, while the dominance of liberal tendencies positions the individual as the agent for their own change, it is the very desire for self-realisation which leads to the collective foraging for a just society (Bhaskar 2001). Socially just change seeks to overturn normative values espoused in everyday practices which value some bodies-and-minds, while debasing the *other*.

Beyond the philosophical re-visioning of a good life and disability, social scientists and health researchers have explored how people with impairments understand a good life in their everyday practices. For instance, the qualitative research of Pols and Limburg (2016), as well as Sakellariou (2015), shows the contextual nature of a good life, which changes over time and space, and in interaction with impairment. They argue, thus, that a good life must be understood as dynamic, as something which changes as someone's values or perspectives change, and which can only be worked towards through ongoing negotiation in everyday life (Sakellariou 2015). This construction of a good life and disability is completely different to normative ideas, such as those in Albrecht and Devlieger's (1999) disability paradox, which – despite reports from many people with impairments – constructs the nature of disability as inherently precluding a good life.

Helen (first author), whose individual and collective subjectivity is the subject/object of this chapter, begins to coalesce understandings of disability activists' desire to live an ordinary life, a good life, a normal life, and how these desires are entangled and enacted in the everyday. As a long-standing self-described disability feminist activist, Helen's life history and engaged everyday practice begins to open up the political imagination which combines *the personal* of disability with the disabled political identity. It is an individualised account, but it is an individualised account which reveals the intensity of internal negotiations of the everyday self emerging with the struggles of being in the world; individual desire is coupled with collective change, self-realisation demands structural change, sexual intimacy and expression challenges heteronormative assumptions, and moments of isolation are entrusted to long-standing friendships.

In all, Helen's narrative enables us to traverse normative notions of the good life as they are lived through a range of everyday experiences and the striving to be valued as a disabled woman growing up in a small rural town of Western Australia. Helen's life narrative, thus, reveals the differing modalities of reflexive experimentation which become a vital strategy to reimage and practice notions of the good life. Helen's embodied practices are illustrative of the diffuse ways in which disability enables the reimaging of inclusive forms of everyday citizenship.

Methodology

The methodological strategy developed for this chapter draws on qualitative approaches grounded in the oral history tradition (Portelli 1991), with the added dimension of friendship, love, and solidarity. This methodology was chosen owing to the collaborative ways in which the writing of another's narrative is never an isolated event, but one shared across a range of temporal and spatial moments of talking (Perks and Thomson 2015). It also embodies, as a practice, many of the desires and associated practices deeply intertwined with Helen's subjectivity. As a methodological practice, it bridges the personal desire to narrate one's life story for change, yet also builds a transformative solidarity learnt through the shared process of *telling* captured across a range of time-scapes (Perks and Thomson 2015). The telling of Helen's narrative emerges from the extended fifteen-year friendship between Helen and Karen (second author), which first began in the early 2000s when both were Western Australian public servants working on committees for the realisation of disability service provision across a range of state policy portfolio areas. The sharing of this experience – working as policy activists inside the state bureaucracy – led to a flourishing long-standing friendship of mutual trust and respect.

Karen and Louisa's (third author) friendship also started at work. While living across the country, Louisa and Karen would meet annually at a national conference and their connection grew through a shared interest in social justice, good teaching, music, and laughter. Years later, Louisa came to work at the university where Karen was based and they worked together developing some online teaching materials. As part of this, Karen introduced Louisa to Helen, with the idea that her story may bring some of the online learnings to life. Louisa interviewed Helen and then transcribed the interview, creating the basis for this story.

The rest of this chapter is divided into two sections. The following section – the body of the chapter – is Helen's life narrative. While drawn from the transcript of the initial interview with Louisa, Helen has worked extensively on, and rewritten, the story. Most of Helen's story is written chronologically, from her rural childhood (when contracting polio meant institutionalisation) to her retirement as a 'self-funded retiree'. Karen and Louisa also asked Helen to draw out certain themes relevant to this book, such as ideas around normalcy, the everyday, and a good life. In the final section, Karen and Louisa reflect on Helen's story and how understanding it can facilitate understandings of disability in her everyday practices.

Helen's story

My very early years, prior to polio

I was born in Nedlands, Western Australia (WA), in 1947.

My mother left school at junior level and became a stenographer with the Commonwealth Department of Shipping and Transport. Back then, women had to relinquish their jobs upon marrying. She is an extremely well-read person and maintains she had read much of Shakespeare before the age of 14.

My father at the time was an accountant with the Vacuum Oil Company, later to become area manager for the North West of WA. In 1951, my father was transferred through his work to Kununoppin (Kunno), a small wheat belt town in rural WA. I was 4 at the time. In 1952, my sister, Carol, was born. My brother didn't arrive on the scene until 1957, well and truly after I had contracted polio.

I have wonderful memories of my time in Kunno. I was a very active, confident, and outgoing young girl. I would play in the wheat silos out on the railway line, chase race-horse goannas and build cubby houses in the bush.

I was a good little cricketer. I loved putting on my whites and the smell of new sand-shoes was intoxicating. I was so good at cricket that a complaint to the headmaster of the school was made by parents of the boys that they did not want to play with me because they could never get me out!

I remember fondly the love of riding my two-wheeler iridescent blue Malvern Star bike. I once rode my bike seven miles to Training (another town) where my father was playing cricket and, needless to say, he was somewhat shocked when I appeared!

As my mother says, I really lived a life of my own. I would wander off without her ever knowing where I was or where I ended up. I'd make my way across the petrol drums and down to the town barber, Eddie Green. The offer of PK chewing gum was the lure. Later in the day, he would put me on his shoulders and take me home. I also signed myself in at the local school. I loved to watch the kids playing 'Farmer in the Dell'. 'Farmer in the Dell' was a song we all sang together holding hands joining ourselves in a circle. The Principal of the school advised Mum that she should formally enrol me, as I was there every day. I took a shine to the high jump and running at the interschool sports. I was a very good runner and I still have my competition shirt with my entry number to this day!

Contracting polio, moving to the institution

I contracted polio three days before my seventh birthday although, at the time, the country doctor did not diagnose me with polio, in spite of one of the biggest epidemics occurring at the time. I was the only kid in the town to have contracted it. There was one other woman on an outlying farm that also contracted polio. To celebrate my birthday, the children could only leave presents on the veranda near my bedroom window. We were quarantined and not permitted to travel to other towns. My parents were not permitted to travel to Northam where Queen Elizabeth the Second was visiting. It was a terrible shock for my parents to realise their first daughter was lying flat in bed, unable to talk or move, something which Mum tells me she has never really gotten over. Interestingly enough, neither Mum, Dad, nor Carol (who was 2 at the time) contracted the virus!

The irony was that, days later, I was transported to the Infectious Diseases Hospital in Perth by my father, the first volunteer to use the new makeshift 'van/ambulance' which the town had purchased. I was in the infectious diseases ward for approximately two weeks. Once the infectious stage subsided, I was then transferred to The Golden Age, another institution, where I spent a short amount of time. Later, I was transferred to Lady Lawley

Cottage (LLC), a convalescing home for young people with a wide range of disabilities. As a result of me contracting polio, my father requested a transfer from Kununoppin to Perth so they could be near me to visit.

Visiting hours were restricted to two hours on a Wednesday and a Sunday. LLC was quite some distance from my home. My mother didn't drive so on Wednesdays, she had to rely on public transport, taking three buses to visit me. Children were not permitted to come into the wards but as time progressed, visits with my siblings took place down in the grounds of the institution.

During my time at LLC, Mum and Dad separated. However, on Sundays, Dad would drive the whole family to visit me and we would meet in the grounds of LLC, which allowed greater time for me to develop a healthy relationship with my brother and sister.

One of the infrequent pleasurable experiences of being in the institution was being involved in the Brownies and Girl Guide movement. The activities we did were the same in many ways to the normal kids and, on occasions, we spent a weekend up at Paxwold (in the hills of WA), a Brownie and Guide camp. We slept in bunk beds, we cooked potatoes in foil in the ashes, and we worked on gaining our badges. These activities were some of the most memorable for me and light me up to this day whenever I think about them. In 1959, I was awarded and presented with the Guide badge for fortitude. At the time, only five other people in WA had received this badge and it, indeed, was a great honour.

In those days, going home was not an option. The medical fraternity, in particular the orthopaedic surgeon to whom I was assigned, had enormous control of my body and my life. I remember Mum having arguments with him about whether or not to sign off on invasive surgery. He would shout her down and tell her that the medical fraternity knew what was best for me. If Mum declined to sign the consent papers for operations, then they sought the signature of my father who was more compliant. Mum could not bear the thought of her daughter being cut up and aesthetically disfigured and being left with permanent scars.

There were no resources available in those days to support me going home anyway. My body no longer belonged to me; it belonged to the surgeons and the establishment. I am of the opinion that many of us were 'guinea pigs' in a relatively new area of medicine (that of orthopaedics). I have a newspaper photograph which depicts me at the age of 13 needing an operation to correct a curvature of my spine. My parents needed to raise money to send me to England because at that stage, the surgeons here had not performed such an operation. We didn't make it to England, as we were unable to raise the funds. Mum tells me that the surgeon 'operated on me with a scalpel in one hand and a manual in the other'! Following the operation, I was encased in a full length plaster cast for 18 months and put out on the veranda of Princess Margaret Hospital (PMH) where the only barrier to the grassed area which lead to the ward opposite were canvas blinds. It was extremely hot in the summer – so much so that I would sweat in the plaster cast and, at one stage, developed chicken pox, necessitating me to insert a ruler down the front of the cast to scratch my terribly itchy spots.

LLC was under the auspices of the Red Cross. Every March, their March Appeal was held to fundraise. For some reason, I was chosen to be the 'cover girl' for their March Appeal magazine. I'm not sure why I was chosen but Mum informs me it was because I was blonde, with an engaging smile, and an outgoing personality.

The wards were divided into separate wards for girls and boys, and we were not permitted to visit each other's area. In the girls' ward, there was an Indigenous girl, Lesleigh, who was there when I arrived. She, like me, had polio and walked on crutches and callipers. Often she would assist me with my walking, by positioning herself behind me and helping me swing through. I don't remember her ever having visitors apart from Sister Dorothy who represented some sort of religious order. I can remember Lesleigh being beaten one day down in the bathroom by one of the Sisters as I could hear her scream. It disturbed me greatly and I comforted her when she returned from the wards. I am not sure what she did that earned such a beating. I have a vague recollection that it might have been about lying. Her cries have never left me. I don't remember any of us White Australian children being so badly treated.[1] Lesleigh eventually left LLC and went to Sister Kates, another institution for teenagers with disability. Some 30 years later, I met up with her. Compared to my life, Lesleigh's life demonstrated that not much has changed for Aboriginal Australians over 200 years. Lesleigh's life illustrated enduring forms of racism and the ongoing denial of opportunities for Aboriginal Australians with disability to live a normal life. The lack of family support, an education, living on the streets, and her children in foster care, she had little chance right from the beginning. Indigenous women didn't even get a look in.

Getting out of the institution, going to mainstream school

I was in LLC from age 8 until I was 16. By the time I turned 16, the older (teenage) girls were being moved into the old Matron's quarters. Once we became teenagers, they had to work out a way of 'rehabilitating us' out to other institutions or, for those of us who had one, a home. I didn't wait around to move to the Matron's quarters. I took it upon myself to ask my treating surgeon if I could go home, to which he cocked his head and said somewhat reservedly 'alright then'. To my mother's surprise, on the following weekend leave, I informed her I had come to stay. She had not been advised of my discharge and, of course, we were not set up at home to accommodate my needs. We just made do and worked things out as we went along.

When I left LLC, Sir George Bedbrook, my treating surgeon, along with the Social Security Department were keen for me to finish my schooling. The institutional schooling was totally inadequate. Sadly, my education was not the main focus then. The authorities were more concerned with my physical rehabilitation, which included occupational therapy, physiotherapy, and attending medical appointments.

All grades from primary to high school took place in one classroom. We older students who graduated to high school had to undertake our studies by correspondence. There was little or no tuition from the teacher. We were pretty much left to our own devices. This lack of support certainly had dire consequences emotionally and academically when I left

LLC and attended a normal high school. I would sometimes end up in tears trying my hardest to understand the maths subjects, particularly geometry and algebra. I remember the teacher Mrs Favas spending some class time with me but to no avail. I failed maths in my first year of high school with a mark of 9/100.

Mum was left to organise this transition from institutional schooling to mainstream schooling. She worked with the Principal of Scarborough Senior High until eventually, in 1963, I was officially enrolled. It was quite unusual in those days for someone with a significant disability to be accepted at a 'normal' school. I was 16 at the time and initially they put me into the first year of high school, usually for 12-year-olds. But they discovered that it was too easy for me and so, I was then put up to second year, but ended up failing this year – only attaining two subjects (English and Art). It was soul-destroying to know I had 'failed' high school, but I also recognised that the institutional education, if you can call it that, had also failed me miserably!

I always felt the need to better myself, get a good education, and then a job because that is what I saw 'normal' kids doing. I came from a family who were relatively well-educated and, as a young girl, I was fond of sport, competition, and winning. I pitted myself against myself. I also had an intense desire to relinquish the 'Invalid Pension' (disability income benefit) as it was then called. Accepting the Pension devastated me. I felt so humiliated and ashamed that all I was worth was eleven pounds ten shillings per fortnight. The money, at the time, did help Mum financially as we were poor and although Dad was supposed to send money, it was haphazard and unpredictable. He was extremely unreliable so the money I received filled that breach. I recall Mum having to scrape a few pennies together from a brown screw top jar, safely stored in the linen press, for emergencies. The irony is sweet.

When I attended the mainstream high school, Scarborough Senior High School, the Manual Arts teacher who lived a street away from me ferried me to and from school. Many of my classes were held up two flights of stairs, which I negotiated with some trepidation. I was on callipers and crutches then, so I could walk but it was quite dangerous. I would leave the classroom about 10 minutes earlier before the bell rang to ensure I didn't have the worry of being tripped by the rush of other students changing rooms. I remember a time falling down one flight and cutting my chin and loosening my bottom teeth. There was no thought in those days of bringing classes downstairs.

The Principal had designated (without consultation I found out) Cheryl, a student who was in my class, to assist me in negotiating the school environment. I was relieved to find that Cheryl was a warm, friendly, and understanding person who took on the challenge with unwavering intent. We developed a very close relationship. I would help her with her English and she would help me with my maths. We talked about normal things like love, music (The Beatles were big then), other students, teachers, homework, and what was happening in our families. We developed a long-lasting friendship away from school. She met my family and I met hers. Her friendship normalised my life in the sense that she was able-bodied and I was participating socially just like my sister and brother. She invited me to her home for meals and eventually to her wedding, and that was the first wedding I had ever attended. She arranged for a family member to pick me up and transport me to the venue. I did make other friends at school but Cheryl was the only one that when I left school, I maintained a long-standing relationship with. Our neighbours were very friendly and supportive and I can remember the older guys across the road from us would carry me over to their house to watch TV. We didn't have a TV at the time and I used to love 'The Untouchables' and 'Dragnet'. Later in my young life, I joined the paraplegic sports group, a different community that provided me with both a social and sporting life. I represented the state at the 9th National Paraplegic Games in Brisbane.

Leaving school, getting work

In 1965, I left school and my treating surgeon engaged the services of the Senior Medical Officer (SMO) at the Commonwealth Department of Social Services with the idea of finding and placing me in some form of [sheltered] employment with a charity organisation. In 1966, I was offered a job making coin wrappers for Good Samaritan Industries. The deal was that I would spend two and a half days making coin wrappers in the factory, and the other two and a half days training for a clerical position. However, prior to being trained in office work, I had to turn out 1,000 coin wrappers each of the two and a half days in the factory. Mum and I met with GSI authorities during which time I tried out on the coin-wrapping machine. GSI employed people with an intellectual disability and I didn't have an intellectual disability, so felt I didn't belong in such an environment. I felt so hurt, defeated, and insulted that they would think that that was all I could do. I became visibly upset and, with Mum's support, I declined the offer.

Following my declination, the SMO wrote to my surgeon informing him that as I declined what he considered to be a 'very good offer', he was of the opinion that unless my 'motivation improved', he would think carefully about further intervention. After my 'refusal' of the offer and for approximately 18 months, I sat at home with Mum gaining a very good general knowledge by watching TV game shows. During this time, we were once again visited by the Social Security Department who were keen to get me off the pension. This time, I enrolled in a typing course, which I later used to gain a part-time position as a medical typist with the Royal Perth Rehabilitation Hospital (RPRH) working for George Bedbrook, my treating surgeon, the guru of orthopaedics. The pay only supplemented my pension but the position reflected a full-time workload. In 1984, I secured, under the Commonwealth Employment Program (CEP), a paid position with DASH (Disabled Advocates and Self-Help).

DASH was established in 1981 by a committee comprising of nine disabled people and one able-bodied person. One of its key objectives was to enhance the degree of control disabled people had over their own services. There was a need for an umbrella group in WA to advocate and lobby for social and political reform of disability services. Its work continues today under the name of PWDWA Inc. (People with Disabilities WA Inc.).

Prior to 1984, I had completed a Diploma in Fine Arts at Claremont Art College that, according to social security, had few job prospects, so no financial support was offered. I then followed that up with my Mature Age Matriculation, taking English and English Literature as my preferred subjects. My aggregate was not scintillating, but the interviewing lecturer when I applied to study Social Work at the Western Australian Institute of Technology, now Curtin University, was generous enough to recommend me for the Social Work Degree as my preferred option.

Having graduated from university with a Social Work degree in 1982, I tried on numerous occasions to find work in the field. Whilst my able-bodied friend who went through university with me was able to secure work quite quickly, I discovered that my disability became a focus used by prospective employers to assess my suitability. I had a higher aggregate than my friend and, yet, I was always unsuccessful. I would apply to disability organisations and on one occasion, I rang the human resources office to enquire as to the reason I didn't get the job. The reply was: 'You would take too long to go to and from the toilet'. And this particular position was in one of our large teaching hospitals! Making that phone call was the catalyst for spurring me on to involve myself in the activist movement here in WA. I thought 'I am not letting them off the hook on this one. I will make them accountable'. I have adopted that philosophy ever since as right from a young age, I have never been enamoured of authority.

In 1982, there wasn't an opportunity to lodge complaints of discrimination on the ground of impairment because in WA, the Equal Opportunity Act had not been enacted, least of all including discrimination on the grounds of impairment and disability. I stopped pursuing formal work for a while and undertook a number of voluntary positions with local government organisations, such as Communicare and Sussex Street Law Centre. I also, without a clue, set up my own small business as a consultant on issues of disability, securing a few contracts from the Health Department and other government agencies. This paved the way for me being invited by the then Premier of the State to become a member of the inaugural Women's Advisory Council to the Premier. This opportunity really broadened my networks and helped me to expand socially and academically.

One thing led to another and I subsequently became involved, by invitation, to participate on a State government committee led by Graham Edwards, a prominent politician who had his legs blown off in Vietnam, to amend the WA Equal Opportunity Act to include the ground of impairment. I then secured a contract with the WA Equal Opportunity Commission to progress the amendments through Parliament, following which I successfully applied for the position of Conciliation Officer with the Commission. I worked at the Commission for 13 years, resolving complaints of discrimination until I was headhunted by the WA Department of Education and Training, now the Department of Training and Workforce Development. I remained there for 10 years, retiring in 2010. I am now a self-funded retiree.

Normalised and alternative activist paths: becoming a disabled activist

My involvement in activism in the 1980s played a part in the setting up of the Disabled Advocates and Self Help (DASH) organisation in Perth, WA. Meeting with and writing to politicians, and getting myself known, were key factors in developing a public persona which led to a range of invitations to participate in various other human rights activities. I attended the inaugural Disabled People's International Conference in Singapore in 1981, *for the International Year of Disabled People (IYDP). In 1980, I demonstrated with 60 of my University colleagues outside parliament house in a silent vigil for the Noonkan-bah Aboriginal issue in WA. Noonkankbah became synonymous with the fight to stop oil drilling on a sacred site in the Kimberley region of WA. This protest was during the Charles Court (Premier of WA) era where upon re-election, he renewed his government's campaign to allow the miners to drill wherever they were entitled by non-Aboriginal law. Protesters, with their mouths gagged and carrying lighted candles, staged a silent vigil outside WA Parliament House over the erosion of the civil rights of Aboriginal people.*

In the late 1980s, I became part of a theatre group called Theatre of Difference. It was really the first time in the arts area where able-bodied people were included with people with disability, not the other way around. Participating in plays and dance had a huge impact on my self-esteem and assisted me to overcome socially induced embarrassment about my disability. It contributed to normalising me within the public eye and I began to develop a pride in who I was and, indeed, who I could become! It added to my experiences of life and gave me confidence to pursue other forms of art to try to explore the more creative side of life beyond a single disabled identity. I even tried my hand at stand-up comedy. I enjoy and get a real kick out of making people laugh. I did perform my own routine a few times at Perth Institute of Performing Arts (PICA) and was paid to do so! My routine centred around sharp wittedness that made jokes about able bodied notions of disability. Here's an example: Question from able-bodied person: 'Were you born like that?' Answer: 'Yes, dickhead, I have always been a woman!' And so it went on.

Whilst at Theatre of Difference, the choreographer introduced me to one of the most extraordinary educational programs in which I have ever participated: The Landmark Forum (LF). The technology used is based on the distinction 'ontology', or the being of being human. In working through LF, which was three days and one evening, initially, I could see how my interpretation of a number of incidents during my life had influenced my constructing a good life from those circumstances, but not necessarily a happy and fulfilling life.

Access to the distinctions in LF gave me the freedom to be fully self-expressed and to be true to my principles and ideals. Fear was no longer in my dictionary and I developed the art of creating possibility for myself where none existed as a disabled woman. The most critical aspect of LF for me is the recognition that choice, personal integrity, and taking responsibility are key elements in having life work powerfully.

During the years between 2008 and 2016, I devoted much of my time, as well as working, to being a board member with DADAA (Disability and Disadvantage in the Arts, Australia), a disability arts organisation for people with disability and mental health issues. With much trepidation and questioning of my own ability, I later became the first woman with a significant disability to chair the organisation. As chair, I was very keen to adopt the affirmative model of disability as the context for administering and delivering our programs. The affirmative model has been developed by the disability arts movement and has, at its core, a principled resistance to the 'personal tragedy' model. Essentially, it is a 'non-tragic' view of disability that encompasses positive identities through the lived experience of disability. This was a role where I could embody my beliefs in the power of language and context in order to transform the public's relationship to disability. It was one of the most rewarding and fulfilling experiences of my long life and as a consequence, I flourished as a human being.

It was through the WA Disability Collective (WADC) that my activism was cata-pulted to new heights! The WADC operated as a local collective working for justice for people with disability through education, action, and community campaigns. The Collective, in partnership with the WA Institute of Advanced Studies UWA, sponsored a number of local, national, and international guest speakers who represented critical social issues.

I received a phone call one day from Karen Soldatic, now Dr Karen Soldatic, who at the time worked for the Disability Services Commission in WA. She had attended a function where I was speaking and suggested we catch up for coffee. Over time, a friendship grew and common sentiments about injustice and discrimination bonded us firmly together. Karen had developed the idea of a disability collective in an effort to ignite and open up a global and more penetrating conversation around the oppression of disabled people. Karen was sounding me out and she later invited me to be a co-founder, for which I will always be eternally grateful.

Fertile ground was instilled through our discussions and many get-togethers spawned in me a global approach to my activism as a whole, but in particular my disability activism. My story was not just 'my story'. I soon recognised, following some struggle with concepts and language, that elements of my story intersected with that of other oppressed groups. This was a powerful insight and gave me access to a more effective way of speaking about the injustices faced by disabled people on a daily basis. I also became acutely aware of how privileged I am to be a disabled person!

They called me 'Helen Everywhere'. The title is important to me because it gives me an identity that expresses the essence of who I am over my physical representation, as a disabled person, which too often is used by others to define me. People know me for my work. I have a distinct presence in the world. I have 'form' other than my disability. I am real and I belong.

Friendships and sexual explorations

When I was in LLC, I tried to establish relationships. Not being certain of my sexuality, I accidently discovered masturbation one day whilst rocking back and forth onto my heel whilst holding onto a bedside table. This was most pleasurable!

At the back of the music class, my boyfriend Danny and I used to explore one another while singing 'Ho row my nut brown maiden'. This was a song on ABC, the afternoon music radio show for children in 1950s. If you were disabled in those days, you were considered to be asexual. Meeting up with Danny was clandestine and precarious for fear of the staff catching us out. The occupational therapy room was a favourite venue or the outside toilet. Nothing much happened as none of us knew much about the mechanics of sex, at least I didn't. There was no fostering of support from the institutional staff to explore our sexuality or, indeed, to have relationships with the opposite gender.

At about the age of 14, I 'fell in love' with one of the nurses. I was a favourite of hers. She would hug me and kiss me when she was on night shift, not in a sexual way for her, but that love and special attention she provided caused me to misinterpret her affection as sexual love. I grew up with little understanding of how affection from someone doesn't necessarily have any connection to wanting to be in a relationship with me, unless it does. There was obviously some concern about our relationship because the Matron asked her to leave the institution because she was 'getting too close to me'. So she did. This happened when I had been admitted to Royal Perth Hospital for an operation and on my return, finding out she had left was devastating to me. I felt completely abandoned and duped. During the ensuing years, she wrote many letters to me and expressed how much she missed me. The letters were filled with what I felt was a longing to be with me. I still have those letters but, of course, they have a totally different meaning for me today, given she has married and adopted a child. Gradually, we lost contact and then one day, I bumped into her at a familiar shopping centre and we rekindled our wonderful friendship. Those old feelings rose once more, which rekindled familiar emotions. My hopes were in vain of course and we, to this day, remain good friends.

From about 20 to 35 [years old] was the most heart-breaking time of my life, trying to form relationships and find that special one. It was very difficult. I remember being attracted to both men and women but in very different ways. I was still trying to work out my sexuality. I remember having a friend who was a quadriplegic and was going out with the local radiographer, and I wondered why I wasn't able to attract someone like she did with such a high-level disability. We were both employed at RPRH and it was an awkward time as we were both working in the same office. I regret being annoyed with her. Nevertheless, we remained close and she continued to offer me valuable guidance in my younger life. Sadly, after her engagement, she committed suicide because she felt she was not able to give her boyfriend what she thought he needed. He, on the other hand, wasn't concerned about her disability at all. He loved her without reservation.

I've got a theory based on my observations and anecdotes. It's easier for men with disabilities to attract non-disabled women, than it is for disabled women to attract non-disabled men. Women with disabilities find it harder to maintain attractiveness, because many men are more demanding of the outward appearance. I suspected I couldn't fulfil on that variable. In fact, when I did have a short relationship with a non-disabled man, one of his mates commented to him 'you can do better than that'. It doesn't matter how you spin it. This experience reinforced my theory.

I've had three long-standing relationships with women. I don't know how I fell into the gay scene. I used to get jealous and possessive because I was afraid to live on my own. Now I've lived on my own for years and years, and I don't know if I could live with someone else now. I've never really found my soulmate.

A few years ago, I had a friendship frolic to acknowledge some of the people who matter to me in my life. They are so willing and available to me that I felt something I could contribute to them would be to arrange a gathering to appreciate and acknowledge them. The afternoon took place out in my beautiful backyard surrounded by native grevilleas, silver princess trees, red and yellow kangaroo paws, and cascading hakeas. A garden designed by my friends no less! My very old dog, Mitzi Gaynor, was mooching around anticipating with hopeful looks for the dropping of some special treats. Birdsong twittered above as we sat comfortably together under the patio eating homemade dips with crackers, cheese, olives, and neatly diced vegetables. My beverage was coconut water or sparkling mineral water. My sister made her popular spinach quiche and before I could ask 'where's the quiche?', it had been devoured by the hungry mob.

I went around to each person individually, acknowledging them for their particular contribution to my life. They were very appreciative and also acknowledged me for my friendship and my contribution to their lives. One of the issues I have struggled with is making requests of people to help me with certain tasks that I am unable to do. I fear appearing as though I am 'using them'. It's a bit of a fine line. However, happily, my friends are more than willing to be invited to support me. Of course, as I said before, I also provide support for them.

A lot of people think that people with disability can't make a contribution to able-bodied friends; able-bodied people, however, have just as many issues. I'm very thankful that I've been able to establish friendships over a period of time. A good sense of humour is always an enticing quality, I think. It's interesting the diverse friends I have.

One of the many stories my sister Carol often tells is the time when driving home from work drinks on a Friday night, somewhat tipsy, I gently nudged the bumper of the car in front of me. To my horror, the guy in the backseat of the car turned around and yelled out 'that's my Aunty Hel'. Of course, he was in stitches and, needless to say, has never forgotten this event. Another story was the time when I hopped into my friend's car, they pulled out of the driveway and were well down the street before we realised we had forgotten my wheelchair!

I also recall the numerous sisterly stories regurgitated about our shopping sprees at Myer Department Store and the lack of changing rooms and my constant beckoning of the manager to make my displeasure known. My complaining went on for years until finally, Myer did provide changing rooms for disabled customers but, to my chagrin, inevitably I would find them full of clothes racks, clothes, and trolleys of various descriptions. You have to laugh!

Conclusion: carving out a 'good life' for myself

When we asked Helen what a good life was, she responded:

> *The one I've got now.*
> *Owning my own home.*
> *Having a good financial set up.*
> *Having a beautiful garden to look on.*
> *Being able to move around freely.*
> *Not having to wait for taxis is a luxury.*

> *I did not carve out this 'good life' alone! I say that not to diminish in any way the struggle I experienced in 'making it', but to acknowledge the many wonderful supporters who, at times, had greater faith and trust in me than I did. I want to express my heartfelt gratitude to those people, professionals, family, and friends for their persistent partnership and patience in my pursuit of a life unexpected!*

But this sense of Helen's own life as a good one has taken individual and collective resistance to the normative. Helen talked extensively about the deficit views of the medical fraternity and society in general, which means she 'really carved out a life for myself'. Influenced by her parents, Helen – from an early age – believed that education would set her free from the social constraints imposed upon her as a rural woman with a disability now relocated within an urban environment. But despite pursuing diverse educational avenues, even within the high quality university sector, Helen continued to find barriers to employment and access. When you live in the world's most isolated city (Perth), the Landmark Forum (LF) provided the opportunity for Helen to explore and interrogate her own stories about herself and other people's perspectives about her life, her tenacity, and her integrity. While Helen knew that she was treated unfairly, we see throughout her life story above how she compares herself to the success of able-bodied friends and colleagues. She needed a way to be in her story differently. LF is not just about knowing something; it is about learning how to be in it differently (Erhard et al. 2014).

Despite potential critiques that LF is a form of corporate or personal development education, LF facilitated Helen to create her own life, to have power and control over it. LF's collective atmosphere of the possibility of change offered a new politics of hope for her own life, spurring on her push for socially just change for disabled people. This negotiation of normative understandings of a good life in the everyday is similar to the ways in which Pols and Limburg (2016) and Sakellariou (2015) describe a good life as emerging for people with disabilities. A good life is not static, but requires the mobilisation of a diversity of resources, and an open understanding of its contextual and changing nature. Helen's life, in turn, exemplifies these qualities of dynamism and transformation. This is accomplished both by mobilising her own resources and the support of others in different ways across her life. Helen is incredibly proud of her individual accomplishments and her independence as an older woman:

> No-one, not even my mother, had any expectations of me. In fact, Mum thought I would always live with her. Where I've got to in life, it's better than a lot of able-bodied people. I'm a lot better off than many able-bodied people my age and my gender. Self-funded retiree! Who's disabled, Babe? I have an impairment, that's obvious, but it doesn't disable me.

Nonetheless, Helen's independence and ownership over her own story have emerged in dialogue with collective action and social supports. As Helen notes, at various points in her life, experiences of discrimination resulted in her needing to resist other people's ableist ideas about her capabilities and her limitations. These experiences of the everyday have spurred on new activist tendencies. Indeed, collective action became a significant part of Helen's life. She worked both as an activist insider within formalised bureaucratic public policy committees and forums, and also through forming new alliances, generating collective networks resulting in new disabled people's organisations, and the formalisation of disability civil society activism into disabled people's own representative organisations.

Helen's individual story clearly benefitted from a range of social supports provided through formalised government initiatives. As Sakellariou (2015) contends, a good life is not something we can simply choose for ourselves, nor is it bestowed upon us. Instead, it is a place which we navigate, creatively traversing the given constraints of our personal lives and the broader social structures which often appear unyielding to our concerns. For example, when Helen did access appropriate paid employment, it was through a disability employment scheme, providing a solid foundation to develop her professional career, gaining recognition for her intellectual prowess. She was also the beneficiary of public housing schemes which enabled disabled people to purchase their own homes, enabling her self-expression of autonomy and security. So while Helen despised receiving the Disability Support Pension, carving out a good life did require an understanding of living in an ableist world alongside a range of non-stigmatising social supports which structurally press against disabled people's oppression.

We conclude with a short poem Helen has written in reflecting upon this chapter:

> We have a unique look.
> This unique look is me!
> I am the only one in the crowd of lookalikes.
> I like the idea of being unique.
> It provides colour, interest and conversation.
> It allows me to be free from the debilitating pursuit of 'able-bodiedness'
>   that once played havoc with my mind and kept me small.
> I often felt that I should look some other way,
> Other than I was.
> The societal pressures expressed through various media to conform to
>   stereotypical bodies no longer holds the emotional charge it once did.
> I own my body, I am proud of its endurance,
> Its shape and its performance! I look after it.
> It's my billboard for my identity.
> It has been the catalyst for making a difference in life.
> It's about educating us to be proud of our bodies!

Dedication (from Helen)

This chapter is dedicated to my courageous younger sister, Carol Jillian Soares (Errington), who died from peritoneal cancer on 28 November 2016, aged 64. Cuz: from the age of 11 and upon my arrival home from the institution, you dedicated yourself to making my life easier. Your natural selfless disposition was a gift to me all throughout my life. You witnessed and understood the discrimination I experienced and you were always my ally in seeking redress. You became a soldier for the cause! You adopted acceptance and hope as your companions for the seven years you lived with cancer and, without complaint, steered us through some of the darkest moments. I carry you with me always and I honour the last words you said to me: 'Live your life'.

Acknowledgements

Karen's contribution to this chapter was supported by an ARC DECRA Fellowship: DE160100478. Helen would particularly like to thank Trevor Bennett for all of his energy and efforts in getting the sixty-year-old photo (Figure 6.1) in this chapter to production requirements.

Note

1 Australia's First Peoples, Aboriginal, and Torres Strait Islander peoples were not granted formal recognition and citizenship until a national referendum held in 1967 to amend the National Constitution, Section 51. Prior to this time, indigenous Australians were not regarded as citizens of the nation and lived in a state of absolute exclusion and severe inequality with no constitutional rights. To this day, they are not recognised within the Constitution as Australia's First Peoples, prior to white invasion by the British in 1788.

References

Albrecht, G. L. and Devlieger, P. J. 1999. The disability paradox: high quality of life against all odds. *Social Science and Medicine* 48(8), pp. 977–988.

Bhaskar, R. 2001. *Critical Realism: Essential Readings*. London: Routledge.

Bickenbach, J., Felder, F. and Schmitz, B. 2014. *Disability and the Good Human Life*. Cambridge: Cambridge University Press.

Campbell, F. K. 2009. *Contours of Ableism: The Production of Disability and Abledness*, New York: Palgrave.

Erhard, W., Jensen, M. and Zaffon, S. 2014. Integrity: a positive model that incorporates the normative phenomena of morality, ethics and legality. *Harvard Business School NOM Working Paper* 10–061. Available at: https://papers.ssrn.com/sol3/papers.cfm?abstract_id=1542759 [Accessed: 23 November 2017].

Goggin, G. 2008. Bioethics, disability, and the good life: remembering Christopher Newell, 1964–2008. *Bioethical Inquiry* 5(4), pp. 235–238.

Goodley, D. 2014. *Dis/ability Studies: Theorising Disablism and Ableism*. London: Routledge.

Hansen, N. and Philo, C. 2007. The normality of doing things differently. *Tijdschrift voor Economische en Sociale Geografie* 98(4), pp. 493–506.

Johnson, K., Walmsley, J. and Wolfe, M. 2010. *People With Intellectual Disabilities: Towards A Good Life?* Bristol: Policy Press.

Kittay, E. 2011. The ethics of care, dependence and disability. *An International Journal of Jurisprudence and Philosophy of Law* 24(1), pp. 49–58.

Kittay, E. 2015. Centering justice on dependency and recovering freedom. *Hypatia* 30(1), pp. 285–291.

Perks, R. and Thomson, A. 2015. *Oral History Reader*. London: Routledge.

Pols, J. and Limburg, S. 2016. A matter of taste? Quality of life in day-to-day living with ALS and a feeding tube. *Culture Medicine and Psychiatry* 40(3), pp. 361–382.

Portelli, A. 1991. *The Death of Luigi Trastulli and Other Stories: Form and Meaning in Oral History*. New York: SUNY Press.

Sakellariou, D. 2015. Towards the construction of a nicer life: subjectivity and the logic of choice. *Anthropology in Action* 22(1), pp. 46–53.

Schaler, J. 2009. *Peter Singer Under Fire: The Moral Iconoclast Faces His Critics*. Chicago: Open Court.

Shakespeare, T. 2013. *Disability Rights and Wrongs*. Routledge: London.

Simplican, S. 2015. *The Capacity Contract: Intellectual Disability and the Question of Citizenship*. Minneapolis: University of Minnesota Press.

Skidelsky, R. and Skidelsky, E. 2013. *How Much Is Enough? Money and the Good Life*. London: Routledge.

Snyder, S. and Mitchell, D. 2006. *Cultural Locations of Disability*. Chicago: University of Chicago Press.

Chapter 7

'I employ a crew that can do life with me'

A young woman's creative self-management of support workers

Nikki Wedgwood, Louisa Smith, and Russell Shuttleworth

Introduction

The concept of care is a highly contested one. In the 1990s, the care literature was shaped by a highly divisive debate about the exploitation of women caregivers on the one hand, and the oppression of care receivers with disabilities on the other (Keith 1992; Morris 1991; Thomas 1993). Early feminist analyses of care (e.g. McIntosh 1981) focused primarily on the unpaid work of (mostly women) carers, conceptualising care as exploitation and, by implication, constructing those they cared for as 'little more than "burdens"' (Fine 2005: 148). In response, disability theorists prioritised the perspective of the person being cared for in their early analyses of care and redefined care as yet another form of oppressing people with disabilities (Keith 1992). Given the largely negative experiences of people with disabilities who had been systematically disempowered by an assumption of passivity and dependence both in and outside of institutions, a clear conceptual distinction was made by disability theorists between caring *about* someone (concern for their welfare) and caring *for* someone (taking charge of them) (Morris 1994: 26). Consequently, there have been several calls to replace the loaded, negative, and imprecise term care with words like support, help, or personal assistance (Shakespeare 2000a; Vasey 2000).

In practice, care work mostly 'invokes different experiences, different meanings, different contexts and multiple relations of power' (Williams 2001: 468). When the focus is less on the two seemingly separate roles of carer and cared for, and more on the caring relationship, it becomes evident that in some situations, the line between carer and cared for is blurred (Walmsley 1993). More nuanced analyses of the relationships of power between care receivers and givers have helped to assuage some of the more dichotomous distinctions made in the literature. As Fine and Glendinning point out, 'dichotomising care and dependency assumes an absence of caring activities on the part of disabled people' (2005: 610). In practice, the relationship between carers and those they support is not necessarily always one-way and oppressive (Kelly 2016). Acknowledgment of such complexities has allowed more sophisticated conceptualisations of the social position of both givers and receivers of care (Fine 2005; Hughes et al.

2005; Kittay 2011). Some scholars argue that *interdependence* is a more accurate, less fraught, conceptualisation of the relationship (Shakespeare 2000b; Walmsley 1993; Watson et al. 2004). Moreover, the 'false dichotomy between care and dependence' obscures the 'common interests of the two parties, both of whom may well experience exclusion from the labour market, poverty and marginalisation' (Walmsley 1993: 139).

The very nature of receiving and giving care has also been brought into question, in particular, whether being *dependent* is necessarily negative or just a natural part of the human condition experienced by everyone at one stage or another, whether it be as children or due to ageing, illness, temporary injury, or permanent disability (Fine and Glendinning 2005; Shakespeare 2000b). Thus, the ideal of independence that denigrates both dependency and care in our society is exposed as 'a mere fiction, not only for people with disability, but for all of us' (Kittay 2011: 51). In short, the care literature of the past three decades has been largely characterised by extensive analyses of the power, autonomy and social status of both givers and receivers of care.

One way of reconciling the concerns of both feminist and disability rights activists (Hurst 2001; Keith 1992) is for people who require assistance with daily living activities to receive funding to employ personal assistants (PAs) or support workers. In many high-income countries, there has been a movement towards such individualised funding to enable people requiring assistance with daily living activities to 'take their place as citizens, participating in society and in personal relationships in a way that non-disabled people take for granted' (Morris 1994: 35–36). On the surface, this practical solution of employing PAs seems to address both the demands of women to have their care work valued by being paid, while also meeting the demands of people with disabilities to control how, when, where and by whom their support is delivered. Certainly, employing PAs to help with daily living activities can be liberating and empowering for people with daily support needs because it allows them:

> [T]o acquire control over many of the mundane but vitally important aspects of everyday existence which, hitherto, were delivered, if at all, to a timetable that suited the 'carer'. This system effectively reverses the balance of power between 'carer' and 'cared for'. . . . The 'cared for' becomes the employer and 'carer' becomes the employee. . . . It offers possibilities for active citizenship that were hitherto constrained. It delivers raw, elemental freedoms that non-disabled people take for granted − a bath when one wants it and so on.
>
> (Hughes et al. 2005: 263)

The direct funding model of personal assistance counters the feminist perspective, which has 'the tendency to underemphasise the agency of the recipient' (Kelly 2016: 30). For instance, individualised funding for personal assistance enables adults with disabilities being cared for by parents to free themselves from infantilising dynamics (Rock 1988). It allows those who were reliant on their partners for assistance to ensure their relationships are no longer defined by the giving and receiving of care, or it can liberate those shackled by uncaring, controlling and/or abusive carers (Morris 1994). For children and adolescents with disabilities, daily access to support workers can provide practical support which enables them to participate in activities with their peer group (Skär and Tam 2001).

For many people with disabilities, receiving government funding for support workers is a vast improvement on familial or agency support (Kelly 2016; Lord and Hutchison 2003), but it is not without its critics (Hayes and Moore 2017). A major critique is that since most support workers are still likely to be women, the direct payments system does little to address feminists concerns, particularly in neoliberal times (Hayes and Moore 2017). It simply creates 'one oppression in the effort to alleviate another' (Kittay 2011: 51). This is because direct payment schemes fail to subvert the existing value system in which care is measured unfavourably against the ideal of

> the autonomous adult male who neither requires nor delivers care. To be a carer or cared for – male or female, disabled or non-disabled in either role – is to be found wanting, to be other in relation to the masculine subject of modernity. . . . Participants in the caring relationship are constructed as the vulnerable, the monstrous and the feminine.
>
> (Hughes et al. 2005: 265)

Some argue that, given their shared oppression, the carer and the cared for need to work together to redefine the relationship so as to further both feminist and disability agendas. To this end, numerous feminist and disability scholars alike have called for an ethic of care (Fine 2005; Fine and Glendinning 2005; Hughes et al. 2005; Shakespeare 2000b; Tronto 1993) which defines caring as positive, universal, and essential to human society: 'When we acknowledge how dependence on another saves us from isolation and provides the connections to another that makes life worthwhile, we can start the process of embracing needed dependencies' (Kittay 2011: 57).

That is the theory. In practice, an ethic of care has yet to revolutionise everyday definitions of dependency and care. In the meantime, the PA system is being established in many high-income countries (Lord and Hutchison 2003), most recently in 2016 in Australia via the National Disability Insurance Scheme (NDIS). Certainly, government-funded individualised care has enhanced the citizenship and social inclusion of many people requiring assistance with daily living activities, but the practice is riddled with everyday dilemmas centred around the relationships of power between the carer and the cared for.

In *The Rough Guide to Managing Personal Assistants*, advice on self-managing support workers is provided by various people with daily support needs, based on their own experiences of employing PAs (Vasey 2000). One of the major dilemmas debated in the guide is how to avoid involving one's support worker in social interactions to such an extent that their presence greatly reduces the social interactions of the person they work for, without taking a strictly utilitarian and dehumanising instrumental approach to one's PA as merely 'a disabled person's arms and legs' (Vasey 2000: 32). Consideration is given to whether there should be strict boundaries between the PA and their employer and, if so, where they should be drawn – how much should PAs know about their employer's private life, friends and vice versa? There is also the 'major issue of dealing with the cost of taking a PA with us wherever we go' (Vasey 2000: 28). Another dilemma is how the need for sexual facilitation is best approached with support workers (also explored in Bahner 2012; Shuttleworth and Taleporos in press) and, even if sexual facilitation is not required, how can spontaneity and romance be maintained when support workers are present?

Clearly, these and other issues need to be discussed openly with one's support workers, but this can be awkward and reduce privacy. The complexity of the relationship, and the large range of contexts in which support workers are needed, means these issues need to be handled differently in various contexts and with each support worker. Therefore, these complex, constant, and ongoing issues cannot be resolved with a one-size-fits-all approach. Given the inherent complexities of the PA system, how do people with significant support needs traverse this fraught relationship at the lived, everyday level, while not just surviving, but thriving, in a disablist society? What follows is a close look at the creative ways in which one young Australian woman, Jay (pseudonym), deftly negotiates the lived complexities of the PA system during her transition to adulthood by developing an approach to self-managing support workers. Her approach, we argue, is implicitly infused with an ethic of care.

Method

The case study presented here is from a larger study on the transition to adulthood of young Australians with disabilities (Smith et al. 2015; Wedgwood 2011; Wedgwood et al. 2013). The main aim of the *Transition Study* was to better understand how, in a disablist society, some young people with disabilities manage and negotiate normative aspects of adulthood, including identity consolidation, achieving emotional and economic independence from parents, and establishing adult relationships outside the family, including peer and sexual relationships. Of the fifty or so young Australians with whom initial life history interviews were conducted, around thirty agreed to a follow-up interview a year or two later. Few of the participants had high daily support needs, probably due to limited time, and of those who were in the study, only Jay talked in great depth and detail about self-managing support workers.

Jay's initial interview lasted just over two hours and the second interview, conducted 18 months later, lasted one and a quarter hours. As part of the broader study, Louisa Smith, who conducted both interviews with Jay, developed the interview transcripts into a life history case study, with the primary focus of analysis being on Jay's transition to adulthood. For this chapter, the transcripts were analysed again from scratch by Nikki Wedgwood, with a particular focus on care. In order to ensure credibility, the other team members reviewed the chapter and, where their analyses differed, were reworked in light of the feedback.

It is important to note that while Jay was happy to participate in the study and to discuss many aspects of her life, she did not want to focus on her experiences of bullying and depression, so as not to reinforce negative ideas about disability:

> We could have a 'poor me party'. I could tell you . . . about my negative experience relating to bullying. I don't want to do that. I want you to see from this interview that, yes, we have negative experiences, but you can turn them around to make something positive out of it and that's what I've chosen to do.

The story presented here reflects Jay's constructive emphasis.

Background

Jay is an only child who lives with her parents (both teachers) in a large regional Australian town. She was 25 years old at the time of the first interview and 27 by the second interview. Jay was born with cerebral palsy and, in her words, 'the part of my brain that was affected is the part that controls movement and, for me, all four of my limbs were affected. So that means I can't walk so I use a . . . wheelchair to move around independently'. When her manual wheelchair was replaced with an electric wheelchair at 14 years old, Jay discovered how some of her physical support needs could be supplemented by technology:

> Before that I used a manual chair which I was not really able to push myself around in, other than around the house and on the flat [ground]. So that kind of showed me how much mobility aid can increase your independence . . . and I remember coming home from school and going, 'I had a good day because I could go to the canteen on my own and didn't have to wait for someone to come and be kind enough to take me'.

Jay feels 'lucky to live in this age of technology', but acknowledges technology cannot meet all of her support needs. A lot of the work Jay does requires computer use but poor motor-control makes typing using a mouse or smart screens difficult, and voice-recognition software does not accurately discern her dysarthric speech. Thus, Jay requires human assistance to participate in the workforce, as is the case for many people with high daily support needs

(Solovieva et al. 2010). Working is a critical aspect of Jay's everyday participation in society (as it is for many people). Support workers, thus, are crucial to her social inclusion: 'I've always been happy to wake up in the morning and feel needed'. Although Jay makes a clear distinction between 'feeling needed' and 'feeling like she needs to prove herself', she explicitly linked workforce participation with wellbeing, noting 'a connection between having meaningful work to do and having a better state of mental health'.

Like several participants in the study, Jay is a disability advocate, which fits her philosophy of making something positive out of her negative experiences. For instance, as part of a preventative education programme, Jay visits primary schools to encourage able-bodied students not to bully students with disabilities:

> I find that a positive way to turn my experience [of being bullied] around. I don't ever tell the kids what happened to me. I might say to them, 'Yes when I was your age I was bullied lots' but then I usually say, 'Okay this is what you can do to make sure that you don't do that' because I see it as my life's responsibility to make sure that kids don't have to go through what I went through.

Typical of Jay's agentic and self-directed approach to life, she has, over time, transformed much of her advocacy into paid work, thus practicing what she preaches about people with disabilities charging for services, like public speaking, they are often expected to do for free. As well as speaking at conferences 'to demonstrate people with disability have value and a voice that needs to be heard', Jay also conducts training on person-centred support and educates community groups about disability awareness. At the time of her first interview, Jay's paid work was fairly erratic but, by the second interview, she was consistently getting three days' work a week (subsidised by a disability pension that varies according to how much paid work she has). One reason Jay was getting more consultancy work was that the Australian government began piloting a direct payments program (NDIS) and, in anticipation of the nationwide roll-out of the scheme, many disability service providers and agencies were keen for her to talk to them about her experiences of self-managing support.

Parental support during childhood

Though Jay requires personal support because of her significant physical impairments, she is perfectly capable of participating in daily living activities socially, emotionally, intellectually, and cognitively. Until she was 16, Jay's parents provided most of the support she required with daily living activities, such as getting in and out of bed, toileting, bathing, dressing, and undressing. Jay feels that her parents' approach to supporting her has shaped her attitudes towards her disability, her support needs, and life in general:

They have encouraged a great sense of independence in me . . . I still require a significant level of physical support to negotiate my daily tasks but because of their influence . . . I feel like I've been given the opportunity to live, for want of a better word, a *normal* life . . . They never said, 'oh, poor you, you have a disability so therefore you have to sit in a corner and watch daytime TV' . . . They have done lots of things . . . to make sure that I am now living a fulfilled life with the confidence to be able to make a difference in the world . . . It hasn't been 'oh, we can't do it', it's been . . . 'okay, how can we do it?' . . . and that's . . . given me the attitude that you can make things happen. So I don't take no for an answer very lightly . . . that kind of gets me through a lot of things where otherwise doors might be closed.

The support her parents provided was not limited to personal care, but also facilitated Jay's social inclusion:

My parents were always very, very willing to make stuff happen for me. So they were more than prepared to go on the [Girl Guides] camping week-ends . . . my Dad would come so he could carry me into the tent and . . . take a fold-out bed for me so that I could be a part of it.

As with many parents of children with disabilities, the support Jay's parents provided also involved advocacy, like fighting for Jay's enrolment in a mainstream primary school. When Jay started school, she went part-time to a 'special' school and part-time to a mainstream school. It took until Jay was in Year 3 (about 8 years old) to achieve full-time integration into a mainstream school (with teacher's aide support). This victory was a hollow one, as Jay was socially isolated and bullied there and, when her parents met with the Principal about the chronic bullying, he said 'I'm getting her ready for the real world'.

Concerned about the effect the school was having on Jay's wellbeing and confidence, her parents sought another mainstream school that would enrol her, which she attended in her last year of primary school (11 years old). In contrast to her previous school, the new school was enabling. When she went on the Year 6 camp, the teachers 'knew that I couldn't do the ski lessons so they hired a skidoo and my best friend suffered from vertigo so she went on the skidoo with me'. The students 'would devise a way for me to play handball with them . . . because I can't throw a ball, they would bounce it into my lap'. Jay found 'friends and social acceptance', was invited on sleepovers, and recalls being excited to tell her mum after her first day at her new school that she got in trouble for talking in class: 'I was really happy about it because I never had anyone to talk to in class before . . . in the new primary school I would just get up to mischief like all the other kids'. Jay was finally experiencing a normal Australian childhood. Her contrasting experiences in the two schools taught Jay that 'it's really important to have staff at school that accept disability and they encourage able-bodied kids to accept someone and to recognise the ways in which we're the same and not always focus on the differences'.

Jay's parents provided support that was not only enabling, but also accommodated Jay's normative need for increasing independence as she got older. Even though her significant requirements for daily living activities meant Jay could not attend her Year 6 camp alone, her parents realised it would be too embarrassing for Jay if they went on camp with her, like they did when she was younger. So that she did not 'miss out on the things that 12 year old girls get up to on school camp', they booked two accessible rooms next to each other, one for Jay and her two best friends and the other for Jay's teacher's aide. Jay believes that the role modelling by her parents of this type of pragmatic, creative, and flexible approach to supporting her social inclusion greatly influenced the way she approached her support needs as a young adult.

Agency care post-school

After high school (which had been fairly uneventful in terms of support), Jay and her parents sought government funding to enable Jay to transition from family care to paid care. For Jay's parents, this meant 'a greater sense of freedom for them because I'm not so reliant on them'. It also created challenges for them because Jay was 'not such a little girl anymore and it is an adaptation and adjustment for everybody'. Switching to agency care was an important part of Jay's transition to adulthood, but this was not without its problems. To begin with, stringent eligibility requirements for government funding as result of neoliberal policies (Grover and Soldatic 2013) meant Jay found the application process difficult:

> [It was] quite intrusive and deficit-focused . . . to get any funding you have to pretty much say you can't get out of bed or do anything. The reality is that I can't get out of bed on my own and do the personal things, but I still can contribute meaningfully to the community . . . You spend all your life up until you leave school, well I did with my family . . . telling me that I could do things . . . Then you go and do your post-school assessment and they're like 'So you can't do this, you can't do that' . . . and you have to bare your soul and all of your insecurities.

Having qualified for government-funded post-school support, Jay found she was expected to fit in with the services provided, rather than the services being tailored to her needs. For instance, when she enrolled in a diploma at a vocational college, she received scribing support for assignments but, unless she booked her scribe two weeks in advance, it was rarely provided at a suitable time. The inflexibility of the service did not suit a young adult who typically did not make plans two weeks in advance. Nor did it suit a young woman who did not want to have a male carer getting her out of bed, toileting, and dressing her in the mornings. As Jay recalls:

You would have random people turning up on your doorstep – sometimes a male – to do your personal care support, even though I had said that maybe that's not something I'd like. And so I would send them away and Mum would do it, and that wasn't really conducive to my independence.

There were other implications, aside from the gender and sexual issues of a young woman having a male providing personal care. Bathing, toileting, and dressing and undressing involve nudity and, therefore, vulnerability; 'bathing is something that is done to people and, as such, involves an aspect of power [involving] social as well as a literal stripping' (Twigg 1997: 64). This power imbalance is heightened by the unfamiliarity of agency staff, whether male or female. In Jay's words: 'You don't even know anything about them or their family but they're showering you and doing that stuff'. While the indignity and disempowerment that comes with needing assistance with personal care can never be totally eliminated, even when carried out by a loved one, they are heightened by the relative anonymity of agency staff. Moreover, agency carers work for, and represent, an agency and therefore, as Jay points out, they 'provide quite impersonal support because they have their professional boundaries to adhere to . . . it's quite clinical and even sterile'.

Self-managed support during the transition to adulthood

After a year and a half of agency support, Jay decided 'with the encouragement of my family . . . to go down the journey of self-managed support'. At the time of her first interview, Jay had been employing and managing her own support workers for three years. Though the introduction of the NDIS (piloted in 2013 and rolled out nationally in 2016) has made self-managed support more widespread, at the time of Jay's interviews, it was a rare practice in Australia.

Jay employs support workers for two to five hours each weekday. Her parents, with whom she still lives, provide most of her weekend and evening support, unless they are away. Although Jay's support is government-funded, it is Jay who interviews, recruits, and trains her support staff. They are primarily answerable to her unless there is a problem, in which case they can contact the agency. As Jay stresses, 'all of my staff feel that they work for me . . . all they feel the agency does is pay them'.

Though Jay acknowledges people need to be paid for the work they do, she does not want any support worker 'who rocks up on the doorstep purely . . . for the money'. Thus, Jay asks potential support workers when she interviews them to think about what they can gain from support work. Jay notes there are many qualities that constitute a good support worker but the main criteria for her are:

We match personality-wise because they do way more for me than personal care; they support me in a work context, they do lots of scribing for me, they need to fit into social occasions . . . They need to be inconspicuous. They need to be able to behave like a friend in some contexts. They need to do quite sensitive things sometimes . . . Good care is done in a respectful way. They need to be able to respect your family as well, particularly when you are living with your family . . . [because they are entering] into your parents' space.

Jay also requires her support workers to be discreet because 'the intimate kind of support that I need' means they are privy to aspects of her life that most people keep private. Jay recalled a very nice agency support worker who tactlessly divulged things to her about other clients, making Jay feel she needed to be very careful what she disclosed to her.

Though Jay believes there is a need for agency care in the community and still uses it occasionally, she has found self-managed support has many advantages over agency care. To begin with, she finds it comforting to 'know who is coming into your house and . . . who is going to see you at 6:30 in the morning with your hair sideways'. Hiring her own staff also enables Jay to ensure her support workers are respectful of her and her family. Though Jay feels she will never 'get used to someone putting me on the loo . . . and . . . waiting for [me]', she much prefers to receive intimate care from staff she has selected than from 'random' agency staff because 'at least you know them, so therefore they are more likely to respect your dignity'. Familiarity also improves safety because 'keeping someone safe comes down to how well you know them and how well they might react to what is going to make [a client] fall or just knowing when they're stable, without having to be told'. Thus, Jay questions the assertion that agency staff with formal qualifications have advantages over unqualified support workers.

Another benefit of self-managed support for Jay is that the relationships she has with her support staff are less rigidly defined by formal boundaries between the *personal* and the *professional*:

That doesn't mean to say I know everything about my workers . . . but . . . the communication is more natural. So it's okay to ask someone what they did on the weekend and it's not like, 'oh, that's breaking my professional boundary, I can't tell you that'.

The blurring of this line engenders an ethic of care among Jay's support workers by enabling them to not only take care *of* Jay in the practical sense, but also to care *about* Jay by getting to know her as a person: 'I have individual rapport with my staff . . . I have a genuine relationship with all of my staff. They all actually care about me'. She says:

Some [support workers] – not that this is what I expect – will do extra things or take me to places because they think that they're going anyway or that I would enjoy it and they actually will sometimes say, 'We don't want you to pay us!' I don't do that as a rule but it has happened. My parents went away recently and one of my ex-staff . . . she was a uni[versity] student and she got a full-time job, but she lives [close by] so she said 'I will come and stay with you every Monday night for the five weeks your parents are gone. I don't want you to pay me because I have a full time job and I just like hanging out with you' . . . It is surprising how many people will, when Mum and Dad are away, [provide support] . . . I've got a friend who lives five minutes away and she's a nurse, so she'll come and put me on the loo and then we'll go for afternoon tea or something. So it's not that formalised kind of support. I think it's because my friends know I really appreciate it but don't expect it, they'll do it more.

The time and energy required by people with disabilities to live an ordinary life is generally greater than that of able-bodied people (Pentland and McColl 1999; Wilkinson-Meyers et al. 2015) and self-managing her support does add to Jay's daily workload: 'Managing one's own support workers is another task. It is quite a drain . . . you do have days where you have a pity-party and you go, "poor me . . . is it going to be this hard all the time?" ' Training new staff is particularly time and energy-consuming:

This afternoon . . . I said to Mum 'I am sick of giving people instructions' because I had someone who has been to me less times and she's less able. She tries very hard and she is a lovely young girl, but she just doesn't have the initiative that some of my other crew have. And I was feeling a little bit frustrated this morning just because I had a lot of things to do and she was slow because she didn't quite know what she was doing, which is understandable. I should be more patient.

However, such inconveniences are temporary and Jay feels the period of breaking in new support workers is a small price to pay:

When I complain about having to train another worker, well the other option is to have someone who is supposedly trained who will be coming to the door . . . but you don't know who . . . to get you out of bed in the morning.

Fostering an ethic of care

Given the social nature of humans, it is not unusual for friendships to develop in the workplace. Unsurprisingly, there is evidence that 'disabled people and their assistants do not experience personal assistance in purely contractual, unemotional and instrumental terms' (Watson et al. 2004: 338). Indeed, 'the act of providing care, especially if repeated routinely over time, in fact, *creates* a relationship'

(Finch and Mason 1993, cited in Watson et al. 2004: 333). Moreover, for many people who require assistance with daily living, interacting with support workers may be one of the few opportunities they have for social interactions and friendships. As Jay points out: 'It can be hard for people with a disability to have positive relationships because they might be more isolated than the general population and then they have less opportunity too to practice how to have a good relationship'. Thus, like other participants in the study with daily physical support needs, Jay sees support workers not just as facilitators of social inclusion in everyday life, but also as a pool of potential friends.

Jay spoke at length in both interviews about how most of her support workers have become her friends and that she usually remains in contact with them after they leave her employ. Jay regularly meets up and has coffee with the woman who was her teacher's aide from 5 to 10 years of age:

> That's another added benefit that I find of the support arrangement that I have . . . I still have great contact with the first person that I ever had four years ago and we still have dinner parties together. She comes and gets me and we go places and she will sit on my interview panel when I'm interviewing . . . I don't pay her for that. We do that as good friends now.

Kelly (2016: 77) uses the phrase 'frien-tendant' to characterise this relationship; not fully employee, nor friend, nor family member, nor stranger, the 'frientendant' is ambiguous: extremely intimate, yet also professional. Jay believes friendship is an important part of good support work: 'It's a more natural relationship . . . I think there should be sociability as well [as support] when it's able to be given'. Although she does not use the phrase ethic of care, both her philosophy and practice seem to acknowledge 'how dependence on another saves us from isolation and provides the connections to another that makes life worthwhile' (Kittay 2011: 57).

Occasionally, Jay's friends have become her support workers. She recalled once, when looking for 'an extra back-up person', asking her friend who was looking for work to join her 'support crew'. At first, her friend declined because 'she didn't want to get paid to hang out with me'. So Jay suggested that her friend do a couple of hours of support work as a trial and, if it did not work, they would 'stay friends and . . . throw the working relationship overboard'. It worked well and at the time of the first interview, her friend had been part of Jay's crew for two years. They were both happy for this arrangement to continue until her friend found full-time work. Despite the deliberate blurring of the personal and the professional, Jay feels having friends do support work and having support workers who become friends 'is okay as long as both parties understand boundaries'. However, it is not quite clear what Jay's boundaries are or how they are set. Although Jay says she only socialises with her friend (who does support work) on days that she is not working for her, namely 'to keep that clear distinction', she adds that her friend 'still does things like she'll come and pick me up in her car because she knows that otherwise, I'll have to get a taxi'.

Given Jay's view of support workers as a potential source of friends, most of the people she employs are around her age. One exception is a woman she has known since she was eight years old and whom she still employs because she 'has history with my family and I and, so, in some contexts, I enjoy her looking after me'. In other contexts, like going speed-dating, she would not take her because 'it would just be awkward, not really appropriate, it'd be like taking your mum!' Having young support workers also provides Jay with connections to the culture of her peers:

> I was only saying to one of my workers the other day . . . 'I need to go out more at night. Where can I go? I need to go to some younger places' and she's like 'oh, we should go to [venue]' and it was really good. I'll be going again . . . that's where I can also use the input of my support workers who are a similar age.

Blurring the line between friends and support workers also allows Jay to negotiate creative and flexible support arrangements when needed. For instance, because paying for formal support by the hour for the duration of a trip can be prohibitively expensive, Jay sometimes negotiates informal support arrangements agreeable to both parties:

> If you want to go away . . . for the weekend, you can negotiate hours because, let's face it, I'm paying for them to fly and we're doing nice things and you can say 'I need this many hours of care so I will pay you between these hours – is that okay?' . . . You couldn't do that in Service Provider Land. . . . You can do that though if you have a human connection and relationship with the person and you've acknowledged that they need to be paid so you're not taking them for a ride . . . you're paying them to have a bit of a holiday.

On another occasion, a family friend accompanied Jay on a trip as her PA in return for flight and accommodation. Being single with grown-up children who have left home, she liked having someone to travel with – a win-win.

Another creative support arrangement made possible by the blurring of lines between support workers and friends is Jay's support circle made up of close friends and past and present support workers who can provide Jay with informal support to supplement her everyday support team. Again, it is not clear how these boundaries between friendship and support are maintained, or if that is even possible or desirable.

Though unsure what the future holds, Jay feels that when she first moves out of home, she would most likely stay in her hometown, 'because that's where my life is at the moment and it makes sense not to live too far away from your family so you can still have informal support and relationships with them'. She envisages something like moving in with a housemate, who would have reduced rent in return for providing a small amount of informal support to supplement the majority of support provided by paid workers.

Support with dating and intimacy

During her first interview, when invited to talk about romantic or sexual relationships, Jay reported:

> Of course I have some desires in that direction and it is something that I would like to happen and yes, it is something that I've given great consideration to. But you can't force it to happen . . . and it's really probably only been since I turned 25 that I've seriously thought about that. I mean, I'm not saying that I haven't considered it or wondered what it might be like when I have a boyfriend, but it's only kind of been in the last couple of months that I've sort of thought, 'okay what will that actually look like?' . . . I will explore that as I get the opportunity to but, yes, I will definitely be open to any kind of experience that I can have in that direction.

Two weeks before her first interview, Jay saw *The Sessions* – a movie based on a true story about a man requiring a ventilator to breathe, who employed a professional sex surrogate to experience sexual intimacy. Jay said the movie 'opened up my eyes to some considerations'. Around that time, Jay had attended a workshop on sexual facilitation for people with significant physical disabilities, after which she asked the young female support worker who was driving her home how she would feel about doing sexual facilitation as part of her job: 'She's fine and that's good . . . it was a good time for me to realise that you do actually need to have a conversation with the people that are supporting you around what their role might be in that'. The hesitancy that significantly disabled people and their support workers often feel in bringing up facilitated sex is understandable given the discomfort many people have about discussing sex publicly. Such awkwardness can also be complicated by an uncertainty with how to manage the complex ethics of this practice in contexts where policy guidelines are not clear (Bahner 2012; Browne and Shuttleworth 2006; Shuttleworth and Taleporos in press).

In her mid-twenties, Jay noticed many of her able-bodied friends were getting boyfriends or marrying and starting families, making her wonder 'what am I doing with my life?' and feeling down and dejected. By the second interview, the crisis had passed but, at the time, it had precipitated some experimentation, prompting her to explore her sexuality through a photo-shoot of herself in lingerie and other things she chose not to disclose in the interview. Jay also experimented with speed-dating. Unlike numerous other study participants who were not keen to date a person with a disability, often for practical reasons, Jay said she did not 'have anything against potentially having a partner who might have a disability' but, nevertheless, 'didn't want to go disability dating . . . I wanted to . . . have a go in the able-bodied world'. Jay took a good friend and support worker with her for scribing and moral support, noting that speed-dating is not something she would have done with an agency carer. She even had to 'work up to' going with one of her own support staff. Because speed-dating involves filling out a scorecard for each date and Jay requires help with scribing, her friend helped her with that after each date but, during the dates, sat discreetly at the bar talking to the bartender. Early debates about the use of support workers considered whether they should merely be the arms and legs of their employers in social situations, particularly on romantic dates (Vasey 2000). However, the support worker who accompanied Jay to the speed-dating event was not merely her scribe (or arms). She also provided moral support and was a sounding-board for Jay, who discussed each date with her before filling in the scorecard.

Jay did meet someone she liked speed-dating but 'it didn't eventuate to anything'. Though Jay said her speed-dating experiences were 'pretty good' and she was glad she did it, she also noted 'I've only been speed-dating twice and I think I've got over it now'. Her plan is to try internet dating next but, at the time of the second interview, she had not got around to putting up a profile. Jay's ultimate hope is to 'find mister almost perfect'.

Conclusion

According to Jay's accounts, the flexible and creative support system she has developed enables her to work, socialise, travel, and maintain ordinary relationships, thus facilitating her transition to adulthood. Self-managing her support gives Jay the independence to access and participate in the world on her terms, a move which can be viewed as empowering, liberating, and inclusive. Yet, in order to determine the merits of any support arrangement, it is critical to explore the social position of both parties in the relationship. We only have Jay's account of the dynamics between her and her support workers, but her anecdotal evidence suggests that the system of direct payments (at least in this case) has not 'abrogate[d] the master/slave relation' (Hughes et al. 2005: 263). Certainly, all of Jay's support workers are female (which she never mentions explicitly, even when listing the qualities she looks for in a support worker). Given her support is government-funded, her support workers would not be highly paid and, obviously, as the person who hires and fires them, Jay has more power over them than they do over her.

However, when examining 'the nature of power within and surrounding care relationships', it is important to make a 'distinction between the inequality of power and the exertion of domination' (Kittay 1995, cited in Fine 2005: 146). Given that many of Jay's support workers occasionally provide unpaid support of their own volition, Jay appears to have fostered largely egalitarian and reciprocal caring relationships with her support crew. Without interviewing her support workers, it is not possible to determine whether they feel they are expected to provide some unpaid support, or whether they feel it improves their chances of remaining employed. However, the fact that most of Jay's support staff become friends with her, and maintain those friendships long after leaving her employ, would seem to indicate that this was not the case. This brings into question the critique that the PA system 'effectively closes off the possibility of an ethic of care and responsibility in which many feminists place much hope' (Hughes et al. 2005: 263).

Sadly, Jay's uncanny talent for fostering an ethic of care in her relationships with her support workers does not pose a broad structural challenge to the way in which care and dependence are socially defined. Not everyone who needs daily personal support receives government funding and, of those who do, few would possess Jay's remarkable knack of inspiring friendship and alliance, while juggling both personal and professional boundaries, in order to self-manage a support crew as adroitly as Jay does. Moreover, boundary maintenance between the personal and professional needs to differ from one person to another because, as Watson et al. (2004: 333) point out, the 'giving and receiving of care . . . is experienced differently at various points in the life-course and on the basis of gender', along with ethnicity, sexuality, and religion. For instance, another *Transition Study* participant who self-managed his support developed romantic feelings for one of his young female support workers. Romance between support workers and their employers is not uncommon, but it can be considered a transgressing of appropriate boundaries. Therefore, it may be viewed negatively, particularly in light of gendered power relations, though this would of course vary depending on the sex and sexuality of the support worker and that of the person with support needs. However, in some instances, care relationships can be viewed pragmatically as a viable avenue for intimacy because people with high support needs experience high levels of sexual exclusion and have few other opportunities to meet potential sexual partners, let alone develop sexual or romantic relationships (Shuttleworth 2000).

Because support work provides a rare opportunity for able-bodied people to get to know the people they work for as fully human beings, support workers are less likely than most to see the person's disability as a disincentive or barrier to getting to know them. Moreover, workplace friendships are commonplace, but the intimate nature of support work makes it even more likely that a support worker and their employer will extend their relationship beyond that of purely employer and employee. It is Jay's success in recognising and fostering this aspect of the relationship with her support workers which is the most crucial and creative component of the management and negotiation of her everyday support needs. Despite Jay's assertion about maintaining boundaries, she also often talks about deliberately blurring the professional with the personal. This goes beyond simply employing friends or paying people to socialise with her. Jay's support workers not only enable her to participate in activities with her peer group (Skär and Tam 2001), but many become part of her peer group.

This ensures that the support she receives goes beyond the contractual obligations of an employee to their employer because it is based on respect for Jay as a person and friend, thus avoiding the many shortfalls of impersonal and sterile agency care, a theme beautifully explored in the film *The Intouchables*. Based on a true story about a quadriplegic man who, sick of clinical interactions with trained carers, hires an untrained and inexperienced male support worker, the film explores the resultant unlikely friendship developing between them based on genuine mutual respect and which, ultimately, results in an unorthodox caring relationship based on an ethic of care.

Jay was not the only study participant with everyday care needs who preferred to employ and train a carer with no formal qualifications than to employ agency staff with formal qualifications, with whom she feels no personal connection. Given the current roll-out of the NDIS scheme in Australia, which allows people with disabilities to determine who they employ to do their care work, the implications of this for the supply and demand of people with formal care qualifications remains to be seen. Jay's account of her success in negotiating what is, for the most part, a win–win for her and her support workers provides an inspiring and detailed account of the everyday negotiations of the potentially fraught PA system. The keys to her success in instilling an ethic of care into her relationships with her support workers are her creativity, empathy, intelligence, and confidence. It was unclear whether Jay's approach to managing her support was influenced by the disability or care literature directly, or perhaps indirectly through her work as a disability advocate and her contact with disability agencies. What was clear, however, was that her highly developed sense of independence, agency and ingenuity mirrored her parents' resourceful and innovative facilitation of her social inclusion as a child. In Jay's own words:

> When you need someone to support you with every aspect of your life, especially in terms of personal care and support . . . I don't let it stop me, I am not stuck at home because of it. I employ a crew that can do life with me.

References

Bahner, J. 2012. Legal rights or simply wishes? The struggle for sexual recognition of people with physical disabilities using personal assistance in Sweden. *Sexuality and Disability* 30(3), pp. 337–356.

Browne, J. and Shuttleworth, R. 2006. My home, your workplace: people with physical disability negotiate their sexual health without crossing professional boundaries. *Disability and Society* 20(4), pp. 375–388.

Fine, M. 2005. Dependency work: a critical exploration of Kittay's perspective on care as a relationship of power. *Health Sociology Review* 14(2), pp. 146–160.

Fine, M. and Glendinning, C. 2005. Dependence, independence or inter-dependence? Revisiting the concepts of 'care' and 'dependency'. *Ageing and Society* 25(4), pp. 601–621.

Grover, C. and Soldatic, K. 2013. Neoliberal restructuring, disabled people and social insecurity in Australia and Britain. *Scandinavian Journal of Disability Research* 15(3), pp. 216–232.

Hayes, L. and Moore, S. 2017. Care in a time of austerity: the electronic monitoring of homecare workers' time. *Gender, Work and Organization* 24(4), pp. 329–344.

Hughes, B., McKie, L., Hopkins, D. and Watson, N. 2005. Love's labours lost? Feminism, the disabled people's movement and an ethic of care. *Sociology* 39(2), pp. 259–275.

Hurst, R. 2001. Rethinking care from a rights perspective. *Global Conference on Rethinking Care*, Oslo, Norway, 22–25 April 2001.

Keith, L. 1992. Who cares wins? Women, caring and disability. *Disability, Handicap and Society* 7(2), pp. 167–175.

Kelly, C. 2016. *Disability Politics and Care: The Challenge of Direct Funding.* Vancouver: University of British Columbia Press.

Kittay, E. 2011. The ethics of care, dependence, and disability. *Ratio Juris* 24(1), pp. 49–58.

Lord, J. and Hutchison, P. 2003. Individualised support and funding: building blocks for capacity building and inclusion. *Disability and Society* 18(1), pp. 71–86.

McIntosh, M. 1981. Feminism and social policy. *Critical Social Policy* 1(1), pp. 32–42.

Morris, J. 1991. 'Us' and 'them'? Feminist research, community care and disability. *Critical Social Policy* 11(33), pp. 22–39.

Morris, J. 1994. Community care or independent living? *Critical Social Policy* 14(40), pp. 24–45.

Pentland, W. and McColl, M. A. 1999. Application of time use research to the study of life with a disability. In: Pentland, W., Harvey, A., Lawton, P. and McColl, M. A. eds. *Time Use Research in the Social Sciences.* New York: Kluwer Academic, pp. 169–188.

Rock, P. 1988. *Food For Thought, The Carers' Movement: Dangers Ahead?* London: Disability Awareness Training and Education for Health.

Shakespeare, T. 2000a. *Help.* Birmingham: Venture.

Shakespeare, T. 2000b. The social relations of care. In: Lewis, G., Gewirtz, S. and Clarke, J. eds. *Rethinking Social Policy.* London: Sage, pp. 52–65.

Shuttleworth, R. 2000. The search for sexual intimacy for men with cerebral palsy. *Sexuality and Disability* 18(4), pp. 263–282.

Shuttleworth, R. and Taleporos, G. In Press. Disability, facilitated sex and sexual participation. *Sexuality and Disability.*

Skär, L. and Tam, M. 2001. My assistant and I: disabled children's and adolescents' roles and relationships to their assistants. *Disability and Society* 16(7), pp. 917–931.

Smith, L., Wedgwood, N., Llewellyn, G. and Shuttleworth, R. 2015. Sport in the lives of young people with intellectual disabilities: negotiating disability, identity and belonging. *Journal of Sport for Development* 3(5), pp. 61–70.

Solovieva, T., Walls, R., Hendricks, D. and Dowler, D. 2010. Workplace personal assistance services for people with disabilities: making productive employment possible. *Journal of Rehabilitation* 76(4), pp. 3–8.

Thomas, C. 1993. De-constructing concepts of care. *Sociology* 27(4), pp. 649–669.

Tronto, J. 1993. *Moral Boundaries: A Political Argument for an Ethic of Care.* London: Sage.

Twigg, J. 1997. Bathing and the politics of care. *Social Policy and Administration* 31(1), pp. 61–72.

Vasey, S. 2000. *The Rough Guide to Managing Personal Assistants.* London: National Centre for Independent Living.

Walmsley, J. 1993. Contradictions in caring: reciprocity and interdependence. *Disability, Handicap and Society* 8(2), pp. 129–141.

Watson, N., McKie, L., Hughes, B., Hopkins, D. and Gregory, S. 2004. (Inter)dependence, needs and care: the potential for disability and feminist theorists to develop an emancipatory model. *Sociology* 38(2), pp. 331–350.

Wedgwood, N. 2011. A person with abilities: the transition to adulthood of a young woman with a severe physical impairment. *YOUNG – Nordic Journal of Youth Research* 19(4), pp. 435–454.

Wedgwood, N., Smith, L., Shuttleworth, R. and Llewellyn, G. 2013. An eye opening experience: a critical turning point in the life of a young woman with a severe visual impairment. *Journal of Social Inclusion* 4(1), pp. 5–23.

Wilkinson-Meyers, L., Brown, P., McNeill, R., Reeve, J., Patston, P. and Baker, R. 2015. To live an ordinary life: resource needs and additional costs for people with a physical impairment. *Disability and Society* 30(7), pp. 976–990.

Williams, F. 2001. In and beyond New Labour: towards a new political ethics of care. *Critical Social Policy* 21(4), pp. 467–493.

Chapter 8

(Re)negotiating normal every day

Phenomenological uncertainty in Parkinson's disease

Narelle Warren and Darshini Ayton

Introduction

Idiopathic in nature, Parkinson's disease (PD) is unpredictable, creating uncertainties in managing and creating a *good life* in the present. Unknowable rates of progression mean that these uncertainties also impact upon people's capacity to imagine – and, therefore, plan for – their future. PD is typically associated with ageing, yet it is diagnosed during a person's working life in about one-tenth of cases and, in such cases, is considered *young-onset* (Schrag et al. 1998). The term young-onset has consistently been poorly defined, ranging anywhere from young adulthood to 60 years of age, although it has been mostly considered to occur between 50 and 60 (Flensborg Damholdt et al. 2012). The atypicality of young-onset variants of PD means that themes of unpredictability, uncertainty, and (lack of) control are especially important for people so diagnosed, not least because the disease trajectory has received limited research attention and, thus, remains unclear. These themes form the focus of this chapter, in which we explore the following question: with no roadmap or template available, how do people with young-onset Parkinson's disease (YOPD) achieve a life of quality and meaning, which has elsewhere – including in this volume – been referred to as the good life (Sakellariou 2016; Warren and Manderson 2015)? How are certainty and, conversely, uncertainty experienced, and what everyday challenges to ideals of control arise for this group of people?

This chapter aims to elucidate notions of what we term 'phenomenological uncertainty' – that is, the sense of uncertainty pervading the everyday lived experience of a subset of Australian women and men diagnosed with YOPD. In doing so, we highlight not only the variations in subjective experience (which we refer to here as the phenomenological experience of illness) *between* individuals with Parkinson's, but more profoundly focus on the fluctuations that occur *within* an individual's experience. In order to lead a life that is satisfying and fulfilling – both of which are components of a good life – participants constantly engaged in processes of internal negotiation to attempt to reconcile ideas of identity, embodiment, and function. This negotiation was especially notable in the experiences of people who experienced PD in an atypical way, particularly when the onset occurs much earlier in the life-course than most people so diagnosed, as we discuss below.

Our focus on phenomenological experience is important, as we are concerned with the meanings that our participants gave to their embodied presents and futures (van Manen 2017). In exploring these meanings and experiences, this chapter draws on the experiences of Australian men and women who were diagnosed with PD while still of working age (and so were considered to have YOPD) who took part in a large, four-year (2012–2015, inclusive) narrative research project in Victoria, Australia, exploring the trajectories of chronicity in neurological conditions (stroke and Parkinson's disease). Fifty-eight men and women living with PD – and, where relevant, their family caregivers, all of Western European descent – took part in the research project. Of these, thirty-two had been diagnosed with YOPD. The majority of participants were interviewed more than once, often over a period of several hours. All were recruited through community-based peer-support organisations, via social networks (both in person through snowball sampling and online), and the Fox Trial Finder website, which seeks to find volunteers for PD-related research (The Michael J. Fox Foundation for Parkinson's Research 2017). Without exception, participants' accounts emphasised the multiple uncertainties that permeated their everyday lives and the effortful work they undertook in attempting to find sense and order in responding to these. Those with YOPD, however, spoke about the challenges they faced every day and how they felt confused, and often deeply concerned, around what their future held, particularly in terms of retirement and family relationships.

Disability as a stand-alone concept was rarely discussed explicitly in participants' accounts, yet permeated everyday bodily management in the present and was something that occupied – and was resisted, as much as people were able to do so – in participants' imaginaries of the future. We term these idealised conceptions of people's anticipated futures their imagined biographies, drawing on both Bury (1982) and Faircloth et al. (2004). Many of our participants spoke of not wanting to 'be a burden' to their family members, especially where they still had young children, in the future; ideas of disability are embedded in these discussions. Indeed, one of the few certainties of PD is the degenerative process, in that people so diagnosed will eventually experience physical and, often, psychological and cognitive disabilities as the condition progresses. The accounts discussed below were explicitly chosen because their accounts challenged the few certainties that accompany PD. In having been diagnosed with young-onset PD in their forties or fifties, participants disrupted the widely held assumption that Parkinson's only affects older people (Warren and Manderson 2015).

Certainty, control, and chronicity

Certainty and control – or lack thereof – are dominant concepts in sociological and anthropological research on chronic disease, including in research on neurodegenerative disability (Nijhof 1995, 1996; Pavey et al. 2013, 2015; Sakellariou 2015). At its essence, having certainty – or at least a sense of it – facilitates some type of prediction about the future, whether that future refers to tomorrow or some years away. It also provides a sense-making mechanism through which experience can be interpreted and responded to. Having such certainty can provide a sense of control over what might otherwise be an out-of-control experience (Seear 2009), profoundly impacting wellbeing and quality of life (Warren and Manderson 2013). Knowing why particular bodily signs, symptoms or forms of expression have occurred not only facilitates the management of everyday life in the present, but also allows for the laying forth of a map of the future ahead (Warren and Manderson 2015). Indeed, Biehl and Locke (2010) argue that it is through such cartographies that people can make sense of the uncharted territories of chronic illness, that is, the bodily realities which seem bewildering and overwhelming, and located in the enormous void within which biomedicine is (largely) silent.

Yet, certainty is often limited in the context of chronic illness and the spectre of uncertainty persists even where there is some predictability inherent in the illness course (Manderson and Smith-Morris 2010; Sakellariou 2016). For the majority of people living with chronicity, uncertainty is the dominant mode of experience. Chronic conditions often do not progress in a linear and uniform way, and are instead characterised by good and bad days (Charmaz 1991). In addition, for the most part, the onset of symptoms – and thus the diagnosis itself – is often unexpected and rates of progression vary subtly from person to person, as may pathways of recovery or responses to particular medication types. Uncertainty problematises the seductive notion – based largely on an acute model of health conditions – that illness course is both predictable and, therefore, amenable to management and cure.

Bodily management practices are shaped by such uncertainties. This occurs in a range of ways, two of which we consider in this chapter. First, temporal fluctuations in bodily status may lead to an experience of phenomenological uncertainty, that is, the uncertainty pervading everyday subjective experience (Sakellariou 2016). Second, such phenomenological uncertainty precedes the deployment of technologies – medications, surgical interventions, and so forth – which may aid in the management of everyday life, but which themselves may give rise to further uncertainties such as side effects, accelerating disablement, or the development of new health problems (Hunt et al. 2012; Mol 2008; Pols 2012). Consideration of such issues is not regularly given weight clinically (Warren and Manderson 2015), but these can have profound implications for people's lives – and those of their family and friends, especially people involved in providing informal care.

Parkinson's disease and (the problem of) control

Parkinson's disease (PD) is the second most common neurodegenerative disease after dementia and related conditions, including Alzheimer's disease, in industrialised settings (Tanner et al. 2008). Because of its vast variability in symptom experience and disease progression (Flensborg Damholdt et al. 2012), people so diagnosed actively seek to manage its variations in their everyday life. While this invokes ideas of normalcy, this is a misnomer. Anecdotally referred to by consumer organisations and movement disorder specialists (a sub-specialisation of neurology) as a *designer disease* (Parkinson's NSW 2017), meaning that it appears differently from person to person, PD is expressed idiopathically: it rarely presents with the same symptoms or progresses in the same way for any two people. Uncertainty is, therefore, a key characteristic of PD (Nijhof 1996), starting before diagnosis, where contestations exist around the natural history of the disease (Braak and Braak 2000; Braak et al. 2004), and continuing through-out the disease course (Warren and Manderson 2015). Below, we draw on our participants' accounts to elucidate the multiple uncertainties of Parkinson's dis-ease, and the associated challenges.

Diagnosis: questioning its truth and moments of certainty

Diagnosis itself is often problematic, and remains open to contestation, occur-ring through processes of exclusion and arrived at through a *best fit* judgment and responsiveness to pharmacological treatment (Warren and Manderson 2015). Four cardinal or hallmark bodily signs are considered indicative of Parkinson's disease: tremor, which is usually unilateral (that is, it affects one side of the body, at least initially); bradykinesia, or difficulty in initiating or maintaining movement; rigidity or stiffness, a type of muscular tightness or resistance to movement; and postural instability, difficulty in maintaining balance during movements (Jankovic 2008). However, only two must be present for a diagnosis to be made, as one study participant (Will, aged 59 years, diagnosed one year earlier) explained:

> [The neurologist] said . . . various Parkies [people with Parkinson's] get various symptoms, you know, you don't get them all.

Unilateral tremor is the most widely recognised symptom, but is not present for approximately one-third of people. This absence produces its own form of uncertainty for some. Darshini interviewed Lisa (aged 47) on multiple occasions about her experience of YOPD and, despite having been diagnosed five years prior, she continued to question whether she really had PD:

DARSHINI: *Are you still in that headspace of not [being] sure if you believe [the neurolo-gist] about your diagnosis?*
LISA: Yeah, particularly if they're like, oh maybe it's MS [multiple sclerosis], and then I think . . .
DARSHINI: *It doesn't fill you with confidence.*
LISA: No. I think that just because there's so much uncertainty about it, and because I don't have the tremors or anything, I just find it hard to, it's not that I don't want to accept it, it's just that I sometimes think I need a bit more concrete proof.

Muscle rigidity and stiffness, with or without tremor, further leads people to question the meaning of, and reasons for, their symptoms because of its ubiquity. As any number of conditions can explain this bodily sign, its presence does not provide the 'concrete proof' that Lisa and other participants sought. However, some certainty can be obtained where this rigidity extends to the facial muscles, leading to the characteristic *Parkinson's mask* (Jankovic 2008) and limiting the range of expressions. Elena described the point at which Andy's (husband) diagnosis became clear for them:

ELENA: [The neurologist] just got [Andy] out in the corridor, walked towards me and then went back in, 'yes you've got it'. And we thought, how can he? How can he tell? And he did a few of these exercises, 'do this, do that'. And the other thing I think is the masked look on the face. That's probably something I didn't, I finally had an a-ha moment, because I often, before he was diagnosed, we'd look at him and think, 'he hasn't responded to that'.

DARSHINI: *Like facial expressions?*

ELENA: Yes, and I'd think, 'he's not listening to me', or 'he didn't think that was funny', or 'he's not affected by that really sad thing'. So I think then I thought, 'oh, that's what's happening'. Because they described it as a masked face that they get.

Related to rigidity and stiffness is bradykinesia, which occurs when a person experiences difficulty in commencing (akinesia) or executing bodily movements. In a smaller number of cases, people with PD may also experience postural instability when undertaking movements on one side of the body, meaning that compensatory balance mechanisms are unable to be effectively deployed. The embodied experience of PD is itself contradictory and gives rise to both uncertainty and frustration. It is difficult to make sense of a body that always moves (as occurs in the case of tremor), but which simultaneously will not get moving (due to akinesia), is slow to move (as occurs with bradykinesia), or has limited range of movements (a result of rigidity and stiffness). Accordingly, the grounding of diagnosis on the confluence of common motor (including the cardinal signs) and non-motor symptoms always leaves open the potential for diagnostic contestation – and gives rise to pervasive experiences of uncertainty (Warren and Manderson 2015), which continue throughout a person's life with PD. What is certain is that diagnosis is a portent of inevitable physical and, for many, cognitive degeneration. Beyond this, however, there is little that can be predicted or known. Consequently, and as we explore below, people with YOPD are forced to reconfigure everyday life as it happens.

The particular uncertainties of young-onset Parkinson's disease

Being diagnosed with YOPD brings with it different impacts, challenges, and outcomes compared to those encountered by a typical (i.e. older) onset population, starting at diagnosis and continuing throughout their life with PD. Disease progression (i.e. degeneration) experienced by people with YOPD is slower than in older populations and is characterised by a series of losses: of valued roles and responsibilities; of physical, social, and cognitive functioning; and largely a consequence of the other types of losses of independence (Charlton and Barrow 2002). The speed with which this occurs is largely unknown until it is looming in the future. Participants in our study discussed how they had initially experienced rapid progression of symptoms – and increasing associated disability – in the early stage after diagnosis before achieving a kind of plateau. Sally (aged 63 years), for example, was diagnosed over twenty years before we met, yet had only recently retired from work because of fatigue. She explained what was going on in her life around the time of diagnosis, which occurred at the same time as she was dealing with considerable stress:

> [When] I was approximately in my 40s, early 40s when I started to, um, uh, feel a sort of stiff, generalised stiffness in – in my body and sometimes a sort of loss of balance, sort of feeling a bit strange . . . I thought I was having a nervous breakdown. Um, it was a difficult time in my life, um, and I just, I just thought it was all psychologically, emotionally induced. Um, so, I didn't take much notice of it for a long time.

Sally described how, although she continued to experience symptom fluctuations over the ensuing two decades, these had largely stopped since she had retired, primarily because she was able to manage her stress:

NARELLE: *Do you find that you have a lot of those sort of fluctuations?*
SALLY: Um, not so much since I stopped working. Um, I stopped working, um, two years ago now . . . Um, I, uh, because I can spend a lot of times be – observing myself now. Observing what's happening, because when I was working, I used to be up at five every morning and I'd, you know, I was just doing, doing, doing and all the time, I was again not – not taking any time to consider myself or my body or anything like that, so I didn't observe myself very well at all. And since I've been able to, now, take – revel in not doing anything, not feeling guilty about it at all, sleeping when I want to sleep, I – I can sort of manage those, that sort of thing much, much better, but it certainly, certainly still happens.

Sally's account challenges more commonly held understandings of an illness trajectory as following a linear pathway. The nature of neurodegeneration as both variable and progressive suggests that, regardless of the rate with which the degeneration occurs, the downward trajectory will fluctuate in terms of bodily functioning and symptoms over time. Such fluctuations also occur in response to affective or personal life circumstances: Sally, for example, experienced disease progression through changes in symptoms that occurred in response to psychological stress:

> Well, most of my life I've been a single mother. It's an enormous amount of stress to keep – to keep, um, the income going and that sort of stuff at a certain level, and [I had] jobs I absolutely hated and all that sort of stuff, so I thought it was – I thought it really was emotionally induced by anger, self-anger and outward anger towards certain people and, um, and the stress of just trying to live day-to-day and being able to cope financially and psychologically and emotionally with my children and stuff like that.

Furthermore, as we discuss below, in addition to these life demands, the very task of managing PD from day to day was both confusing and stressful. Unsurprisingly, as reflected in Sally's account of the complex demands placed upon her life, younger people experience significant negative social and psychological condition-related impacts (Schrag and Schott 2006); they will, for example, live longer with PD and experience the onset of disability earlier in the life-course. They also may be responsible, financially and emotionally, for the wellbeing of dependent others, particularly their children. Accordingly, they report higher psychosocial need, higher caregiver demand and burden, poorer quality of life, and greater incidence of depression and anxiety (Knipe et al. 2011). The body is central here, both in terms of the expression of symptoms and as the focus of daily activities (Warren and Manderson 2008), while simultaneously representing (embodying) the degeneration occurring within the brain. Bodily monitoring becomes heightened as a strategy to harness or slow decline, and may result in hyper-surveillance, where everything is interpreted as a sign of degeneration. This process too may shape expectations and understandings of the potentiality of the future (Manderson 2011; Manderson and Smith-Morris 2010).

Phenomenological uncertainty

The uncertainties commencing at the moment of diagnosis extend throughout people's lives with PD, shaping their everyday experiences and requiring ongoing negotiation. In the following section, we draw upon several illustrative case studies – selected because of their evocative accounts as well as their generalisability – in order to elucidate these embodied and interpersonal challenges.

Embodying idiosyncrasy: YOPD and how it occurs 'between lives'

In his work on the subjectivities of care of motor neurone disease (MND), Sakellariou (2016) highlights the way in which neurodegenerative disability is experienced by spouses, as two individuals who are touched by and who experience

MND, yet who are neither fully independent nor fully enmeshed. He terms this intersubjective experience of MND as occurring 'between lives' (2016: 1905). This positioning of disability as occurring between lives provides a lens for examining the idiosyncratic experience of YOPD beyond social comparison. Participants in our study looked to the experiences of others with PD to try and work out what was happening to them, and to provide a frame of reference for making informed decisions about their own health and future. But this is not always possible, as Sally, who we met earlier, made explicit. Her sister was also diagnosed with PD some years after Sally, yet despite both experiencing a young-onset variant, they each had a profoundly different experience:

SALLY: She's six years younger than me, but she had some – she had severe epilepsy and she developed hers a lot later than me. Her, um, everybody's symptoms are so different, as you would know, and her medication can be quite different to mine, too of course, and she's got the epilepsy on top of that. But, it's – it's been a very strange disease to get your head around because, uh, sometimes you think you haven't got it, sometimes you thought – trick-trying to talk yourself into the fact that you haven't, you know, 'I can't have it because mine isn't progressing the same way', as some-body else you know who's got it is. And for me, I find it difficult at times to even, I don't know if I'm delusional or not or I'm just thick, but I some – I find it very difficult, because mine is so slow, my sy – my progression is very slow, um, and I have a very low tolerance . . . to my medication so I only have to take quite a small amount of my medication in comparison to other people again that I know . . . And mine lasts, of course, different lengths of time to other people, my side effects are different to other peoples' and all – because everything's so different you – sometimes you delude yourself into thinking you haven't got it. Um, and you think – sometimes you think it's psychological, it's, you know, all that sort of stuff, so it's very – it's a very – for me it's a very complicated and very confusing disease.

NARELLE: *Even though you've had it now for a long period of time?*

SALLY: Yeah, I'm still, still, still trying to find things out about it, still trying to compare myself with other people . . . It's just – it's just very complicated and because there isn't like, nor – like, there's so many things – if you have so many other diseases, you can sit down with someone who's got it and is practically identical.

This variability leads to a lack of shared experience between any two people with PD. For Sally and her sister, key differences occurred in terms of age at onset, rate of progression (whereby Sally had a much slower progression than her sister), the medications taken, the amount of medication required and the time before wearing off occurs, and in the side effects experienced. In contrast to couples where MND is co-constructed and held up between lives (Sakel-lariou 2016), YOPD falls between lives – little connects two people in terms of condition-related experience beyond the disease label and, potentially, some shared symptoms. Sally continues, comparing her physical appearance to her sister's some fifteen years after diagnosis, to further highlight these differences:

> I mean, she's [Sally's sister is] younger than me, she's about ten years younger than me, and her sh – I mean to me, whether again I'm delusional or kidding myself or I'm too vain, I think she looks much more like a Parkinson's person than I do.

In highlighting this notion of 'a Parkinson's person', Sally emphasised the significance of the visual markers of PD – stooped posture, shuffling gait, or the typical *Parkinson's mask* with the associated limited expressive capacity of the face (*hypomimia*) (Jankovic 2008) – for self-identification and social interactions. While on one hand, she was proud of not displaying the visible effects of PD, Sally's own status as *unusual* (Garland-Thomson 2009) gave rise to new uncertainties. In particular, the lack of commonality with others – which Sally's narrative illustrates – disrupted the sense-making that participants sought. They wanted to know what was going to come next so that they could make meaningful relational and affective decisions, as well as refine how they went about managing their condition. Such lack of certainty about what their bodily signs meant *for them* created a type of phenomenological knife's edge, in which they were never sure which way they would go. She compared the phenomenological experience of PD with that of returned soldiers suffering from shellshock (now referred to as post-traumatic stress disorder), the only frame of reference that she had to understand the embodiment of the cognitive and emotional changes that accompany the condition:

> So, it's very much like, like, something that's instilled in your body and you can't quite get it out again . . . Like, one day you can feel, and so you can do everything, you can do your housework, you can go for a walk, you can do anything. And the next day you wake up and no – no reason that you can think of, you can barely walk or you can – you – the anxiety's there and you don't know why it's there because there's nothing to create it, so it's all those sort of things.

Evident from Sally's account here is the sense of not being in control of her body, but rather feeling that something else was making the decisions that she was living. This resonates with Frank's (1995) work on illness narratives, where the very process of illness demands that the ill person surrender their energy, time, and will to deal with their embodied needs:

> It seems to mostly affect my left side, my right side doesn't seem to be affected, which is great because I am right-handed. But, like, sometimes

I – I can't write anymore, um, I have to, um, print. Um, my left side shakes quite noticeably at times and, uh, it shakes more on – if I'm – it depends on what – when I have, you know, when I have to take my next medication, that sort of stuff, but my main symptoms are my walking. I freeze . . . if I'm going through doorways, my peripheral vision seems to get affected and I freeze and I start staggering and I can't move forward or back and I just tend to go [indicates a collapse] . . . like that. So, it's my – it's definitely my walking, you know, I tend to do the moving on the spot stuff, with the freezing but then, um, the cramps and the pain, um, like they're with – and then the side effects are I get a shooting headaches that just, they're – they're just very quick and extremely sharp and it feels kind of like the – the back of my head, it feels like somebody's put a knife just quickly into my head and then it goes away, and then it'll do it again really sharply. Um, my – I get dystonia of the inside of my neck and also of the outside where I have a lot of neck pain and I get, um, shoulder pain on – down this side, but that's also 'cause of the shakes and the stiffness and the muscles, but I also get a shooting nerve pain that goes down – that shoots from there down to there, feels like somebody's hit you. It's the same pain that you get when you hit your funny bone, and um, I get very stiff legs and very stiff musc – tight muscles all over, and my feet get a – just – I remember reading and thinking – that Michael J. Fox [actor diagnosed with Parkinson's at 29, in 1991, and the most widely recognised face of the disease] was saying that he – in the morning when he gets out of bed, because his feet are so stiff, he sounds like he's a horse going across the bedroom floor because you can't flex your feet . . . the other side effects are I get very, um, very dry mouth, extremely dry mouth, um, which reminds me, um, and very dry – dry eyes, so I have eye drops for my eyes as well. Um, espec – I get a lot of nausea with my medication. So, you gotta be careful when you take that. Um, I'm a vegetarian so protein affects you, your medication too, so you gotta be very careful about how much protein you have in your diet and stuff like that.

Good days and bad days characterised Sally's experience. For the most part, she was unable to predict in advance what sorts of day would lie ahead in the short term. Instead, it was only when she woke each day that she would know. To help make this less disruptive to her life, Sally engaged in daily mindfulness techniques and takes medication, which she would 'tinker with' depending on her bodily state each day to manage her illness. This was not straightforward, and she spent considerable time working out how to achieve a sense of control over her PD. Unlike the illness narratives that Frank (1995) discussed, there was no possibility of restitution or recovery. Simultaneously, the quest could never be fulfilled. Chaos was the perpetual state of being. For Sally, everyday life was not laid out ahead of her but, rather, is configured as it happens.

'Parkies' days: the fluctuations within experience

The temporalities of chronicity themselves provided a source of uncertainty in PD. Because it persists over extended periods of time, embodied fluctuations of the condition play out in terms of *good days* and *bad days* (Charmaz 1991). But PD also disrupts this binary, which is typically understood as capturing the everyday chronic illness experience (Charmaz 1991; Manderson and Smith-Morris 2010), to introduce a third, PD-specific form of daily fluctuation: the Parkinson's (or Parkie's, as Will – introduced earlier – more frequently called it after the first mention) day. Highlighting the day-to-day unpredictability, Will explained: 'You have good days and bad days and some days you just have a Parkinson's day, like there's no particular rhyme or reason why you're not feeling particularly energetic but you just aren't'. He continued, explaining that these *Parkinson's days* were characterised by a type of fatigue, notable for the associated sense of ennui. The purpose of medication, in his eyes, was at least partly to deal with these not infrequent days:

> I'd find that I could sleep in most days but I actually don't . . . Quite often I just lay there and listen to the [radio] on the phone, and get out of bed about 8:30–8:45 and muck around. [Later] I find if I'm feeling weary, even if I don't sleep, I very rarely sleep but if I just lay down and have a rest, half an hour or so and I feel okay . . . The Levodopa or whatever it is, I've only been on it, well its two months now I suppose . . . For some people, that Levodopa, it can make them very sick. I've had no issues with it and it just brightens you up. It makes your joints work better and your legs and arms work better and that sort of stuff . . . Takes the stiffness away.

Participants described the Parkies day as neither a good day, in which they felt upbeat and optimistic, nor a bad day, where their symptoms were inescapable and dominated their thoughts. Instead, the Parkies day was one characterised by a sense of ennui, in which they felt devoid of all emotion. Because Parkies days occurred even when things were going well and with some frequency, although they had little rhythm in terms of when they arose, they presented new challenges in terms of working out how to deal with these days as they arose:

WILL: I've been sort of, hanging around home, and sort of got used to it [Parkinson's days]. I, it's sort of hard to describe, but you, you sort of . . . my, one of the big problems is the cognitive, being able to sort of think through things and that sort of thing is fettered, quite often, um, and again, that can be a side effect of the drugs, it's also a side effect of the Parkinson's, so . . .

NARELLE: *So, when you mean fettered, do you mean like cloudy, slower?*

WILL: Yeah, just like never being able to think clearly and um . . . and its things like I, since I've been off work I've been saying things like 'oh, I'm gonna de-clutter the house'. You know, and every day when I wake up, I'm gonna de-clutter the house. I haven't touched the bloody thing yet [after

12 months since finishing work], so, but that will happen, you know . . . I just can't be bothered.

In illustrating his Parkies days, Will described how all drive or motivation was missing, and he was unable to participate in the everyday family life, despite being the stay-at-home parent. Because his plans for the day ahead were disrupted by the Parkies day, Will – like other people in our study – was forced to reassess what he could achieve in light of his embodied experience. This was characterised by its immediacy; because people were unable to predict how they were going to feel and when, they could not make concrete plans, even for the short-term future. The inability to plan for the here-and-now meant that they needed to be responsive to newly emerging bodily sensations. When imagining the future, this became even more crystallised.

The limitations of anticipation: PD futures

From about eight months after her diagnosis, Freya (56 years) met with Narelle (first author) on three occasions over a twenty-month period. Freya was well aware of PD as her mother had been diagnosed eight years earlier but, because of her relatively young age at diagnosis (54 years), she anticipated that her PD would progress slowly:

FREYA: My mother has it so I've been watching her go downhill and she has severe dementia so . . . and I started to feel there was something wrong with me. I think that part of me was watching the way she was moving and thinking that my body was the same. So it was only a thought I had once I realised that I had it, once I had a diagnosis . . .

NARELLE: *How long since she was diagnosed?*

FREYA: I think she's only had it really for 8 years but then she may have had it much longer, as she would have ignored her health.

NARELLE: *Seeing your mum, where she is 8 years after diagnosis? Does that playin to some of your fears about what will happen to your future?*

FREYA: Oh yes, it does naturally, and the worst of it, I think for her is the dementia, so, but, ah, but it also helps you make plans. I mean, they say that Parkinson's is never the same for each person, and I have been reading about, um, early onset, and I think that you are not necessarily going to develop dementia so [try] keeping your mind active and healthy.

Six months after our initial interview, Freya still took comfort in the information that suggested *typical* progression of YOPD was slower than in older onset (i.e. for her mother):

FREYA: I don't [have dyskinesia] and I've been told that you don't necessarily develop it even if you're on medication for 6 or 7 years, so that was a worry of mine that I would develop it, but I may not, and part of that was the thought of trying to stay in the workforce, but, um, so who knows?

NARELLE: *I remember you saying your mum also has Parkinson's, and does she have the same type of Parkinson's that you have or is hers quite different?*

FREYA: I'm not sure, I don't think so. I mean for one thing she's got Lewy bodies dementia now, so I hope I don't get that, but um her attitude, I mean she's much older than me and she didn't do physio, she didn't learn about the disease or anything. She wasn't very good at taking medication even from the start so, so hopefully having a different attitude makes a difference, but I probably try and get more out of life than she did when she first found out. But um, but I've been told that it's probably not genetic even though my mother has it, but if it was to be, I would have developed it at the same age as her probably, not much younger.

By the time of our last meeting, nearly two years after we first met, it was clear that Freya's PD had progressed much faster than she – or her consulting neurologist – had anticipated. She had recently undergone deep brain stimulation surgery because her tremors had worsened to the point that she found work difficult and she could no longer walk. After the surgery, she was not experiencing much change in her symptoms, although her pain was alleviated, and her communication was significantly affected as she now had a much softer voice and more broken speech. When we asked her to reflect on her feelings about her disease progression, the following exchange resulted:

NARELLE: *I remember from the first interview we had that you said it was important for you to keep in mind that your mum's Parkinson's journey wasn't your Parkinson's journey. Because I imagine that could be – that your experience of Parkinson's was quite different to her – her experience.*

FREYA: Yes, but we're not so sure now. Um, I asked my neurologist – one of the questions I asked him the other day . . . was whether I had, um, postural instability gait disorder. And he didn't know what he meant – what I meant.

NARELLE: *Really?*

FREYA: Yeah. I used the acronym, and, um, he asked me to explain the acronym . . . But, um, that – that's linked to higher likelihood of dementia and, uh, fast progression of the disease, which I've been experiencing. So, it all clicks. I finally got him to admit that my progression has been faster, after three years.

NARELLE: *Because you've only been diagnosed – not quite three years now, haven't you?*

FREYA: Yeah. I was just asking how many good years I have left. And he wouldn't answer me. [I asked] . . . given that if I do have [postural instability], um, if it's true that dementia is more outlined for that, how can I prevent dementia? And the next question was, if I do have that, how many good years do

I have? Will I end up in a nursing home? And he answered the first two, didn't get any further than that.

By contrasting Freya's narrative with that of Sally – and even with Will's – it is evident that, even across these three cases, there is considerable variability in experiences of PD. The uncertainty that accompanies PD trajectories over time, as Freya's narrative shows, means that little can be predicted and ideas of progression are continually disrupted and reconstructed. Importantly, the rehearsal of potential futures that occurs with each revision of condition progression means that little can be counted on. Uncertainty is pervasive, compelling renegotiation not only of everyday life – as explained above – but also of the mundane ideas about the future.

Unfolding uncertainty

The undermining of the certainties of chronic disease experience and progression, and disruptive illness narratives as occurring in cases of YOPD, challenges hegemonic biomedical categorisations and opens up new ways of dealing with bodies and negotiating individuals' everyday lives. Such temporalities of illness are deeply shaped by structural, relational, and cultural dimensions, all of which are manifest in social and spatial contexts. In this chapter, we have focused on the everyday subjective experiences of one neurodegenerative condition – Parkinson's disease (PD) – to consider the individual biographic contexts of illness. Opportunities and personal life circumstances play a role in shaping how people respond across days, weeks, and months to produce possibilities of both the here-and-now and the future; these materialities of context (Wolf-Meyer and Taussig 2010) vary not only across settings, but by the nature of the conditions under study. People with YOPD strive to live a good life, taking into account the limitations imposed by their illness, and to achieve the type of life that they had imagined (their imagined biographies). Yet it is because of the peculiarities of PD, which varies not only between people but in a more baffling sense, within one's own experience, that they are compelled to undertake a range of everyday negotiations with themselves to achieve a *good life* – the sense of *who I am* and *who I will be*.

Acknowledgements

Narelle Warren was supported by a National Health and Medical Research Council Australian Research Training Award (part-time, grant number 606785), and has received funding support from UCB Australia. The authors would like to thank Victor McConvey from Parkinson's Victoria and Dr Arup Bhattacharya and Sheree Ambrosini from the Goulburn Valley Health Service for giving us the opportunity to present this at their Parkinson's community events. As a result, our findings were informally discussed among people living with Parkinson's and this assisted in the refining of ideas.

References

Biehl, J. and Locke, P. 2010. Deleuze and the anthropology of becoming. *Current Anthropology* 51(3), pp. 317–351.

Braak, H. and Braak, E. 2000. Pathoanatomy of Parkinson's disease. *Journal of Neurology* 247(2), pp. 113–110.

Braak, H., Ghebremedhin, E., Rüb, U., Bratzke, H. and Del Tredici, K. 2004. Stages in the development of Parkinson's disease-related pathology. *Cell and Tissue Research* 318(1), pp. 121–134.

Bury, M. 1982. Chronic illness as biographical disruption. *Sociology of Health and Illness* 4(2), pp. 167–182.

Charlton, G. S. and Barrow, C. J. 2002. Coping and self-help group membership in Parkinson's disease: an exploratory qualitative study. *Health and Social Care in the Community* 10(6), pp. 472–478.

Charmaz, K. 1991. *Good Days, Bad Days: The Self in Chronic Illness and Time.* New Brunswick, NJ: Rutgers University Press.

Faircloth, C. A., Boylstein, C., Rittman, M., Young, M. E. and Gubruim, J. 2004. Sudden illness and biographical flow in narratives of stroke recovery. *Sociology of Health and Illness* 26(2), pp. 242–261.

Flensborg Damholdt, M., Shevlin, M., Borghammer, P., Larsen, L. and Ostergaard, K. 2012. Clinical heterogeneity in Parkinson's disease revisited: a latent profile analysis. *Acta Neurologica Scandinavica* 125(5), pp. 311–318.

Frank, A. 1995. *The Wounded Storyteller: Body, Illness, and Ethics.* Chicago: University of Chicago Press.

Garland-Thomson, R. 2009. *Staring: How We Look.* New York: Oxford University Press.

Hunt, L. M., Kriener, M. and Brody, H. 2012. The changing face of chronic illness management in primary care: a qualitative study of underlying influences and unintended outcomes. *Annals of Family Medicine* 10(5), pp. 452–460.

Jankovic, J. 2008. Parkinson's disease: clinical features and diagnosis. *Journal of Neurology, Neurosurgery and Psychiatry* 79(4), pp. 368–376.

Knipe, M.D.W., Wickremaratchi, M. M., Wyatt-Haines, E., Morris, H. W. and Ben-Shlomo, Y. 2011. Quality of life in young- compared with late-onset Parkinson's disease. *Movement Disorders* 26(11), pp. 2011–2018.

Manderson, L. 2011. *Surface Tensions: Surgery, Bodily Boundaries and the Social Self.* Walnut Creek, CA: Left Coast Press.

Manderson, L. and Smith-Morris, C. 2010. Chronicity and the experience of illness. In: Manderson, L. and Smith-Morris, C. eds. *Chronic Conditions, Fluid States: Chronicity and the Anthropology of Illness.* New Brunswick, NJ: Rutgers University Press, pp. 1–18.

The Michael J. Fox Foundation for Parkinson's Research 2017. About Fox Trial Finder. *The Michael J. Fox Foundation for Parkinson's Research* [Online]. Available at: https://foxtrial finder.michaeljfox.org/ [Accessed: 23 November 2017].

Mol, A. 2008. *The Logic of Care: Health and the Problem of Patient Choice.* London: Routledge.

Nijhof, G. 1995. Parkinson's disease as a problem of shame in public appearance. *Sociology of Health and Illness* 17(2), pp. 193–205.

Nijhof, G. 1996. Uncertainty and lack of trust with Parkinson's disease. *European Journal of Public Health* 6(1), pp. 58–63.

Parkinson's NSW. 2017. Symptoms and complications. *Parkinson's NSW* [Online]. Available at: www.parkinsonsnsw.org.au/about-parkinsons-disease/symptoms-and-complications/ [Accessed: 23 November 2017].

Pavey, A., Allen-Collinson, J. and Pavey, T. 2013. Lived experience of diagnosis delivery in Motor Neurone Disease: a sociological-phenomenological study. *Sociological Research Online* 18(2), p. 11.

Pavey, A., Warren, N. and Allen-Collinson, J. 2015. 'It gives me my freedom': technology and responding to bodily limitations in Motor Neuron Disease. *Medical Anthropology* 34(5), pp. 442–455.

Pols, J. 2012. *Care at a Distance: On the Closeness of Technology*. Amsterdam: Amsterdam University Press.

Sakellariou, D. 2015. Home modifications and ways of living well. *Medical Anthropology* 34(5), pp. 456–469.

Sakellariou, D. 2016. Enacting subjectivities through practices of care: a story of living with Motor Neuron Disease. *Qualitative Health Research* 26(14), pp. 1902–1910.

Schrag, A., Ben-Shlomo, Y., Brown, R., Marsden, C. D. and Quinn, N. 1998. Young-onset Parkinson's disease revisited: clinical features, natural history, and mortality. *Movement Disorders* 13(6), pp. 885–894.

Schrag, A. and Schott, J. M. 2006. Epidemiological, clinical, and genetic characteristics of early-onset Parkinsonism. *The Lancet Neurology* 4(5), pp. 355–363.

Seear, K. 2009. 'Standing up to the beast': contradictory notions of control, un/certainty and risk in the endometriosis self-help literature. *Critical Public Health* 19(1), pp. 45–58.

Tanner, C. M., Brandabur, M. and Dorsey, E. R. 2008. Parkinson's disease: a global view. *Parkinson Report* (Spring), pp. 9–11.

Van Manen, M. 2017. But is it phenomenology? *Qualitative Health Research* 27(6), pp. 775–779.

Warren, N. and Manderson, L. 2008. Constructing hope: dis/continuity and the narrative construction of recovery in the rehabilitation unit. *Journal of Contemporary Ethnography* 37(2), pp. 180–201.

Warren, N. and Manderson, L. 2013. Reframing disability and quality of life: contextual nuances. In: Warren, N. and Manderson, L. eds. *Reframing Quality of Life and Physical Disability: Global Perspectives*. Social Indicators Research 54. Dordrecht: Springer, pp. 1–16.

Warren, N. and Manderson, L. 2015. Credibility and the inexplicable: Parkinson's disease and assumed diagnosis in contemporary Australia. In: Smith-Morris, C. ed. *Diagnostic Controversy: Cultural Perspectives on Competing Knowledge in Healthcare*. New York: Routledge, pp. 127–146.

Wolf-Meyer, M. and Taussig, K. S. 2010. Extremities: thresholds of human embodiment. *Medical Anthropology* 29(2), pp. 113–128.

Part IV

Global disability politics

Chapter 9

Ethical (dis)enchantment, afflictive kinship, and Ebola exceptionalism

Maria Berghs

Introduction: 'Ebola is over. When are you coming?'

> Ebola was like another war. War and Ebola are the same. War killed us and Ebola killed us. The suffering came back. For example, food suffering. Ebola took the person who looked after me, my uncle in Kenema. He died, he had a business there, but I did not see the body. They just took him. . . . I don't mean uncle like that. He was my family. He traded in banana, cassava, and palm oil and helped with the children's school fees. So, it's like the war. Ebola kills the people close to you. Now people here are provoking me again. I will have those close discussions and the memories make me cry. . . . I give you permission to write about it because those differences from the war are coming back. People say I am not a 'real' war-wounded. I used to be a rebel wife of the colonel [name]. The community are now talking about it. The issue is the fear business. They will tell any man that gets close to me. . . . I have those problems you are talking about. The inside and outside. I can keep a man for short times but never long times. . . . Yes, it is like the community shames him. He will not feel like a man.

The above vignette comes from an interview undertaken in late 2016 with 33-year-old Fatmata.[1] Following the Ebola crisis (what I shall call post-Ebola), I had been invited back to Sierra Leone by a non-governmental organisation that worked with people who had been wounded during the country's ten-year civil war (1991–2002). I had heard stories like Fatmata's many times when I had done research with people who call themselves *amputee* and *war wounded* in 2008–2009, 2011, and 2013 (Berghs 2016c; Conteh and Berghs 2014).[2] Fatmata's story was similar to those of other young girls that had been captured during the war by the rebels and made into *rebel wives*. Due to her visible physical impairment, she was viewed as a person with war wounds, and she could hide her other identity as a former rebel wife.

However, this conversation took place post-Ebola and, for several reasons, it was unusual. First, Fatmata elucidates some of the background to the context of understanding what impairment, disability, and disablement mean. For ordinary people, like Fatmata, life post-Ebola is viewed against the backdrop of past suffering and the loss of a life that she and others have known, such as war and Ebola. These are life-taking violent events which become embodied and seep into the everyday. Second, Fatmata notes the importance of kinship relationships and also newer associational communities created in society based on impairment, disease, or disability, like being *war wounded*. These concepts are ambivalent in that they promote belonging, but also seem to exclude through naming. Third, Fatmata relates the disruptive power of gossip and rumours for her gendered identity, the veracity of her wounds, and her relations in a community. She notes how ethical relationships are made of performative practices (showing kinship), moral actions (giving help), and discourses (community talk). Fourth, she explains the importance of secrecy to contain violence in her everyday life and why public naming by a community can have different emotional affects and effects, for example, in that a man is both shamed and his masculinity questioned by associating with her. Lastly, she exposes how disablement is connected to her visible and invisible injuries, almost as if there is still a moral contagion or poison through her past relationship to violence. What happened to her in the war represents a violation of the social rules for the community and she is still viewed as being socially polluted.[3] Fatmata also does something very unusual in giving me permission to write about how these differences from the war are coming back and refusing to keep the discussions about her past closed or in a private domestic sphere.

This conversation reminded me theoretically of the work of Veena Das, namely because of the emphasis on how morality, contagion (linked to violence), and disablement affect the everyday. Das (2015a, 2015b) explains that the focus on 'ordinary ethics' means uncovering the way in which ethics becomes embodied and enacted in language as part of the everyday. For Das (2015a: 117), it is a person's 'attentiveness to the other within the small events of everyday life as the expression of the moral'. Fatmata, thus, describes ordinary ethics in terms of the performance of virtues of her uncle in keeping ties of kinship, responsibilities of care, and obligations of sociality through small acts, such as the payment of school fees. Fatmata also describes how ordinary ethics can become undone through other actions, like public gossip about her impairment.

I begin this chapter by giving some theoretical background to what disability means in Sierra Leone and why I believe it is linked to morality. Second, I elucidate some of the background to Ebola to explain why *ethical unmaking* becomes implicated, and explain how austerity is of concern for people post-Ebola. By ethical unmaking, I mean the description of processes whereby social pollution and stigma are no longer contained by family or kinship. Instead, bonds of social belonging, caring, and responsibilities that encompass personhood as moral become undone. I elucidate how the meaning of disability still affects people's everyday lives post-Ebola and how disablement is displayed as afflictive kinship. Lastly, I give two examples of public ways in which international organisations try to repair social ethics and contain stigma which, in turn, instead create disablement.

Theoretical background

Das and Addlakha (2001: 511) explain how concepts of disease and disability have become correlated to 'postmodern forms of sociality'. Associational communities or groups, for example, are created based on various definitions linked to biosocial, biopolitical, or biovalued 'understandings of disease, impairment orientated or disability formations' (Das and Addlakha 2001: 511). They argue that (2001: 530):

> We need ethnographies of performance, tracking disability through utterances that have a perlocutionary force, such as rumour or gossip, to evaluate whether biosociality is to be understood primarily in terms of affiliative, associative communities, or whether postmodern forms of sociality demand a reimagining of filiative community as well.

For Das and Addlakha, what it means to belong, in terms of citizenship, is publically constructed. By contrast, kinship is 'the sphere in which the family has to confront ways of disciplining and containing contagion and stigma' (2001: 512). Hence, disability and impairment are not located in a body, but 'within a network of social and kinship relations' (Das and Addlakha 2001: 512). Disability and impairment, indeed, are discursively formed and demarked through definitions linked to 'notions of defect that mark other social categories such as gender' (Das and Addlakha 2001: 514).

In Sierra Leone, impairments can be physical, sensory, or cognitive, but may be interpreted in a myriad of ways. In the various ethnic groups in the country (i.e. Mende, Temne, Limba, Fula), impairment can also be socially and spiritually constructed and linked to ideas of misfortune, social defect, and/or moral worthiness, which in turn are linked to emotional states such as honour, shame, or abjection (Berghs 2016c). They locate impairment within moral economies of blame linked to kinship (ancestors), necessitating actions of social repair or purification to ensure social belonging again (Berghs and Dos Santos-Zingale 2011). By contrast, disability is constructed as a global signifier linked to impairment, for example, as viewed in terms of a medical identity, such as *amputee*, or defined by international human rights frameworks, such as *persons with disabilities*. For instance, understandings of poliomyelitis (polio) are morally ambivalent and can become disabling. In certain parts of Sierra Leone, people still believe that the cause of polio is linked to witchcraft. The witchcraft accusation focuses on a bodily sacrifice having been made in exchange for blessings or good fortune (*baraka*) that will lead to political position or riches (Berghs 2016c; Berghs and Dos Santos-Zingale 2011). It mimics the colonial history of the Atlantic slave trade where African bodies and body parts are exchanged for wealth and power (Shaw 2002). Witchcraft is connected to disharmony of kinship relations and most accusations focus symbolically on women.[4] Van de Grijspaarde et al. (2013) have illustrated how the distribution of witchcraft accusations in Sierra Leone is linked to normative ambiguity in communities where patriarchal power and patrimonial systems are under threat. Schneider (2016) too has illustrated how the naming of very ill children, whose survival is uncertain as *ogbanje*[5] spirits, is understood as penalising women's societal misdeeds.

While social remedies can be sought to repair relationships and restore moral order, people who have had polio may still be viewed as signifiers of the immoral spiritual sacrifices that their kin have made. In the capital city of Freetown, people who have had polio relate that they have been abandoned by their families and many view themselves as living on the margins of society. Szanto (2015) argues that this is exemplified in how they are involved in activities like blacksmithing. In West African culture, blacksmiths embody a liminal identity as straddling the world of material and occult immaterial (McNaughton 1993). This is why some people who have had polio prefer to be called *persons with disabilities* because of the link to public discourses on citizenship, equality, and rights (Berghs 2016c). Yet, when you ask people in Sierra Leone who have an impairment what that means for them, they will typically not use the term disability or disabled, but say something linked to explaining feelings of moral abjection (akin to Fatmata) or abandonment, such as stating 'I am useless'. This is related to the importance of performing obligations of kinship as embodied, for example, so that others accept their caring roles or work, and value this as contributing to the wellbeing of the group.

I argue that this is why in order to understand impairment, disease, and disability in Sierra Leone, there is a need to understand morality or ethics. Disability is discursive, enacted, and becomes embodied. The way in which those processes act together involves both morality and ethics and, as such, it is hard to disentangle the two in terms of giving conceptual definitions, as Zigon (2009) espouses. Instead, morality and ethics are viewed as emerging in the everyday where making such distinctions does not always work (Das et al. 2015; Lambek 2010). As Al-Mohammad and Peluso (2012: 54) state, it makes more sense to think of an 'ethical rough ground' where violence and the mundane have to be conceptualised together. Morality and ethics cannot be disentangled, but become spontaneously embodied in our habits, dispositions, and interactions and, thus, are ordinary. The ascription of any form of visible and invisible impairment can become moralised (positively and negatively) as part of global, local, and hybrid moral economies, that is, 'the production, distribution, circulation, and use of moral sentiments, emotions and values, and norms and obligations in social space' (Fassin 2009: 37).

I suggest that the way in which impairment is ascribed and becomes moralised is termed disability. So, for example, when someone with an impairment describes feeling 'useless', they are not just describing a utile form of discrimination (disablement), but they are also describing an emotional state linked to a normative claim about how society is constructed. They are describing what the quotidian is or how they are regarded in the everyday that makes up the 'social customs and norms' (Fassin 2009: 37). The word 'useless' is important because it illustrates a lack of intentionality towards what is deemed by others as the norm of being. In Fatmata's case, moral policing is leading to an unequal status in society and confrontation with a moral inchoate, over which she has no control. By inchoate, I mean to indicate how ethical boundaries and material, spiritual, and embodied belongings are unmade via the ways in which we live social life. Before explaining how this happens, I will provide some background to the Ebola epidemic in Sierra Leone and how that became linked to humanitarian action.

'Ebola e do so'[6]

On 7 November 2016, Sierra Leone celebrated one year of being declared Ebola-free by the World Health Organization (WHO). Ebola, a viral haemorrhagic fever, is also known as Ebola virus disease (EVD)[7] and describes a severe and highly infectious virus initially spread zoonotically, but then primarily spread anthroponotically, through contact with bodily fluids (Brown and Kelly 2014; Leach and Scoones 2013). The Ebola epidemic started in Guinea in December 2013 and spread geographically from rural areas to the urban centres of Guinea, Sierra Leone, and Liberia via internal and external trading networks and porous borders of neighbouring West African countries with close historical, economic, political, social, and cultural links (Leach 2015; Richards 2016).

Despite warnings by non-governmental organisations, including Médecins Sans Frontières (MSF),[8] early responses to the epidemic were marked by local and global institutional failures to assess its seriousness (Kamradt-Scott 2016; MSF 2014; Philips and Markham 2014). EVD is deadly, and survival from the disease is correlated to timely access to quality healthcare. As in other African countries affected by Ebola, Guinea, Sierra Leone, and Liberia are resource-rich countries with deeply rooted local and global inequalities which have led to civil conflict and political upheaval, resulting in historical mistrust towards ruling classes and elites (Leach 2015). This extends to ineffective health systems and government hospitals which are underfunded, require reimbursement and bribes, lack equipment, do not have well-trained nor well-paid staff, and cannot ensure access to basic medicines (Berghs 2016b). People, thus, rely on a medical pluralism of formal and informal care from indigenous healing from secret societies or healers, medicines they can buy, or what is available but unregulated on the local markets, as well as health and limited social care they can access through religious, charitable, and non-governmental organisations (NGOs) (Berghs 2016b). This pluralistic and mainly informal system continued to play a big role in the way in which people dealt with managing illness during the Ebola epidemic (McLean et al. 2016).

As Ebola developed into a major humanitarian crisis with global implications in terms of biosecurity, a Public Health Emergency of International Concern (PHEIC) was declared in August 2014 by the WHO. A WHO Ebola Response

Team was implemented and by September, the United Nations (UN) Security Council lobbied for emergency and militarised interventions (Farrar and Piot 2014). A UN Mission for Emergency Ebola Response (UNMEER) was set up to bolster the WHO and aid coordination of international efforts. Initially, the emergency aid and military responses in these countries were organised along colonial lines, with the Americans in Liberia, French in Guinea, and British in Sierra Leone aiding NGOs and civil society in those countries. For example, the UK's National Health Service (NHS) worked with the Ministry of Defence (MoD) and Department of International Development (DfID) in an emergency medical response called *Operation Gritrock*. Early interventions focused on strengthening the health system by ensuring the presence of Ebola Treatment Centres (ETC), Community Care Centres (CCC), and logistics. Logistics

Figure 9.1 Walls in western Freetown

Figure 9.2 Walls in western Freetown

included ambulances, training staff in infection control and prevention, providing patients with effective care or palliative treatment, containing Ebola through quarantine measures, contact tracing, surveillance, ensuring public health education about Ebola, and effective community outreach and sensitisation. These interventions often brought in sharp relief dilemmas between ethical actions and human rights, as well as collective and individual responsibilities for public health that depended on the cooperation of individual people who had Ebola (Calain and Poncin 2015; MSF 2015).

This was because the Ebola epidemic also represented a humanitarian paradigm shift. The epidemic was the first time that experimental and untested diagnostics, treatments, and vaccines that had not been tested on humans were given the ethical green light and fast-tracked during a medical emergency (Cohen and Kupferschmidt 2014; MSF 2015). This instantiated new types of humanitarian collaborations between philanthropic funding bodies, international institutions, universities, military, NGOs, the diaspora, local governments, civil societies, and the pharmaceutical industries to ensure acceleration, innovation, and funding of research (Wellcome Trust and CIDPRAP 2015). As a successful vaccine and ethical trial method were found (Henao-Restrepo et al. 2015), these new collaborative research platforms acted as future blueprints of development of emergency clinical research during epidemics and pandemics (Piot el al. 2017; WHO 2016a).

Presently, the West African countries of Sierra Leone, Guinea, and Liberia are recovering from one of the deadliest outbreaks of Ebola that the world has ever seen. According to the WHO, the epidemic affected 28,616 people, with 11,310 deaths and over 10,000 survivors (WHO 2016b). Sierra Leone was particularly badly affected with the most cumulative cases of EVD (14,124 people), although Richards (2016: 21) argues that it had the lowest death rate of the West-African countries. In total, 3,956 people died and 10,168 survived but are living with clinical sequelae (i.e. neurological, visual, and musculoskeletal) and psychosocial issues in what is being termed post-EVD or post-Ebola syndrome (WHO 2015). By 2016, Sierra Leone had seen no new cases for over a year. However, flare-ups were still expected, but vaccines are being successfully trialled (Geisbert 2017). In the following section, I illustrate how Ebola affected everyday life and undid *ordinary ethics* (Das 2015b) for many people in Sierra Leone.

Ethical spheres of unmaking personhood

In October 2016, I was primarily working in two districts of the country: the Western-Urban district, which includes the capital city of Freetown, and the Bombali district, where many amputee and war-wounded people had been relocated. Post-conflict, people who had been wounded in the war had been segregated in a camp in Freetown to treat their injuries and later they were resettled all over the country in what were colloquially described as amputee camps.[9] A colonial history of segregated institutional settings, such as day workshops or schools, meant that disabled people still tended to live together according to impairment. For instance, post-conflict people who had polio lived in created segregated communities (Berghs and Dos Santos-Zingale 2011). Many Sierra Leoneans felt that this *sequestration*, in terms of Giddens's (1991) understanding of spatially locating people as different, of people with war wounds was morally wrong and they should have been reintegrated back into their villages (Berghs 2016c).

People who were wounded during the war also saw their injuries as political, not linked to conceptions of impairment needing moral containment, and thus adhered to medical identifiers (Berghs 2016c). Yet, for many disabled people with impairments or injuries that were morally ambivalent, living in segregated communities meant access to non-governmental resources that allowed for inclusion. As a community leader, Sam explained: 'I am respected because I have a house and land'. While some of these settlements had been isolated, out-of-reach ghettos in 2008, they were physically integrated into urban settings in 2016. I visited a total of nine of these resettlement sites belonging to people who called themselves *amputee* and *war wounded*, and a segregated resettlement of people who had had polio. I interviewed thirty people who called themselves amputee or war wounded as a result of the past civil war. I was also taken to different sites linked to the Ebola epidemic and talked to non-governmental organisations, community leaders, and government officials about the impact of austerity measures.

Before the Ebola epidemic, Sierra Leone was internationally viewed as a *donor darling* (Vitalis Pemunta 2012), recovering well from a ten-year civil war and making a democratic and neoliberal transition to development. Ebola seemed to interrupt that trajectory and rebuilding the nation state was once again required. In 2015, the government of Sierra Leone set out a post-Ebola strategy for recovery to rebuild the health care system (Green 2016). However, in late 2016, the economy was still struggling because of its dependence on commodity markets which had collapsed. Bilateral donor funding to the government had also been cut back among recriminations over corruption and a lack of focus on rebuilding sectors affected by the epidemic, such as health and agriculture. The government had, therefore, been forced to implement austerity measures which led to inflation, with rising food prices and fuel hikes upsetting recovery efforts. It is against this background that people related how Ebola had affected them. A 50-year-old woman, Zainab, explained:

> It brought the suffering from the war back. The hardship. . . . Every day we saw plenty of bodies in (name of place). It was more fearful because it was the unseen enemy. . . . Ebola retraumatised.

Generally, several layers of ethical unmaking of social norms necessary for kinship were referenced. People did not recall a moral breakdown, but described difficulties of not performing their social obligations of reciprocity or responsibilities of care (Das 2015b). A 60-year-old man, David, stated:

> It was more fearful than the war because it is an invisible fight. . . . It was very difficult because of the restriction of movement. No visiting your neighbour. No touching. We could also not sustain ourselves.

They explain the unmaking of a relational ethics of caregiving, in that Ebola mainly affected the caregivers, such as the mother in family, female healer in a village, and healthcare professionals in hospitals. The ethical dilemmas facing frontline healthcare workers and those involved in conducting research have rightly been given a lot of attention in the literature (Calain and Poncin 2015; Cohen and Kupferschmidt 2014; MSF 2015), but all Sierra Leoneans faced dilemmas linked to caregiving acts and access to healthcare (Yamanis et al. 2016). For example, a 30-year-old man, who wished to remain anonymous because of the stigma linked to hiding family members who were ill during the epidemic, poignantly related:

> My small boy had malaria but we were not sure. So, I locked him in his room. I did not let my wife look after him until we were sure the fever, vomiting and diarrhoea were not Ebola. It was terrible. We were so afraid. My wife was crying so much.

Ebola also undid the secret society ethics[10] and religious norms that govern practices around life and death. Most attention during the Ebola epidemic was given to rites of death because of the dangers of infection linked to transporting bodies and religious rituals, such as washing corpses or the stigma facing burial workers (Richards 2016; Richards et al. 2015). However, people I talked to mainly mentioned the loss of the rites of embodied life-giving, such as restrictions on seeking healing or accessing hospitals. A group of women in one community explained that the *okadas* (motorcycle taxis) would not transport sick people unless you paid them a lot of money. In the same vein, they mentioned difficulties of ensuring women could give birth safely (Black 2015), how they heard women who had survived Ebola lost their babies, how many children lost their parents, and the fosterage of orphans (Evans and Popova 2015). A related issue often brought up in several communities I visited, and by NGOs, was how many teenage girls became pregnant during the epidemic because they were not in school. There was generally felt to be an increase of sexual exploitation of young girls and gendered violence in society. One community leader said that 'I feel the violence has come back'. The government ban on pregnant girls in schools in terms of loss of rights was never brought up (Amnesty International 2015).

Generally, all people I met talked about the unmaking of collective ethics of social customs, courtesy, and love for each other owing to the Ebola crisis, with subsequently profound effects on those affected. Radio and other programmes giving information about Ebola had seemingly focused on sensitising communities, but messages were directed towards individuals neglecting social responsibilities of care. As a 40-year-old community leader, Sam, stated when explaining handwashing messages: 'You have to prevent, yourself'. Similarly, during a long drive, my taxi driver Ibrahim explained how people stopped greeting each other by shaking hands and putting on seatbelts in his taxi because they were scared of the 'sweat' of the virus. While eating out of one bowl had been common, people told me how they did not want to share such meals during the epidemic. Several people stated that they did not pray close to their friends in the mosque but kept their distance. People gave examples of how they disregarded showing neighbourly affection, and stopped social visits to relatives during quarantines or the country's three day lockdown. One lady described how they were initially afraid of hugging loved ones who had survived Ebola. Especially calling the emergency phone number to report Ebola was sometimes viewed as unneighbourly and recriminations in communities exist to this day (Yamanis et al. 2016). Disabled people also mentioned the lack of ability to go begging. Sam related: 'The blind [sic] have to go out. They demonstrated and went on a rampage when they could not'. Mathew, a 20-year-old man, stated that the 'sympathy' for disabled people was not there during Ebola, meaning that non-disabled people did not give them money.

Lastly, Ebola was unmaking all people's efforts towards late modernity's promises of development and the global ethics of state-building. This is why some people felt that it had been part of their civic duty to get involved in aiding the Ebola response. Schools, universities, and formal and informal businesses closed during the epidemic which meant that people often lacked choices. Yet, that there were people who profited from Ebola is still viewed with suspicion. For instance, Edward (head of the Amputee and War-Wounded Association – AWWA) told me:

> Waterloo was where the Ebola Treatment Centre (ETC), the containment area for the ambulances and all those places were located. That's also where they built the Ebola houses, those mansions. Those are the ones that profited. Nobody wanted to live here, now they are around us.

Thus, for Edward, the Ebola crisis called into question the idea of fairness of global justice as it becomes localised (Dawson 2015). Invoking discourses of national duty and the performance of citizenship is a way in which people try to contain that suspicion. The reason why this becomes emotionally ambivalent is correlated to an ethical disenchantment with the idea of neoliberal development as bringing prosperity and a *good life*, and sacrifices being rewarded. The government and global institutions are used to informing communities in Sierra Leone around ideas of state-building as good, in terms of, for example, how reintegration of former ex-combatants will aid peace. Neoliberal economic policies become intimately linked to the work of state-building and security. However, as I have illustrated above, during Ebola and now post-Ebola, policies were felt to be preventing ordinary ethics (Das 2015b). Ethics for international

NGO professionals and civil society were instead framed within aspirational values and social mores that they brought with them, such as public health messages or human rights values. They were also linked to teleological espousals of Western life, wherein economic development and individual capacity building is needed to gain social mobility and success. This is why Fatmata stated that the differences from the war were also coming back in terms of the undoing of social norms and customs. Ordinary ethics allows for those small acts that sustain life which, if they are prevented, can lead to further impairment and trauma for people. In the following section, I explain how disabled people in Sierra Leone try to uphold life and deal with neoliberal values through an afflictive kinship and differential disability.

Disability as disablement: growing afflictive kinship

> I think it is leprosy? I am not sure? I remember seeing similar cases as a nurse in Liberia. Is she on medication? Did you touch her?
>
> (Sarah)

Earlier in the chapter, I explained how the ethics of everyday life and collective performances of kinship were publically unmade during the Ebola epidemic. I also explained why kinship was important in terms of the containment of stigma in the private realm (Das and Addlakha 2001). In this section, I will focus more on life post-Ebola and what that tells us about the creation of disability and disablement. As Fatmata stated, the way in which she held her life together was achieved through access to resources (emotional, physical, financial, spiritual, etc.) which changed over time and affected her (re)habituation and disposition. While a community association based on impairment (Das and Addlakha 2001) could be successful in terms of access to resources, it did not always mean further recognition by family, nor were the ties of kinship ensured. For example, when I visited an association for people who had polio located on a large compound with skills training, microfinance, and a bakery business, I noted the following:

> When I asked Alpha, the young man who was showing me the administrative offices and computers, if his family came to visit and were proud of him, he said that they would not have 'those thoughts', although some families came to visit.

My fieldnotes did not record any problems with Ebola survivors, but I still noted problems with inclusion:

> In one of these settlements of 20 houses that had been affected by Ebola, people were described by an NGO as generally to be 'doing well'. The settlement had lost a young woman, Aminata, and two of her family members. A young infant had survived and was being fostered by Aminata's relative in

a nearby village. Her neighbours explained how the house was put under quarantine and then decontaminated with chlorine. The community had also been 'sensitised' about Ebola so they did not have issues with stigma, nor with people living in the house now. Instead, people in the community complained about discrepancies in food aid during Ebola, noting how they were still easy targets of corruption. Despite the fact that people had small livestock, were engaging in petty trading, and the harvest season meant people were working with crops, overall everyone I met stated that they felt that they had to 'strain'.

Sam explained that there was a general 'unease' because of differences coming back and being exacerbated by austerity. When Sam stated that their land ownership was still being contested, another man explained that the landowning families were 'jealous' of amputees. A man of 60 years, Abdul, stated:

> Since Ebola, there has been no progress. Look how you find us. The lights and roads are not reaching us. The night time the place is dark and thieves come. They steal our domestic animals. When we try to stop them, they threaten us.

Another community leader, John, explained that Ebola meant the closure of schools and loss of employment and, so, people found other ways of survival. Post-Ebola, he noted that this had continued because parents could not pay the school fees:

> Young boys go into violence. Young girls go into a promiscuous life. Parents are trying their best, but the peer-group has a negative influence.

According to John, these youth were also giving the community a bad name, with recriminations from their neighbours. Furthermore, a health focus on Ebola had neglected other health and social care issues across the life-course. For example, a young girl stated 'we need nets for malaria'. An older man in his sixties, Pa Ibrahim, explained how he needed his wheelchair fixed. Similarly, Mami Fatu, an older lady in her sixties, said: 'I am no longer able to farm. I have a sickness but don't understand it. It is giving me problems in my eyes and look at my hands. The colour is going'.

Health and rehabilitative needs were secondary concerns because interactions between inflation and post-Ebola issues meant unemployment and food insecurity had to become priorities. This was confirmed in two other communities I visited, where people related the difficulties of rebuilding lives because of austerity. Ali, a middle-aged man who was a tailor, stated: 'Business is a communal affair. If other people are not able to pay for your services, you can't live'. All heads of communities that I met argued that they wanted better leadership, community projects to ensure employment, and a reopening of the government reparations programme for victims of the war. Resentment against the government and their association was also expressed as well as to a football team in Freetown that they accused of corruption, able-bodied control, and making money from Ebola. People used charitable understandings of disability and bureaucratic policy discourses of development, disability inclusion, and Ebola education as goods in society to write projects and gain funding. Post-Ebola, this was more difficult because disability was not viewed as connected to Ebola, nor linked to rebuilding the health system (Berghs 2016b).

In the Western-urban district, people gave more explicit expression to how disability as disablement existed in society. In many settlements, houses were in a poor state of repair and, in one place, a school was closed because the government had stopped paying the teachers. They explained having to strain in daily life in stronger Krio words such as *tranga* and having to *dreg* for work. A double amputee in his late thirties, Ibrahim, explained: 'We are still being kept out of jobs because people do not see us as whole. We are still begging in the streets and paying for the school fees in that way'. Their experiences of Ebola were also different, with many more people in their neighbouring communities and extended families affected. More psycho-social and health issues were reported because of the close density that they now lived with their neighbours. Again, issues were not with Ebola survivors, who lived nearby and, for example, used their health clinics. They did not feel stigma was a problem because they had been *sensitised* and they felt everyone had suffered *that time*. Instead, I noted:

> Due to their proximity to the main roads to the former ETC and living closer to affected communities, they related they had constantly heard the ambulance sirens. Especially the sounds of the sirens had brought back the memories of the war and emotional distress.

In one community, the 50-year-old chairlady stated that they were glad Ebola was 'done', but did not understand why I was asking questions about it. She was more worried about the impact of government austerity measures. It was a continuous worry for her to make ends meet. People noted that they were no longer anxious about increases in price of a bag of rice, but were thinking in terms of a cup and how many times per week they could afford to buy rice. Tamba, an elderly man over 60, stated:

> I have so much pain but I can't afford to buy the medicines. What is really causing me problems is the fact that I am a stranger here. Who is going to look after me? My neighbours cannot help me anymore.[11]

Illnesses, diseases, psycho-social issues, and disability as disablement were not described in terms of 'routine ups and downs of life' (Das 2015a: 37), but in a continuum of physical and psycho-social affliction and disablement that people did not normalise – but had to go to the background of their concerns because of the immediacy of managing daily life during austerity. People decried the fact that they had to 'suffer' and 'strain', but had no other options than to try and 'bear life together' in a kind of afflictive kinship. Relatedness was no longer in terms of associational community of impairment or disability, but in terms of the maladies and poverty they were exposed to. While living together was a way in which they could ethically uphold life, it also brought out tensions and differences in identities linked to impairment, gender, age, and ethnicity. However, while people were trying to ensure ordinary ethics post-Ebola, for instance, in terms of caring for each other and showing neighbourly love, austerity measures were unmaking those efforts. The ties of kinship that normally would contain violence, contagion, and stigma were also no longer functioning, nor were public discourses on citizenship and rights linked to disability and health. Impairment was being moralised in a negative way as disability and disablement was occurring in terms of global abandonment. In the next section, I examine if global attempts to repair the social ethics in terms of moral bioeconomy can contain this stigma, and if Ebola survivors also face disablement and disability.

Clinical (bio)economies: extractive Ebola exceptionalism

In this section, I examine two examples of public ways in which international organisations try to repair social ethics and contain stigma in terms of a moral bioeconomy. The first example is the creation of a cemetery to ensure a proper burial for people who died from Ebola. The second is the formation and naming of a biosocial association based on Ebola survivorship. In my fieldnotes, they are both linked, but I illustrate how both methods to contain violence, contagion, and stigma only ensure the opposite.

A common refrain I heard post-Ebola was that disabled people did not know where their neighbours or family members, who had died, had gone or if they had religious burials. For example, Mohammed, a man in his fifties, related a troubling memory: 'They took my brother away. I do not know where he is buried'. Proper burials are necessary social customs to honour ancestors (Richards 2016). Despite the fact that a burial site existed, people felt that their roles in burial practices, for example, as family members, had been taken away from them. Their presence in the performance of rituals of death had been ignored. Thus, I was invited to visit the Paloko cemetery:

> Edward had last been there during the epidemic with journalists in 2014. He stated he had seen a big burial pit but that a bigger cemetery was being built by an NGO nearby. This was clearly marked along the main road but we had to drive through several villages and behind a school to get to the site. There we were greeted by people who were looking after the cemetery. The caretaker offered to show us around. We saw hundreds of graves in plots for children, women, men – and according to if they had been buried

with a coffin. All of the graves had the same inscription: *In Loving Memory*. We were told that if people were looking for family members, there was a map with the names of people. We said our prayers and gave thanks for a dignified burial place. On the way back to Freetown, we were stuck in traffic because of Chinese road construction when we saw the sign of the headquarters of Sierra Leone Association of Ebola Survivors (SLAES). A bunch of young men were hanging out behind the sign watching the traffic on their second floor balcony. Impulsively, we decided to stop and go talk to them. Edward and I had read an article in the press where SLAES compared their advocacy for better healthcare, socio-economic programmes, and inclusion in society to that of the lobbying that the victims of the war had done (Cham 2016). Having just come from Paloko, we wanted to thank people and Edward knew I also wanted to ask about clinical research.

Both victims of the war and people who had Ebola were identified through medicalised identities that marked them (i.e. war wounds or EVD). These collective markers of identity were mainly institutionally given. For example, amputees were initially viewed in medical terms, as the name suggests, then as *victims* in transitional justice, and now in terms of disability by government, NGOs, and charities, therefore closing appeals to the state for reparations (Berghs 2016a). Different bureaucratic classifications engender new norms and dispositions as well as responsibilities to such people in society. They were never viewed as *survivors* or by other identities which, in ordinary life, were more important, such as in Fatmata's case. By contrast, people who had EVD and lived through the most severe forms of the disease were an exceptional category and classified as survivors and, thus, in terms of an Ebola biosocial identity and future (Berghs 2016b).

At SLAES, we were met by Yusuf Kabba in his office. He was the president of the association and related that the association's concerns for its members, who were mainly young people, were about employment. Connecting current UN policy discourses on sustainable development to Ebola survivors, he argued that while they were being given some of the same skills training and start-up kits that victims of the war had received, this was not done in a sustainable way. Yusuf related that he felt that AWWA was not organised soon enough after the war, so their leadership was unable to advocate strongly. He noted that he felt 'pity' for the victims and sorry for the way they had been treated by the government. They did not intend to make the same mistakes, which is why they had protested against the governmental neglect of their health. Yusuf and his friends noted that it was also SLAES that had engaged in a lot of sensitisation or educational activities, and had made a big impact on ending the overt discrimination Ebola survivors experienced. In my fieldnotes, I noted that medical treatment as research was viewed as discriminatory:

> I asked about medical treatment and Yusuf grew angry, stating they were currently partaking in research because they had 'no choice'. He said that

they were 'not happy' and 'tired' of science. Yusuf reminded me of a frustrated chairman who I had met in the past and who was very cynical of researchers in Sierra Leone and their motives. He grudgingly answered my questions but it was clear he felt disdain. By science, they meant the research that was being done *on* them which was linked to foreign researchers like myself. Yusuf had been advocating on this form of 'discrimination'. He noted how science was 'disturbing their minds' and gave the example of semen testing. He explained that scientific explanations of how long Ebola could live in the body were incorrect, noting how they were told the virus could live in bodily fluids like semen for 6 months, then a year, and now science could not give them an end date. The young men around him shook their heads in agreement when he stated that they had their traditions and cultural norms which went against donating semen. While the young men had obviously had many conversations about socio-cultural norms linked to masculinity and sexuality in research, I noted Edward becoming uncomfortable about talk that I knew he felt belonged to the domestic sphere. I apologised to SLAES and changed the subject.

Getting involved in research and testing a vaccine for Ebola is normatively framed as rationally and morally the right thing to do by the global community (Piot et al. 2017). The pursuit of science, even in its experimental forms, is viewed institutionally as a collective good for public health. In Sierra Leone, Ebola research becomes biomedically linked to health, development, and security of the nation state, similar to earlier peacebuilding and transitional justice discourses. Ebola survivors are expected to want to *fight back*, for example, by getting involved in clinical trials or plasma studies (Enserink 2015), which calls into question the framing of individual ethical choices, informed decision-making, and the ability of people to refuse involvement in science (Holt 2016). Likewise, the screening of Ebola survivors is viewed as necessary to their health, and their involvement in science understood in terms of present individual and collective global future benefit.

Yusuf and the other survivors, while aware of those issues, questioned the way in which they were being viewed strictly in terms of a biosocial identity and felt there was an ambiguity around choices. Screening and research framed as a normative good meant refusal would arouse moral and practical policing. They questioned the ontological status of the Ebola virus as a disease and the empirical foundations of that science. Instead, Ebola was viewed in terms of chronicity or shifting impairments. While they had been diagnosed with EVD syndrome, there was no real diagnostic sequela, future prognosis, or categorical measurement of how much Ebola was in the body and what bodily fluids it was carried in (and for how long). Instead, they all highlighted fluctuating bodily problems with, for example, joint pain, cognitive impairment, or vision loss in terms of disability, but they did not use that word. They questioned why and how issues like vision loss become permanent in some people if they had *survived*

Ebola. Yusuf quoted some of the research evidence from Uganda and asked why science did not know how long Ebola survivors would be affected, calling into question the idea of surviving Ebola, scientific research, and medical diagnosis. Their final message, as it has been with other people I talked to Sierra Leone, was that for them, employment was currently more important, in terms of helping them psycho-socially, to rebuild their futures and improve their health and overall wellbeing. It was employment that they knew would lead to integration into society again, thereby countering any notion of disability and disablement.

I thought scientists and other researchers would be interested in following the survivors for the rest of their lives, in terms of biosocially understanding Ebola and ensuring mainstreaming in services. As we were driving back to Freetown, I asked Edward what he thought. He grew cynical and said: 'They will forget about them, unless they can make money from them'. He was pointing to their utility in the global economy. For him, Ebola becomes an exceptional medical category linked to recuperation of biological resources that take primacy, but are perceived as linked to an extractive bodily economy (Shaw 2002). Ebola survivors currently have a utile biological value, so are a part of a biomedical moral economy. However, this does not mean that they are immune from discrimination. Edward noted that they are only viewed globally in utilitarian terms of efficacy of future biovalue. Yusuf understood this, which was why rebuilding life socially was more urgent because that is where usefulness as personhood is morally located.

Conclusion: ethical decontamination

In this chapter, I have elucidated what is meant by disability and disablement in Sierra Leone. I noted how disability is linked to an ascription of moral force to impairment. I have explained how this becomes linked to understanding ordinary ethics (Das 2015b) and how the Ebola epidemic affected not only the creation of impairment, but increased disability and disablement in society post-Ebola in terms of a new afflictive kinship. Public ways in which international organisations try to repair social ethics and contain stigma in terms of a moral bioeconomy do not function and only created more discrimination in society, especially for Ebola survivors. I also tried to find a word to describe the disenchantment of post-Ebola life, what that means, and the pace and messy temporal fluidity of ethical making and unmaking (Das 2015a, 2015b) that become inchoate because the public and private boundaries of ethical life no longer function. During the writing of this chapter, I looked through some pictures that I had taken of the Hastings Decontamination Site.

The place had been empty and people described being 'fearful' of going near it. Fatmata had used a similar expression to describe why people did not want to come close to her, almost as if she was still contaminated by what was perceived as an immoral past. I was thinking about the explanations I had been given by James of the differing sites and cleaning of ambulances, and the

Figure 9.3 Decontamination site tent

stripping, shedding, and burning of all materials that had possibly been infected by the virus long after the end of Ebola. James was a Sierra Leonean in his thirties who I had met by chance and had been involved in the *Ebola effort*. Like many Sierra Leoneans, he told me he thought it was part of his 'moral duty' to get involved. I told him about why I was in the country and explained that the main question people asked me linked to Ebola was where the 'Ebola money' had gone. James stated he too was having difficulties making ends meet and had wondered about Ebola money, but that I would not like his questions. He, thus, asked to stay anonymous, but he wanted me to write about this issue. He said it was easy to blame the government, but he also felt the international community were culpable because 'not all donated money went directly to the government'. We had a long discussion where he raised many questions, for example, about inequalities of local and international salaries, access to equipment and vaccines, whether DfID had donated all of the materials to the Sierra Leonean people, and why they burnt unused donated items like medicines and pallets of baby wipes. I said that I had no answers to these questions, but he insisted I write about them.

People like Fatmata, Yusuf, and James had all emphasised that I *had* to bring out of the private and personal sphere the silencing of *their* disablement in its multiple local and global neoliberal forms. I think this is where the ordinary ethics of everyday people becomes ethically exceptional, in that they are trying to wrest back control through perlocutionary force over what is defined by outsiders and insiders as contagion. They are, it seems, engaging in a kind of meta-ethics or extraordinary ethics, where they take up moral actions of repair and ethical decontamination.

Notes

1 All names in this article are fictional unless the person is a public figure.
2 I undertook fieldwork in Sierra Leone in 2008, 2009, and 2011. This was based on a PhD study about the reintegration of people who call themselves amputee and war wounded. In 2013, I was involved in aiding the Amputee and War-Wounded Association (AWWA) to conduct research about reparations. I was invited back in 2016 to learn how Ebola had affected AWWA and disabled people. I also met with voluntary, non-governmental organisations and universities that had supported me on a research bid linked to (bio)ethics and Ebola survivors. After meeting with survivors themselves and taking their advice, I decided not to pursue this research further. In 2017, I was working on a Newton-funded project linked to sickle cell. Sierra Leoneans described this as a neglected public health issue and 'good' work.
3 Stark (2006) has described how girls who were raped during the conflict now describe their moral luck being altered in terms of *misfortune* or social pollution because of the violations against the rules of the secret societies. She describes this as *noro*. I have only heard of social pollution or bad luck in this context.
4 In Sierra Leone, it is a woman who leaves her maternal home to go to her husband's house or village. She is, thus, viewed as an *outsider* to the patrilineage.
5 A Nigerian Igbo word meaning spirit children who come and go. *Ogbanjes* are also viewed as malicious spirits whose behaviour lies outside of the conventional norms and, as such, they can be subjected to social criticisms.
6 This Krio expression of admonition means something akin to 'Ebola, that's enough!' or 'It's enough now'.
7 I will use the term *Ebola* because that was what was being used by people in Sierra Leone.
8 Also known as Doctors without Borders.
9 Settlements could have as little as four houses near a village and, in other places, more than twenty houses could be built together, but outside the nearest urban centre. Houses were intended to primarily benefit victims of the civil war, especially people who had been amputated or gained war wounds. However, due to internal corruption, disabled people and other people who gained injuries or lost limbs also benefitted.
10 There are male and female secret societies in Sierra Leone and with different names according to the ethnic groups they are associated with. For instance, in the south of the country among the Mende people, it is the female *Sande* and male *Poro*. Initiation rites are secret and usually happen around adolescence. Initiation, while comprising bodily techniques and rituals such as circumcision, is viewed mainly in terms of training that is necessary to enter into moral sociality and understanding the responsibilities of what it means to be an adult man or woman. In Sande, non-initiates outside of the secret knowledge (*hale*) are known as *kpowa*. They are 'foolish' people who not do have the skills of adulthood. The word can also mean mental illness.
11 Tamba was from Kono; he was a stranger in the area where he was living. This meant that his extended family did not live around him to be able to help him in times of economic hardship.

References

Al-Mohammad, H. and Peluso, D. 2012. Ethics and the 'rough ground' of the everyday: the overlappings of life in postinvasion Iraq. *HAU: Journal of Ethnographic Theory*, 2(2), pp. 42–58.

Amnesty International. 2015. *Shamed and Blamed: Pregnant Girls' Rights at Risk in Sierra Leone*. London: Amnesty International.

Berghs, M. 2016a. Local and global phantoms: reparations national memory and sacrifice in Sierra Leone. In: Devlieger, P., Rusch, F., Brown, S. and Strickfaden, M. eds. *Rethinking Disability: World Perspectives in Culture and Society*. Antwerp: Garant, pp. 275–292.

Berghs, M. 2016b. Neoliberal policy, chronic corruption and disablement: biosecurity, bio-social risks and the creation of 'Ebola survivors'? *Disability and Society* 31(2), pp. 275–279.

Berghs, M. 2016c. *War and Embodied Memory: Becoming Disabled in Sierra Leone*. London: Routledge.

Berghs, M. and Dos Santos-Zingale, M. 2011. A comparative analysis: everyday experiences of disability in Sierra Leone. *Africa Today* 58(2), pp. 18–40.

Black, B. O. 2015. Obstetrics in the time of Ebola: challenges and dilemmas in providing life-saving care during a deadly epidemic. *Obstetric Anaesthesia Digest* 35(4), pp. 180–181.

Brown, H. and Kelly, A. H. 2014. Material proximities and hotspots: toward an anthropology of viral haemorrhagic fevers. *Medical Anthropology Quarterly* 28(2), pp. 280–303.

Calain, P. and Poncin, M. 2015. Reaching out to Ebola victims: coercion, persuasion or an appeal for self-sacrifice? *Social Science and Medicine* 147, pp. 126–133.

Cham, K. 2016. Sierra Leone Ebola survivors protest neglect. *Africa Review* [Online]. Available at: www.africareview.com/news/Sierra-Leone-Ebola-survivors-protest-neglect/979180-3146590-7h8ibd/index.html [Accessed: 23 November 2017].

Cohen, J. and Kupferschmidt, K. 2014. Ebola vaccine trials raise ethical issues. *Science* 346(6207), pp. 289–290.

Conteh, E. and Berghs, M. 2014. '*Mi At Don Poil': A Report on Reparations in Sierra Leone for Amputee and War-Wounded People*. Freetown: Amputee and War-Wounded Association.

Das, V. 2015a. *Affliction: Health, Disease, Poverty*. New York: Fordham University Press.

Das, V. 2015b. *What Does Ordinary Ethics Look Like? Four Lectures on Ethics: Anthropological Perspectives*. Chicago: HAU Books.

Das, V. and Addlakha, R. 2001. Disability and domestic citizenship: voice, gender, and the making of the subject. *Public Culture* 13(3), pp. 511–531.

Das, V., Al-Mohammad, H., Robbins, J. and Stafford, C. 2015. There is no such thing as the good: the 2013 meeting of the Group for Debates in Anthropological Theory. *Critique of Anthropology* 35(4), pp. 430–480.

Dawson, A. J. 2015. Ebola: what it tells us about medical ethics. *Journal of Medical Ethics* 41(1), pp. 107–110.

Enserink, M. 2015. Ebola survivors fight back in plasma studies. *Science* 348(6236), pp. 742–743.

Evans, D. K. and Popova, A. 2015. West African Ebola crisis and orphans. *The Lancet* 385(9972), pp. 945–946.

Farrar, J. J. and Piot, P. 2014. The Ebola emergency – immediate action, ongoing strategy. *New England Journal of Medicine* 371, pp. 1545–1546.

Fassin, D. 2009. Moral economies revisited. *Annales. Histoire, Sciences Sociales* 64(6), pp. 1237–1266.

Geisbert, T. W. 2017. First Ebola virus vaccine to protect human beings? *The Lancet* 389(10068), pp. 479–480.

Giddens, A. 1991. *Modernity and Self-Identity: Self and Society in the Late Modern Age*. Stanford: Stanford University Press.

Green, A. 2016. West African countries focus on post-Ebola recovery plans. *The Lancet* 388(10059), pp. 2463–2465.

Henao-Restrepo, A. M., Longini, I. M., Egger, M., Dean, N. E., Edmunds, W. J., Camacho, A., Carroll, M. W., Doumbia, M., Draguez, B., Duraffour, S. and Enwere, G. 2015. Efficacy and effectiveness of an rVSV-vectored vaccine expressing Ebola surface glycoprotein: interim results from the Guinea ring vaccination cluster-randomised trial. *The Lancet* 386(9996), pp. 857–866.

Holt, K. 2016. Ebola vaccine trial in Sierra Leone battles against fear and logistics. *The Guardian* [Online]. Available at: www.theguardian.com/global-development/2016/mar/10/ebola-vaccine-trial-sierra-leone-fear-logistics-immunisations [Accessed: 23 November 2017].

Kamradt-Scott, A. 2016. WHO's to blame? The World Health Organization and the 2014 Ebola outbreak in West Africa. *Third World Quarterly* 37(3), pp. 401–418.

Lambek, M. 2010. *Ordinary Ethics: Anthropology, Language and Action*. New York: Fordham University Press.

Leach, M. 2015. The Ebola crisis and post 2015 development. *Journal of International Development* 27(6), pp. 816–834.

Leach, M. and Scoones, I. 2013. The social and political lives of zoonotic disease models: narratives, science and policy. *Social Science and Medicine* 88, pp. 10–17.

McLean, K. E., Abramowitz, S. A., Ball, J. D., Monger, J., Tehoungue, K., McKune, S. L., Fallah, M. and Omidian, P. A. 2016. Community-based reports of morbidity, mortality, and health-seeking behaviours in four Monrovia communities during the West African Ebola epidemic. *Global Public Health* [Early View].

McNaughton, P. R. 1993. *The Mande Blacksmiths: Knowledge, Power, and Art in West Africa*. Bloomington: Indiana University Press.

Médecins Sans Frontières (MSF). 2014. Global bio-disaster response urgently needed in Ebola fight. *MSF* [Online]. Available at: www.msf.org/en/article/global-bio-disaster-response-urgently-needed-ebola-fight [Accessed: 23 November 2017].

Médecins Sans Frontières (MSF). 2015. *Pushed to the Limit and Beyond: A Year Into the Largest Ever Ebola Outbreak*. Geneva: MSF.

Philips, M. and Markham, Á. 2014. Ebola: a failure of international collective action. *The Lancet* 384(9949), p. 1181.

Piot, P., Coltart, C.E.M. and Atkins, K. E. 2017. Preface: the 2013–2016 West African Ebola epidemic: data, decision-making and disease control. *Philosophical Transactions of the Philosophical Society B* 372(1721), pp. 20170020.

Richards, P. 2016. *Ebola. How a People's Science Helped End an Epidemic*. London: Zed Books.

Richards, P., Amara, J., Ferme, M.C., Kamara, P., Mokuwa, E., Sheriff, A.I., Suluku, R. and Voors, M. 2015. Social pathways for Ebola virus disease in rural Sierra Leone, and some implications for containment. *PLOS Neglected Tropical Diseases* 9(4), p. e0003567.

Schneider, L. T. 2016. The ogbanje who wanted to stay: the occult, belonging, family and therapy in Sierra Leone. *Ethnography* 18(2), pp. 133–152.

Shaw, R. 2002. *Memories of the Slave Trade: Ritual and the Historical Imagination in Sierra Leone*. Chicago: University of Chicago Press.

Stark, L., 2006. Cleansing the wounds of war: an examination of traditional healing, psychosocial health and reintegration in Sierra Leone. *Intervention* 4(3), pp. 206–218.

Szanto, D. 2015. *Where Parallel Worlds Meet: Civil Society and Civic Agency. Politicising Polio in Sierra Leone*. Unpublished PhD Thesis. University of Pécs, Hungary.

Van de Grijspaarde, H., Voors, M., Bulte, E. and Richards, P. 2013. Who believes in witches? Institutional flux in Sierra Leone. *African Affairs* 112(446), pp. 22–47.

Vitalis Pemunta, N. 2012. Neoliberal peace and the development deficit in post-conflict Sierra Leone. *International Journal of Development Issues* 11(3), pp. 192–207.

Wellcome Trust and Centre for Infectious Disease Research and Policy. 2015. *Recommendations for Accelerating the Development of Ebola Vaccines, Report and Analysis*. Minneapolis: University of Minnesota.

World Health Organization. 2015. *WHO Meeting on Survivors of Ebola Virus Disease: Clinical Care of EVD Survivors, Freetown, 3–4 August 2015: Meeting Report*. Geneva: WHO.

World Health Organization. 2016a. *An R&D Blueprint for Action to Prevent Epidemics: Plan of Action, May 2016.* Geneva: WHO.

World Health Organization. 2016b. Ebola situation report. *WHO* [Online]. Available at: http://apps.who.int/ebola/ebola-situation-reports [Accessed: 23 November 2017].

Yamanis, T., Nolan, E. and Shepler, S. 2016. Fears and misperceptions of the Ebola response system during the 2014–2015 Outbreak in Sierra Leone. *PLOS Neglected Tropical Diseases* 10(10), p. e0005077.

Zigon, J. 2009. Morality and personal experience: the moral conceptions of a Muscovite man. *Ethos* 37(1), pp. 78–101.

Chapter 10

Disability and healthcare in everyday life

Hannah Kuper, Goli Hashemi, and Mary Wickenden

Introduction

Discussing the topic of health in relation to disability can raise red flags. There is concern among many people with disabilities[1] that they are seen both by lay people and professionals as *ill* and as having purely health-related problems. The wide range of exclusions that they face in their everyday life are perceived to be a result of these health problems alone, without consideration of the disabling impact of society. Paying attention only to the purely biological differences or difficulties (the impairment) that a person with a disability has does not sufficiently recognise many of their concerns and experiences. Health, however, is an important concern for everyone. Maintaining good health may be particularly important for people with disabilities, as they are already in a marginalised position in society, so that poor health can heighten risks of morbidity and early mortality (Callaway et al. 2015). Disability, health, and healthcare are interrelated and complex issues, and there has been little critical reflection on the links between them. In this chapter, we explore issues around everyday health and access to healthcare for people with disabilities. We illustrate our main points using case studies, providing qualitative data gathered from research in international settings, allowing consideration of the perspectives of people with disabilities living in different cultural contexts and various levels of provision.

Both disability and health have had varying definitions and are used differently by lay people and experts from different disciplines. It is therefore important to first lay out the theoretical underpinning of the relationship between disability and health. The medical (or individual) model of disability is criticised for equating disability solely with health conditions, focusing just on individuals' impairments as the cause of disability, while ignoring society's disabling role (Donoghue 2003; Shakespeare 2004). This model may be both a cause and a consequence of the simplistic conflation of disability and ill health. The social model responds to these concerns by conceptualising disability as an outcome of society's lack of acceptance of individual difference and failure to adapt to different types of needs and provide opportunities for inclusion. People are disabled not by their physical, sensory, or cognitive difference from an assumed *normal*, but by society itself (Oliver and Barnes 2012). A concern with this model in its purest form, however, is that it ignores the impact of impairment by focusing solely on societal factors (Shakespeare 2013; Thomas 2007).

In recent years, the prevailing model for conceptualising disability within health arenas has been the International Classification of Functioning, Disability and Health (ICF), developed by the World Health Organization (WHO 2001). Influenced by changes in the conceptualisation of disability and social model thinking, the ICF describes disability as resulting from the interaction between an individual's impairments and contextual factors, including the attitudinal, social, and physical environment (WHO 2011). A health condition (e.g. diabetes) may lead to an impairment (e.g. sensory deficits) and consequent difficulties in carrying out activities (e.g. difficulty walking due to decreased balance and sensation in the feet). An underlying health condition is therefore a necessary feature of disability, but it is only part of the story. The person's limitations in activities may be exacerbated by personal factors (e.g. age, gender, and genetics), socio-economic factors (e.g. wealth, education, and social support), and contextual factors (e.g. social support, assistive devices, accessibility of the environment, inclusive laws, policies, and attitudes). These factors can operate at individual, family, community, or societal levels. It is the interaction between them that disables the person, not just the presence of a health condition or impairment alone. The manifestation of these interactions, if they are predominantly negative, is that the person's participation in aspects of everyday life on an equal basis with others may be compromised. For example, they may have poorer access to education, work, leisure, and community life. The health condition itself is necessary, but not sufficient on its own, to lead to disability. This conceptualisation of disability through the ICF model will guide the discussions in this chapter.

There are two interrelated issues to explore around health and the everyday lives of people with disabilities. The first is whether people with disabilities have increased vulnerability to poor health, and the second is whether people with disabilities experience greater difficulties in accessing healthcare and engaging in health-related activities. Both issues may have substantial effects on the everyday lives of people with disabilities and whether they would describe themselves as ill or healthy. In terms of the first issue, there is abundant evidence that on average, people with disabilities have worse health than people without disabilities. Chronic conditions such as obesity, hypertension, diabetes, and mental health conditions are more common among people with disabilities in both high-income (AIHW 2010; Froehlich-Grobe et al. 2016; Reichard et al. 2011) and low-income countries (Kuper et al. 2014). People with disabilities are also more likely to self-report that their health is worse than people without disabilities (Altman and Bernstein 2008).

There are several pathways which can explain this association. People with disabilities often have a disadvantaged and marginalised structural position in society, which may make them vulnerable to worse health than others. Specifically, people with disabilities are on average poorer than those without disabilities (Banks and Polack 2014) and social deprivation is well known to impact negatively on general health through a multitude of routes including poorer diet, unhealthier living conditions, and poorer access to care (Marmot and Wilkinson 2003; Marmot 2005). People with disabilities are also frequently excluded from employment, which is linked to worsening mental health and poor physical health, and premature death (Marmot 2010). The health condition underlying the person's impairment may have further negative or secondary health consequences beyond the impairment itself. As an example, spinal cord injury survivors, who have consequent mobility impairments, are more vulnerable to pressure sores, respiratory illnesses, and urinary tract infections. Finally, disability is most common in older people, and older people are more likely to experience ill health (Hogan et al. 1999; Tas et al. 2007).

In any case, vulnerability to poor health among people with disabilities is a major concern. It may impact on their everyday lives in various ways (Callaway et al. 2015). Poor health may limit participation in employment, education, and social life, perpetuating exclusion, and causing a spiral into further ill health. Poor health and its consequences may also result in poverty, suffering, lower quality of life, further morbidity, and early mortality (Callaway et al. 2015; Mannan and MacLachlan 2013; Shakespeare and Kleine 2013; Swartz and Bantjes 2016; UN 2006). Directions of causation between disability and ill health are, therefore, not linear and are often difficult to establish.

There are several important points to keep in mind when considering access to healthcare by people with disabilities. Importantly, the right to access healthcare is enshrined within the UN Convention on the Rights of Persons with Disabilities, as well as in national laws of most countries. Not all people need the same level or type of care, yet they should all receive the level and quality of care they need. These services should cover the full spectrum including 'promotive, preventive, curative and rehabilitative health services' of good quality without incurring financial hardship (WHO 2017b: n.p.). Everyone, regardless of their impairments or disability status, requires general healthcare services. These include health promotion and preventative measures, such as immunisations and nutritional or family planning advice. People may also need treatment of a range of general conditions that may affect anyone, including sexual and reproductive health, minor or major injuries, infections, and the management of non-communicable diseases. These needs will change over the life-course. People with disabilities may also need specific and specialised healthcare related to their underlying impairment. This includes access to medication, surgery, psychological therapies, assistive devices, and therapeutic rehabilitation. Such services usually do not focus primarily on *cure*, but on preventing secondary impairments and optimising function, so that the person can live as pain-free and actively as possible. In many instances, the need for healthcare cannot be easily divided into the general and specialist. Indeed, individual needs are often complex and require an integrated approach to care.

If it is true that people with disabilities are at risk of poor health, then it follows that they have an increased need for health services. This pattern is clear from the World Health Surveys, conducted across 51 countries, where people with disabilities were consistently significantly more likely to seek inpatient or outpatient care (WHO 2011). However, seeking healthcare services does not always equate with good access and quality of care, and the literature is rich with examples of people with disabilities facing great difficulties in this respect (Burke et al. 2017; Eide et al. 2015; Grech 2015; Maart and Jelsma 2014; Pereira and de Carvalho Fortes 2010; Peta 2017; Rotarou and Sakellariou 2017; Saulo et al. 2012). The barriers to accessing healthcare are varied and complex, depending on the context, and can include physical inaccessibility, difficulties with communication, stigma, financial barriers, and inadequate training and facilities at healthcare services.

Even when healthcare is accessed, people with disabilities often report that the quality of care they receive is inappropriate. They report experiencing negative and discriminatory attitudes and lack of recognition of their particular needs (Burke et al. 2017; Eide et al. 2015; Pereira and de Carvalho Fortes 2010; Peta 2017). There is also abundant evidence that people with disabilities pay more to access services, due to higher costs of transport, the need for a companion to accompany them, or because higher fees are charged (Eide et al. 2015; Grech 2015; Rotarou and Sakellariou 2017). Lack of access to quality, affordable healthcare can mean that people with disabilities may experience unnecessarily poor health, which will impact on their everyday life through difficulties in participation and functioning. This vicious circle makes treatment more difficult and leads to further poor health, decreased social participation, and exacerbated poverty.

Much of the literature on disability and health focuses on single aspects of this relationship in one context. For instance, studies investigating barriers to healthcare tend to focus on specific issues (e.g. transport or stigma) or certain components of healthcare needs (e.g. sexual or reproductive health, or dental care), rather than critically exploring the issues more broadly. To fill this gap, we have used data from four different sources to explore the interrelationship between disability and everyday health. We use case studies to illustrate the complex nature of these associations and how they impact on people's everyday lives.

Method

In this chapter, we present qualitative data gathered as part of research studies in the UK, Malawi, Guatemala, and through clinical experiences in the US. These sources were selected to present different perspectives from adults and children with disabilities, and people living in high- and low-income settings. We have also included the reflections of service providers, as while individual people with disabilities will be the experts of their particular situation, clinicians often have a broad overview of many of the difficulties disabled people experience in accessing healthcare. The analysis sets out to provide key illustrations which will allow critical reflection on access to health in the everyday lives of people with disabilities in different settings, and the types of issues and questions that arise.

Study samples

The UK research drawn on was an ethnographic study of the lives of nine disabled teenagers who had severe spastic quadriplegic cerebral palsy and used alternative and augmentative communication (AAC). The key participants (six girls and three boys) were aged between 10 and 16 at the start of the study. The main focus was on the young people's own perceptions of their lives and issues around identity. The ethnographic fieldwork lasted for two years and all data were collected and analysed by Mary Wickenden (2007–2009). The main method was extensive participant observation in the teenagers' schools, homes, and other settings (Wickenden 2011). This involved the researcher observing and joining in with activities that the teenagers were doing in these contexts for a period of a month or more for each individual. Innovative techniques included using visual methods (pictures and symbols), and also carrying out approximately ten specially adapted extended narrative conversations with each participant focusing on a range of topics, including: 'important people', 'friendships', 'my body', 'my kit', 'my dreams', 'who helps me and who I help', and 'my life story'. Each conversation was represented visually with drawing and writing (by MW), and these records were kept in a personal file for each teenager so that they could review and revise their data regularly.

All nine key participants had severe difficulties with producing speech (seven had no speech) and two were also deaf. However, they had broadly *normal* cognitive abilities. They communicated using a mixture of low- and high-tech communication aids (computer aided vocal output systems, communication books and charts, alphabet boards, gesture, signs) which they combined and switched between according to the situation and the skills and responses of their conversation partners. All used a power wheelchair and could operate a computer mouse either directly or through adapted switches (two could walk a short distance).

The data from Malawi is taken from a study carried out in 2013–2015 which aimed to design a participatory approach to evaluation of Community Based Rehabilitation (CBR) programmes which, in Malawi, are run by a government supported agency (MACOHA [Malawi Council for the Handicapped]). A new methodology and tools were developed and trialled in four sites (two in Malawi, two in Uganda) over a two-year period. The study was undertaken in collaboration with local government, international non-governmental organisations (INGOs), and disabled people's organisation (DPO) partners. The result was *PIE* (Participatory Inclusion Evaluation), an approach which involves collecting in-depth information about many aspects of disabled adults and children's lives directly from them and their families, and from other stakeholders, during focus group discussions, individual interviews, and through telling stories (Post et al. 2016). Teams of local researchers collected data from informants over a three-week period. This was followed by a period of analysis, community validation, and report writing. Although some secondary quantitative data were collated, the main emphasis was on collecting qualitative data from the local community about the effectiveness and impact (mainly focusing on quality and access) of the CBR programmes.

The researchers used a range of visualisation methods and consensus making activities to discuss various aspects of service provision and support that was provided in the district for disabled people. Participants were asked to discuss and evaluate the kinds of support and services they had experience in the five broad WHO CBR component headings of health, education, livelihoods, social, and empowerment (WHO 2017a). The data collected from disabled children focused more broadly on the extent to which they felt socially included, as well as their perceptions about who helped them.

The data from Guatemala were collected in 2016 as part of a national study of disability carried out among adults and children. The study's objectives were to: develop an estimate of national and regional disability prevalence; to explore the lived experience of disability in terms of socio-economic status, quality of life, participation, health, and opportunities to go to school and work among people with and without disabilities; and to explore cultural, ideological, and social interpretations, and responses to disability. A small sample of participants during the quantitative portion of the study (household surveys), who lived in households with disabled family members, were further interviewed on their access to healthcare services and what access to health meant for them. In total, five participants were interviewed. They included participants from rural areas in the departments of Guatemala and Sololá.

Finally, anecdotal case studies from the US healthcare system are presented. These are based on the experiences of a clinician working in an outpatient rehabilitation setting in Northern California from 2013–2015, focusing on the clinician's understanding and struggles with each of the unique circumstances faced by her clients.

Joint data analysis

The authors jointly discussed the conceptual framework for the association between health, disability, and access to health, using the ICF (WHO 2001) as a starting point. They then examined their available data from the different sources to identify examples where the relationship between health and disability arose. Context is clearly very important to these associations, and so the data are presented as a series of case studies from different settings to explore these issues critically and in-depth. Three different domains were considered: the contextual factors influencing the relationship of health and disability; factors promoting or impeding access to healthcare among people with disabilities; and the impact of accessing healthcare on the everyday lives of people with disabilities. All names and identifying features have been changed in the case studies to ensure anonymity.

Case study 1: children with disabilities in Malawi and the UK

The influence of context and environment is clearly illustrated by two study participants, one from the UK study (Jesse) and one in Malawi (Martha). The girls have severe cerebral palsy of similar severity, but live in very different cultural contexts. Jesse is a 12-year-old girl living in a well-resourced high-income setting in England (Wickenden 2011). Despite having severe functional difficulties in both mobility and with speech, she reports that she is 'not disabled' because she 'does everything her friends do'. This self-perception is attributed to the fact that she has a supportive family and is equipped with a power wheelchair, both high- and low-tech communication aids, and other equipment (e.g. adapted bathroom and computer). She attends a mainstream school where she accesses the mainstream curriculum supported by an assistant, and goes to the local inclusive sports club (Wickenden 2011). The findings from the UK study found that children like Jesse know they are different in some ways that other people notice, but describe themselves as *normal teenagers* and want to be treated as such. They hate being seen as ill, weak, vulnerable, or unable to do things that their non-disabled siblings and peers do.

In contrast, Martha is a 12-year-old girl who has a very different experience. She has similar impairments to Jesse. However, she lives in a resource-poor setting in rural Malawi. Her impairment was not identified by the health services until she was 5, although her family noticed her difficulties with activities, such as sitting, walking, feeding, and talking. These differences may have been understood negatively by her family and community, because she was reportedly not taken out of the house or to school and, so, has become excluded from her community. She has not been offered specific rehabilitation to improve her posture and feeding, has no special seating, and spends most of her time lying down. She has no adapted communication system, either low- or high-tech, so she cannot express her needs or opinions. She is at risk for pressure sores, chest infections, dislocated hips, contractures, and other secondary impacts of her original health condition. Her family find it difficult to look after her, with daily activities such as feeding, toileting, and bathing being particularly frustrating and physically hard work for her carers (Wickenden 2011).

In relation to health, Jesse has access to both mainstream and specialist health services when needed, both because she lives in a high-resource setting and because of her supportive family environment. Her primary care doctor (GP) knows her well and states she is no more ill than her two non-disabled siblings (Wickenden 2011). She also has regular access to orthopaedic and neurological specialists, physiotherapists, and speech and language therapists, all of whom provide impairment-specific input from time to time as needed.

In Martha's case, she appears to have had no access to any of the different possible levels of healthcare, whether general or specialist. If Martha becomes ill with a general illness, such as malaria or a stomach bug, her parents often do not take her to the clinic for testing and treatment (Wickenden et al. 2017). They say it is too difficult to get her there because transport is inaccessible and when they do go, the nurses are unfriendly and say that she is not a priority and a waste of resources (Wickenden et al. 2017). In addition, because she does not attend school, she has not been immunised or included in local nutrition and other preventative health programmes that her siblings and peers received. Martha does not receive good quality or equitable treatment, because of physical and attitudinal barriers in the health service and because of lack of resources in Malawi. Her right to health, both specialised and general, is being denied.

The two cases illustrate how the link between disability and health depends on context. The extent to which both disabled people themselves and others focus on their health condition, and their impairment itself, varies greatly. We see here a contrast between the two girls, arising from various interacting situation-specific factors. A supportive family may be particularly important for children with disabilities, as they are the facilitators to the uptake of healthcare as well as to participation in society. The impact of access to healthcare or lack of it in the everyday lives of people with disabilities is clearly demonstrated by the cases of Jesse and Martha. Jesse aspires to go to university and run a business. Her parents and sisters see and treat her as an equal member of the family, and they actively advocate for her inclusion, especially if this is denied by others (Wickenden 2011). A key facilitating factor contributing to this high level of inclusion appears to be Jesse having access to mainstream and specialist health services when needed. In contrast, Martha's situation illustrates a reinforcing vicious circle of exclusion and violation of rights, and a lack of specialist healthcare services contributing to restricted access to school and the community. A lack of visibility through not attending school further reduces her access to healthcare and other services and opportunities.

Case study 2: a household of people with disabilities in Guatemala

The experience of disability is often evident at the household level, impacting on siblings, spouses, children, or parents as well as the person with impairments him/herself. This makes it important to consider the perspectives of carers and families when exploring issues around disability and access to health at the household level. In a poor area around Guatemala City, Lucia, a 60-year-old woman, lives with her husband, father, daughter, and grandchildren. They live in a two-storey house with nine steps to get to the alley that leads to the street. Lucia identifies herself as the primary caregiver for two disabled family members, her husband who is in his 80s and her father in his 90s. Lucia's father is blind, has difficulty walking, and requires help when moving around the house.

He does not have any mobility aids and needs help to move around due to fear of falling. Lucia's husband had a stroke some years ago, and while he can use a walking stick for short distances, he holds on to walls and furniture to move around the house, has very poor balance, and is prone to falls. Lucia says both men are fearful of being left home alone and also of leaving the house. This is likely to be related to the nature of their impairments, a lack of assistive devices, and an inaccessible physical environment, making them more vulnerable to falls and injury.

Lucia states that while the family can access healthcare services in the community, the energy and the cost involved in getting to a doctor for either herself or the two men is so hard that she saves it for emergencies only. During the interview, while crying, Lucia states that:

> You know I have diabetes myself but thank God, neither them or I have gotten very sick over the past years as I don't know what I would do . . . I can't leave them alone. . . . I can't even go to the doctor myself.

She admits that neither her husband nor father have been to a doctor for over a year because:

> It is too difficult to take them . . . we need to help them get out of the house, the steps are very difficult for all of us . . . get them into a wheelchair in the alley . . . then use the wheelchair to take them to the street where they can get into a car.

Both men may have other undiagnosed secondary complications such as diabetes, high blood pressure, or cholesterol, or age-related conditions that are not treated or managed. These conditions can further decrease quality of life, participation, and raise the risk of early mortality. Lucia adds, for instance, that 'I only pray that they don't get the flu'. This scenario demonstrates how both people with disabilities and their caregivers with limited supports face physical and financial barriers and are likely to avoid going to the doctor until there is an emergency. Lucia admits that because of the difficulties of access, their need for healthcare is not sufficiently prioritised in relation to the other competing demands of the family. This case illustrates that Lucia and her family are experiencing a violation of their right to healthcare, which has arisen from a lack of social support, poverty, and lack of assistive devices. Their inability to leave the house will also have negative social and psychological consequences for Lucia, her husband, and father, due to isolation and marginalisation. This is particularly true for Lucia who was crying throughout the entire interview, while repeatedly thanking God for keeping all three of them safe from serious illness and the flu. This highlights the complexity and interconnectedness of disability, health, and social participation, and how this can have an impact on the entire household.

Case study 3: a healthcare provider in the US

Magda works as a therapist serving a diverse community in the East Bay region of Northern California. She has been involved in a number of situations while trying to help adults with disability manage their daily life and access rehabilitation services and assistive devices in the area. While her stories are not from her client's perspectives, they provide insight into the daily challenges faced by many people with disabilities living in the region. The cases present her with a number of dilemmas and challenges as a clinician when working with her clients due to structural barriers related to specific eligibility requirements for receiving particular services or assistive devices.

John is a 67-year-old man living with a history of diabetes with severe neuropathy and chronic lung disease. Up to two to three years ago, prior to his visit with Magda, John was independent in most of his everyday activities and while he had two adult sons, he lived alone and enjoyed having his autonomy. Unfortunately, his condition declined rapidly over the past few years. While he is still able to move around at home using a walker with a seat, he can no longer manage getting around the community independently. John now has to rely on his sons or his neighbours for all activities outside of his home such as shopping, going to the park or library, and visiting the doctor.

John wants a motorised scooter that would enable him to go out and return to being independent in the community so that he can retain his independence. As John lives on government disability income, he cannot afford to buy a motorised scooter and hopes that his visit with Magda will facilitate getting funding for it through his social services. While Magda believes that John would benefit from a scooter, his social insurance plan only covers the cost if he requires it to manoeuvre inside his apartment. According to John and his sons, this is his third attempt at applying for a scooter, yet the reality of the eligibility criteria will still result in his case being denied for the third time. According to the system, John is not yet *disabled enough* to qualify for a scooter. Valuing his independence and recognising how busy other people are, John and his sons admit that he avoids going out as much as he would like and does not visit the doctor for what he considers 'non-essential appointments' (e.g. annual checks and the flu vaccine). As one of John's sons describes:

> The only reason he let us bring him today is because it may help him get a scooter, he is too worried about being a burden to us. We would be happy to help him.

John is experiencing a violation of his right to healthcare. This case study also shows the importance of both social support and assistive devices in the uptake of healthcare services, as barriers do not work in isolation, but are reinforcing. While using a motorised scooter would allow him independence, another impact of its absence is to limit his use of healthcare services. He is less likely to go out and has become more sedentary in his lifestyle, which, in itself, is problematic for his overall health. John is also at an increased risk of social isolation. Lack of access to assistive devices and rehabilitation therefore contribute to a vicious circle, limiting access to further healthcare as well as impeding general wellbeing and social participation.

Magda also works with clients who rely on disability transport services. These are publicly funded wheelchair accessible rides for people who need assistance to get in and out of a vehicle. While the service enables community members to get out of their home and go shopping or to a medical appointment on their own, it also presents various challenges related to scheduling and logistics which have serious consequences. For example, Doris is a 55 year-old woman who experienced a stroke eight years ago. The stroke affected Doris' left side and as a result, she requires the use of a manual wheelchair for most functional mobility, specifically when leaving home. For Doris to go anywhere, she is reliant on the disability transport services. Magda noted that although Doris expressed a high desire for rehabilitation, she seemed to miss a lot of appointments. One day, Magda noticed that Doris was a few hours early for her appointment and was still waiting for her ride at the end of the day at the entrance of the hospital. It emerged that the transport pickups were either too early or late, and did not wait more than a couple of minutes at the pick-up points, even if they arrive early. This meant that Doris had to plan her entire day around the transport schedule and give herself plenty of extra time on both sides of her appointments. Unlike the other cases discussed, Doris did have access to assistive devices that she needed and services to help her with transport. However, it took her a lot of time and energy to reach her medical appointments, and so was disadvantaged compared to people without disabilities when seeking healthcare.

Discussion

The case studies demonstrate the vulnerability of people with disabilities to poor health, which arises from a complex jigsaw puzzle of individual, social, structural, and service-related factors. This vulnerability is also shown in the general medical literature. It is important to emphasise that it is not the *fault* of people with disabilities that they may have poorer health (Helman 2007), but that this arises from the many embedded and seemingly intractable structural inequalities that they face. The evidence base about the relationships and interactions between illness, health, and disability is also far from complete; it is restricted mainly to high-income countries and is not always consistent in its claims (Horner-Johnson et al. 2010). Although disability is precipitated by a health condition or impairment, a distinction should be made between these underlying factors and any ill health people may also experience. Many types of impairment are stable and permanent from a medical point of view, meaning that the conditions are stable and there are no cures for the condition. The disabled person is, to a large extent (apart from in the early stages of adapting to a newly acquired impairment), psychologically and practically accommodated to their type of body or mind. To them, their difference is normal, and therein lies a paradox for others interacting with them (Watson 2002).

This permanency in an altered state can be challenging both for health professionals, whose raison d'être is curing people, and for people in the community who find such difference bewildering, embarrassing, or threatening (Shakespeare 1994). Too often, people (though usually not disabled people) equate disability with illness and or a disease, and this risks falling back into the potentially pathologising stance of the medical model of disability, with the expectation that the healthcare community is responsible for treating and possibly *curing* it. This belief system, in turn, diminishes or disregards the importance of the many contextual factors that contribute to the disabling process and the poor health experienced by some people with disabilities.

On the one hand, it is important that disabled people get equal access to good quality healthcare when they need it. On the other, overly medicalised views of disabled people which prioritise and privilege the health-related aspects of their experience are unwelcome by them. Many disabled people say that their impairment is not the only, or indeed the most important, defining aspect of them, and that too much interest is given to it rather than other parts of their identity (Watson 2002). Although other people might see the disabled person as different and as ill, their way of moving, thinking, communicating, or perceiving is normal for them and their families.

The case studies show the challenges that people with disabilities, in both high- and low-income settings, can face in accessing healthcare services, and allow for an exploration of the interaction between different barriers facing individuals and how they reinforce each other. For instance, in the case of Martha, her disability means that she is excluded from school, and so has poorer access to healthcare. It also highlights examples where barriers can be overcome, and this is usually because multiple domains are tackled – such as Jesse who had a supportive family, access to a range of assistive devices, and a positive policy environment around her. The use of case studies rather than traditional barrier assessment highlights a more fundamental underlying issue in accessing healthcare, that is, the disadvantaged and marginalised structural position in society of many people with disabilities. This can be true in both rich and poor countries. At the extremes, this is as a result of a fundamental lack of recognition of disabled people as citizens with the same rights as others (Meekosha and Soldatic 2011). They are easily subject to some severe forms of rejection and neglect which are perpetuated and embedded at a range of levels within society from within the family, through community level up to national policy (Shakespeare 2012; Swartz and Bantjes 2016).

These kinds of discrimination can be described as form of *structural violence* as conceptualised by Farmer (2005), although this term has not been used very often in relation to disability. This institutionalised disadvantage implies that the difficulty is in the system, not in the person. Endemic discrimination then sanctions the denial of both everyday general healthcare and good special-ist help and provision of assistive devices to disabled people. The result is often compromising their chances of keeping well and having a *good life*, something it is often wrongly assumed they cannot have in any case (Albrecht and Devlieger 1999; Mackenzie and Leach Scully 2007).

The literature is rich in highlighting the range of barriers facing people with disabilities in relation to access to healthcare, which is also demonstrated in our case studies. Physical barriers to accessing healthcare are the easiest to visualise and understand, most obviously inaccessible buildings (Mudrick et al. 2012; Popplewell et al. 2014), but also inaccessible toilets or lack of appropriate equip-ment (Drainoni et al. 2006; Lim et al. 2015; Smith et al. 2004; WHO 2011). Not so obvious perhaps is the lack of accessible transport, or local facilities, which can limit people with disabilities' access to health services. These failures may be due to logistical aspects, lack of inclusive policies and planning, or few resources to meet the additional costs related to adapted transportation and the distance needed to travel. Social barriers related to human interactions and misconcep-tions are also important. People with disabilities may lack confidence that they will be positively received – as illustrated in Martha's family. An unwelcome response from healthcare staff will discourage people from seeking further help. Health promotion messages may not reach people with particular impairments, such as people with hearing or visual impairments if they are only produced in one format (Kuenberg et al. 2016; Pereira and de Carvalho Fortes 2010; Saulo et al. 2012; Ubido et al. 2002). There may also be misconceptions that people with disabilities do not require certain types of information, due to stigma or misinformed assumptions. For example, people with disabilities may not be provided with education on contraception or sexual health promotion as they are assumed not to be sexually active (Kiani 2009; Peta 2017; Smith et al. 2004). Financial barriers should also not be overlooked. People with disabilities are on average more likely to be poor and, as a result, additional costs of healthcare make it unattainable. They are more likely to report that they cannot afford healthcare than their non-disabled peers (WHO 2011). In countries without free access to healthcare, a key driver is the lack of affordable healthcare or insur-ance coverage (Reichard et al. 2017).

Overall, these diverse barriers may translate into poor access to healthcare services (Centers for Disease Control and Prevention 2010; Diab and Johnston 2004; Iezzoni et al. 2000; Reichard et al. 2011; WHO 2001). This exclusion may operate across different sub-specialities within health, including uptake of preventative measures such as cervical and breast cancer screening (Horner-Johnson et al. 2013; Wu et al. 2012), adherence to anti-hypertensive drugs (Park et al. 2008), or attendance at routine health examinations (Chun et al. 2012). Given that access to healthcare is difficult to conceptualise and measure, the evidence base needs further data and strengthening. In particular, better metrics need to be developed to assess access to health. Studies measuring health condi-tions in terms of serious illness often show that most people will seek care in these instances, including people with disabilities (Kuper et al. 2014; Mactaggart et al. 2016). In contrast, if health conditions are measured in relation to *any illness in the past week*, many people will likely not have sought care; this is often appropriate in the case of mild self-limiting conditions. More nuanced scales are needed in order to measure access to healthcare, and people's decision-making rationales in relation to seeking it. More data is also needed to compare access to services between people with and without disabilities, and how this varies by gender and over the life-course.

The quality of the healthcare encounter is also an important consideration, including disabled people's perceptions of treatment by health professionals (de Vries McClintock et al. 2016; Shakespeare and Kleine 2013). According to the WHO (2011), people with disabilities are twice as likely to find the healthcare provider's skills inadequate to meet their needs, four times more likely to report being treated poorly, and nearly three times more likely to report being denied care. This poor quality care may occur for a variety of reasons, prominent among which is difficulties in communication (Eide et al. 2015; Pereira and de Carvalho Fortes 2010; Siddique 2014; Ubido et al. 2002). People with disabilities may face stigma and discrimination, or be afraid that they will do so when accessing healthcare. This is particularly apparent among people with mental health or intellectual impairments (Al-Zboon and Hatmal 2016; Ali et al. 2013; Chadwick et al. 2012; Clifton et al. 2016; Micheal and Richardson 2008). People with disabilities may have multiple and complex health needs, requiring coordinated care across different specialities, something often not achieved in reality (Al-Zboon and Hatmal 2016; Ali et al. 2013; Chadwick et al. 2012; Clifton et al. 2016; Shakespeare and Klein 2013). This can result in people with multiple impairments or complex needs being denied access to the quality care they need (Clifton et al. 2016; Morris 2004).

What is, as yet, unexplored in the literature, although clearly demonstrated in the case studies in this chapter, is the more distal and long-term effects of lack of healthcare for people with disabilities, including on social participation and wellbeing. For instance, Martha's experience of living in Malawi showed a feedback loop, where a violation of the right to assistive devices led to lack of a school place and, in turn, missing out on other aspects of healthcare provided at school. In contrast, fulfilling the right to health of people with disabilities may lead to an upward spiral of enhanced inclusion, as it did with Jesse.

Improving access to healthcare among people with disabilities is urgently needed, and is a key priority of the WHO Global Disability Action Plan (WHO 2014). Ensuring good quality access to healthcare for all will require innovative solutions to be developed using evidence-based techniques. The United Nations Convention on the Rights of People with Disabilities outlines four main concerns that need to be addressed in ensuring the right to health, among others. Services should be accessible, including the full spectrum of physical, communication, and social accessibility. Furthermore, these services must be affordable and available close to where people live. The quality of the services must be as good for people with disabilities as for those without. Solutions must target different aspects of healthcare provision, including physical modifications to facilities (e.g. installing ramps, handrails, wide doors) and using equipment with universal design features (e.g. adjustable examination tables). Less obviously, it is also important to develop alternative modes for communication (e.g. sign language, communication technology, pictures, symbols, easy-read, Braille) and offer different modes for delivering services (e.g. outreach or extra time for consultation). There is also a need to train healthcare staff on disability awareness and responsiveness, and provide health education for people with disabilities. The development of these interventions will require a participatory approach, working in partnership with people with disabilities, to ensure that the solutions are appropriate for people with a range of impairments and needs. It is through these combined efforts that the right to healthcare will be fulfilled for people with disabilities, which can lead to an upward spiral towards full participation and healthy everyday lives.

Conclusions

Overall, we have shown that the social model of disability and the ICF serve as useful theoretical frameworks for considering the health and wellbeing of people with disabilities in a broad way in a range of contexts globally. Although both encourage a movement away from a purely health dominated view of disability, good health and healthcare remain important for disabled people. A human rights model of disability is perhaps a more powerful tool, emphasising equity and (alongside other entitlements) a right to a variety of types of healthcare as needed by the individual. Disabled people need both specialist healthcare, related to their impairment, and general healthcare accessed through mainstream routes within their communities, alongside their neighbours. Regardless of the type of healthcare, it needs to be of good quality, timely, accessible, respectful, and responsive to individuals' needs. Disabled people often resist being labelled as vulnerable or seen as unhealthy or sick, but the reality is that many are vulnerable to poor health. This is sometimes a consequence of their structural position as an excluded group and the likelihood of being poor, as well as linked to their impairment and its effects. Nevertheless, their everyday health needs to be assured by the provision of equitable health services which recognise their needs and rights in the context of disablement and while living ordinary lives alongside their peers.

Note

1 We use the terms *people with disabilities* and *disabled people* interchangeably, while understanding that these phrases have different socio-political connotations and are favoured by different groups in different contexts.

References

AIHW. 2010. *Health of Australians With Disability: Health Status and Risk Factors.* Australia: AIHW.

Albrecht, G. L. and Devlieger, P. J. 1999. The disability paradox: high quality of life against all odds. *Social Science and Medicine* 48(8), pp. 977–988.

Ali, A., Scior, K., Ratti, V., Strydom, A., King, M. and Hassiotis, A. 2013. Discrimination and other barriers to accessing healthcare: perspectives of patients with mild and moderate intellectual disability and their carers. *PLOS ONE* 8(8), p. e70855.

Altman, B. M. and Bernstein, A. 2008. *Disability and Health in the United States, 2001–2005.* Hyattsville, MD: National Centre for Health Statistics.

Al-Zboon, E. and Hatmal, M. M. 2016. Attitudes of dentists toward persons with intellectual disabilities in Jordanian hospitals. *Special Care in Dentistry* 36(1), pp. 25–31.

Banks, L. M. and Polack, S. 2014. *The Economic Costs of Exclusion and Gains of Inclusion of People With Disabilities.* London. International Centre for Evidence in Disability.

Burke, E., Kébé, F., Flink, I., van Reeuwijk, M. and le May, A. 2017. A qualitative study to explore the barriers and enablers for young people with disabilities to access sexual and reproductive health services in Senegal. *Reproductive Health Matters* 25(50), pp. 43–54.

Callaway, L., Barclay, L., McDonald, R., Farnworth, L. and Casey, J. 2015. Secondary health conditions experienced by people with spinal cord injury within community living: implications for a National Disability Insurance Scheme. *Australian Occupational Therapy Journal* 62(4), pp. 246–254.

Centers for Disease Control and Prevention. 2010. Delayed or forgone medical care because of cost concerns among adults aged 18–64 years, by disability and health insurance coverage status – National Health Interview Survey, United States, 2009. *Morbidity and Mortality Weekly Report* 59(44), p. 1456.

Chadwick, A., Street, C., McAndrew, S. and Deacon, M. 2012. Minding our own bodies: reviewing the literature regarding the perceptions of service users diagnosed with serious mental illness on barriers to accessing physical healthcare. *International Journal of Mental Health Nursing* 21(3), pp. 211–219.

Chun, S. M., Hwang, B., Park, J. H. and Shin, H. I. 2012. Implications of sociodemographic factors and health examination rate for people with disabilities. *Archives of Physical Medicine and Rehabilitation* 93(7), pp. 1161–1166.

Clifton, A., Burgess, C. and Clement, S. 2016. Influences on uptake of cancer screening in mental health service users: a qualitative study. *BMC Health Services Research* 16(257), pp. 1–12.

de Vries McClintock, H. F., Barg, F. K., Katz, S. P., Stineman, M. G., Krueger, A., Colletti, P. M., Boellstorff, T. and Bogner, H. R. 2016. Health care experiences and perceptions among people with and without disabilities. *Disability and Health Journal* 9(1), pp. 74–82.

Diab, M. E. and Johnston, M. V. 2004. Relationships between level of disability and receipt of preventive health services. *Archives of Physical Medicine and Rehabilitation* 85(5), pp. 749–757.

Donoghue, C. 2003. Challenging the authority of the medical definition of disability: an analysis of the resistance to the social constructionist paradigm. *Disability and Society* 18(2), pp. 199–208.

Drainoni, M., Lee-Hood, E., Tobias, C., Bachman, S. S., Andrew, J. and Maisels, L. 2006. Cross-disability experiences of barriers to health-care access: consumer perspectives. *Journal of Disability Policy Studies* 17(2), pp. 101–115.

Eide, A. H., Mannan, H., Khogali M, van Rooy, G., Swartz, L., Munthali, A., Hem, K. G., MacLachlan, M. and Dyrstad, K. 2015. Perceived barriers for accessing health services among individuals with disability in four African countries. *PLOS ONE* 10(5), p. e0125915.

Farmer, P. 2005. *Pathologies of Power: Health, Human Rights, and the New War on the Poor.* Berkeley: University of California Press.

Froehlich-Grobe, K., Jones, D., Businelle, M. S., Kendzor, D. E. and Balasubramanian, B. A. 2016. Impact of disability and chronic conditions on health. *Disability Health Journal* 9(4), pp. 600–608.

Grech, S. 2015. *Disability and Poverty in the Global South: Renegotiating Development in Guatemala.* Basingstoke: Palgrave Macmillan.

Helman, C. 2007. *Culture Health and Illness.* Abingdon: CRC Press.

Hogan, D. B., Ebly, E. M. and Fung, T. S. 1999. Disease, disability, and age in cognitively intact seniors: results from the Canadian study of health and aging. *Journal of Gerontology and Biological Science and Medical Science* 54(2), pp. M77–M82.

Horner-Johnson, W., Dobbertin, K., Lee, J. C., Andresen, E. M. and Expert Panel on Disability and Health Disparities. 2013. Disparities in chronic conditions and health status by type of disability. *Disability and Health Journal* 6(4), pp. 280–286.

Horner-Johnson, W., McGee, M. G., Michael, Y. L., Rosso, A. L. and Wisdom, J. P. 2010. Aging with a disability: a systematic review of cardiovascular disease and osteoporosis among women aging with a physical disability. *Maturitas* 68(1), pp. 65–72.

Iezzoni, L. I., McCarthy, E. P., Davis, R. B. and Siebens, H. 2000. Mobility impairments and use of screening and preventive services. *American Journal of Public Health* 90(6), pp. 955–961.

Kiani, S. 2009. Women with disabilities in the North West province of Cameroon: resilient and deserving of greater attention. *Disability and Society* 24(4), pp. 517–531.

Kuenberg, A., Fellinger, P. and Fellinger, J. 2016. Healthcare access among deaf people. *Journal of Deaf Studies and Deaf Education* 21(1), pp. 1–10.

Kuper, H., Monteath-van Dok, A., Wing, K., Danguah, L., Evans, J., Zuurmond, M. and Gallinetti, J. 2014. The impact of disability on the lives of children: cross-sectional data including 8,900 children with disabilities and 898,834 children without disabilities across 30 countries. *PLOS ONE* 9(9), p. e107300.

Lim, N. G., Lee, J. Y., Park, J. O., Lee, A. J. and Oh, J. 2015. Pregnancy, prenatal care and delivery of mothers with disabilities in Korea. *Journal of Korean Medical Science* 30(2), pp. 127–132.

Maart, S. and Jelsma, J. 2014. Disability and access to healthcare: a community based descriptive study. *Disability and Rehabilitation* 36(18), pp. 1489–1493.

Mackenzie, C. and Leach Scully, J. 2007. Moral imagination, disability and embodiment. *Journal of Applied Philosophy* 24(4), pp. 335–351.

Mactaggart, I., Kuper, H., Murthy, G. V., Sagar, J., Oye, J. and Polack, S. 2016. Assessing health and rehabilitation needs of people with disabilities in Cameroon and India. *Disability and Rehabilitation* 38(18), pp. 1757–1764.

Mannan, H. and MacLachlan, M. 2013. Disability and health: a research agenda. *Social Inclusion* 1(1), pp. 37–45.

Marmot, M. 2005. Social determinants of health inequalities. *Lancet* 365(9464), pp. 1099–1104.

Marmot, M. 2010. *Fair Society, Healthy Lives: The Marmot Review.* London: Institute for Health Equity.

Marmot, M. and Wilkinson, R. G. 2003. *Social Determinants of Health: The Solid Facts.* Geneva: World Health Organization.

Meekosha, H. and Soldatic, K. 2011. Human rights and the Global South: the case of disability. *Third World Quarterly* 32(8), pp. 1383–1397.

Micheal, J. and Richardson, A. 2008. Healthcare for all: the Independent inquiry into access to healthcare for people with learning disabilities. *Tizard Learning Disability Review* 13(4), pp. 28–34.

Morris, J. 2004. *Services for People With Physical Impairments and Mental Health Support Needs.* York: Joseph Rowntree Foundation.

Mudrick, N. R., Breslin, M. L., Liang, M. and Yee, S. 2012. Physical accessibility in primary healthcare settings: results from California on-site reviews. *Disability and Health Journal* 5(3), pp. 159–167.

Oliver, M. and Barnes, C. 2012. *The New Politics of Disablement.* Basingstoke: Palgrave.

Park, J. H., Lee, S. Y., Kim, S. Y., Shin, Y. and Kim, S. Y. 2008. Disparities in antihypertensive medication adherence in persons with disabilities and without disabilities: results of a Korean population-based study. *Archives of Physical Medicine and Rehabilitation* 89(8), pp. 1460–1467.

Pereira, P.C.A. and de Carvalho Fortes, P. A. 2010. Communication and information barriers to health assistance for deaf patients. *American Annals of the Deaf* 155(1), pp. 31–37.

Peta, C. 2017. Disability is not asexuality: the childbearing experiences and aspirations of women with disability in Zimbabwe. *Reproductive Health Matters* 25(50), pp. 10–19.

Popplewell, N.T.A., Rechel, B.P.D. and Abel, G. A. 2014. How do adults with physical disability experience primary care? A nationwide cross-sectional survey of access among patients in England. *BMJ Open* 4, p. e004714.

Post, E., Cornielje, H., Andrae, K., Maarse, A., Schneider, M. and Wickenden, M. 2016. Participatory inclusion evaluation: a flexible approach to building the evidence base on the impact of community-based rehabilitation and inclusive development programmes. *Knowledge Management for Development Journal* 11(2), pp. 7–26.

Reichard, A., Stolzle, H. and Fox, M. H. 2011. Health disparities among adults with physical disabilities or cognitive limitations compared to individuals with no disabilities in the United States. *Disability and Health Journal* 4(2), pp. 59–67.

Reichard, A., Stransky, M., Phillips, K., McClain, M. and Drum, C. 2017. Prevalence and reasons for delaying and foregoing necessary care by the presence and type of disability among working-age adults. *Disability and Health Journal* 10(1), pp. 39–47.

Rotarou, E. and Sakellariou, D. 2017. Inequalities in access to healthcare for people with disabilities in Chile: the limits of universal health coverage. *Critical Public Health* 27(5), pp. 604–616.

Saulo, B., Walakira, E. and Darj, E. 2012. Access to healthcare for disabled persons: how are blind people reached by HIV services? *Sexual and Reproductive Healthcare: Official Journal of the Swedish Association of Midwives* 3(1), pp. 49–53.

Shakespeare, T. 1994. Cultural representation of disabled people: dustbins for disavowal? *Disability and Society* 9(3), pp. 283–299.

Shakespeare, T. 2004. Social models of disability and other life strategies. *Scandinavian Journal of Disability Research* 6(1), pp. 8–20.

Shakespeare, T. 2012. Still a health issue. *Disability and Health Journal* 5(3), pp. 129–131.

Shakespeare, T. 2013. *Disability Rights and Wrongs.* Abingdon: Routledge.

Shakespeare, T. and Kleine, I. 2013. Educating health professionals about disability: a review of interventions. *Health and Social Care Education* 2(2), pp. 20–37.

Siddique, H. 2014. Deaf couple angry with hospital over lack of interpreter during birth of son. *The Guardian* [Online]. Available at: www.theguardian.com/society/2014/jan/19/deaf-couple-lack-interpreter-birth-university-college-hospital-london [Accessed: 23 November 2017].

Smith, E., Murray, S. F., Yousafzai, A. K. and Kasonka, L. 2004. Barriers to accessing safe motherhood and reproductive health services: the situation of women with disabilities in Lusaka, Zambia. *Disability and Rehabilitation* 26(2), pp. 121–127.

Swartz, L. and Bantjes, J. 2016. Disability and global health. In: Grech, S. and Soldatic, K. eds. *Disability in the Global South.* Switzerland: Springer, pp. 21–33.

Tas, Ü., Verhagen, A. P., Bierma-Zeinstra, S. M., Odding, E. and Koes, B. W. 2007. Prognostic factors of disability in older people: a systematic review. *British Journal of General Practice* 57(537), pp. 319–323.

Thomas, C. 2007. *Sociologies of Disability and Illness: Contested Ideas in Disability Studies and Medical Sociology.* Basingstoke: Palgrave Macmillan.

Ubido, J., Huntington, J. and Warburton, D. 2002. Inequalities in access to healthcare faced by women who are deaf. *Health and Social Care in Community* 10(4), pp. 247–253.

UN. 2006. *Convention on the Rights of Persons With Disabilities and Optional Protocol.* New York: United Nations.

Watson, N. 2002. Well I know this is going to sound very strange to you but I don't see myself as a disabled person: identity and disability. *Disability and Society* 17(5), pp. 509–527.

WHO. 2001. *International Classification of Functioning, Disability and Health.* Geneva: World Health Organization.

WHO. 2011. *World Report on Disability.* Geneva: World Health Organization.

WHO. 2014. *Draft WHO Global Disability Action Plan 2014–2021: Better Health For All People With Disability.* Geneva: World Health Organization.

WHO. 2017a. *About the Community-Based Rehabilitation (CBR) Matrix: Disability and Rehabilitation.* Geneva: World Health Organization.

WHO. 2017b. Universal health coverage. *Health Systems.* Available at: www.who.int/health-systems/universal_health_coverage/en/ [Accessed: 11 August 2017].

Wickenden, M. 2011. Whose voice is that? Issues of identity, voice and representation arising in an ethnographic study of the lives of disabled teenagers who use augmentative and alternative communication (AAC). *Disability Studies Quarterly* 31(4).

Wickenden, M., Cornielje, H. and Nkwenge, P. 2017. The PIE model and tools: meeting the need for a systematic and participatory approach to evaluating the impact of CBR. In: Nganwa, A. B., Sserunkuma, M. C. and Mbugua, P. K. eds. *CBR Guidelines: A Bridge to Inclusive Society Beyond the 2015 Development Framework.* Uganda: CBR Africa, pp. 24–41.

Wu, L. W., Lin, L. P., Chen, S. F., Hsu, S. W., Loh, C. H., Wu, C. L. and Lon, J. D. 2012. Knowledge and attitudes regarding cervical cancer screening among women with physical disabilities living in the community. *Research in Developmental Disabilities* 33(2), pp. 376–381.

Index

Note: Page numbers in *italics* indicate figures.